Underhill's Principles of
the Law of Partnership

UPTO CH 8.

Underhill's Principles of the Law of Partnership

Twelfth edition

E. R. Hardy Ivamy LLB, PhD, LLD

of the Middle Temple, Barrister
Professor of Law in the University of London

with a chapter on Partnership Taxation by

D. R. Jones LLB Solicitor,

Principal Lecturer at the College of Law

London
Butterworths
1986

United Kingdom	Butterworth & Co (Publishers) Ltd, 88 Kingsway, LONDON WC2B 6AB and 61A North Castle Street, EDINBURGH EH2 3LJ
Australia	Butterworths Pty Ltd, SYDNEY, MELBOURNE, BRISBANE, ADELAIDE, PERTH, CANBERRA and HOBART
Canada	Butterworths. A Division of Reed Inc, TORONTO and VANCOUVER
New Zealand	Butterworths of New Zealand Ltd, WELLINGTON and AUCKLAND
Singapore	Butterworth & Co (Asia) Pte Ltd, SINGAPORE
South Africa	Butterworth Publishers (Pty) Ltd, DURBAN and PRETORIA
USA	Butterworth Legal Publishers, ST PAUL, Minnesota, SEATTLE, Washington, BOSTON, Massachusetts, AUSTIN, Texas and D & S Publishers, CLEARWATER, Florida

© Butterworth & Co (Publishers) Ltd 1986

British Library Cataloguing in Publication Data

Underhill, *Sir*, Arthur
 Underhill's principles of the law of
 partnership.—12th ed.
 1. Partnership—England
 I. Title   II. Jones, D. R. (Dai R.)
 III. Ivamy, E. R. Hardy. Principles of
 the law of partnership
 344.206′682   KD2051

ISBN Hardcover 0 406 66907 4
ISBN Softcover 0 406 66908 2

Phototypeset by Cotswold Typesetting Ltd, Gloucester
and printed in Great Britain by Butler & Tanner Ltd, Frome and London

Preface

The purpose of this new edition is the same as that of the last one, that is to provide 'merely a broad sketch giving the salient features of the subject'.

Once again the text has been entirely re-set. The size of the type is now larger to improve readability.

As regards the summaries of the decided cases the opportunity of referring in the footnotes to my 'Casebook on Partnership' (2nd edn, 1982) has been taken so that the reader can conveniently read extracts of the judgments illustrating the points concerned.

The principal change in the new edition is the repeal of the Registration of Business Names Act 1916 and its replacement by the Business Names Act 1985 and the relevant regulations. This has necessitated the complete rewriting of Chapter 13, which is now headed 'Business Names'.

Chapter 12 ('Partnership Taxation') has again been written by Mr. D. R. Jones, Principal Lecturer at the College of Law.

The Appendices now include the Business Names Act 1985, the Company and Business Names Regulations 1981 (S.I. 1981/1685), the Partnership (Unrestricted Size) No. 5 Regulations 1982 (S.I. 1982/530) and the Company and Business Names (Amendment) Regulations 1982 (S.I. 1982/1653).

I should like to thank the staff of Butterworths for undertaking the arduous job of preparing the Index and the list of cases and table of statutes, and for seeing the book through the press.

University College London   E R Hardy Ivamy
March 1986

v

Contents

CHAPTER 5
Persons liable by 'holding out'

CHAPTER 6
Procedure in action by or against partners

CHAPTER 7
Dissolution of partnership   79

CHAPTER 8
Consequences of dissolution of partnership

CHAPTER 9
The insolvency of some or all of the partners

CHAPTER 10
Bankruptcy procedure 112

CHAPTER 11
Limited partnerships

CHAPTER 12
Partnership taxation

CHAPTER 13
Business Names

APPENDICES

APPENDIX A
Statutes

APPENDIX B
Statutory instruments

APPENDIX C
Rules of the Supreme Court

Table of statutes

References in this Table to *Statutes* are to Halsbury's Statutes of England (Fourth Edition) showing the volume and page at which the annotated text of the Act will be found. Page references printed in **bold** type indicate where the Act is set out in part or in full.

List of cases

Chapter 1

The nature of partnership

First of all it is necessary to define the word 'partnership'[1]. There are various rules for determining the existence of a partnership[2]. A partnership may be conveniently contrasted with a limited company[3].

The definition of partnership

The Partnership Act 1890, s 1(1) defines 'partnership' in the following way:

> Partnership is the relation which subsists between persons carrying on a business in common with a view of profit.

The Act then goes on the state[4] that the relation between the members of any company or association which is

(1) registered under the Companies Act 1862 or any other Act for the time being in force and relating to the registration of joint stock companies[5]; or
(2) formed or incorporated by or in pursuance of any other Act of Parliament or letters patent or royal charter; or
(3) a company engaged in working mines within and subject to the jurisdiction of the Stannaries[6],

is not a partnership.

The definition given above is neat and epigrammatic and no doubt puts the matter in a nutshell. But it is easier to concoct an epigram than

1 See below.
2 See pp 5–12, below.
3 See pp 12–14, below.
4 Partnership Act 1890, s 1(2).
5 The Act at present in force is the Companies Act 1985.
6 The Stannaries are in Cornwall and the companies concerned are subject to the exclusive jurisdiction of a local court known as the Stannaries Court. See generally Halsbury *Laws of England* (4th edn) vol 7, paras 1773–1803, and *Dunbar v Harvey* [1913] 2 Ch 530.

to interpret it and as Lord MacNaghten remarked, it is one thing to put a case in a nutshell and another to keep it there[7].

The question 'What is a partner?' is one of no mere academic interest because if the relation of partnership exists in point of law, then, unless the partnership is a 'limited partnership'[8] in which case the ordinary rules are somewhat modified, whatever may be the arrangements between the partners inter se as to how the losses are to be borne, and however much the partners may have repudiated the notion of partnership, each partner will, as between himself and the creditors of the firm[9], be liable to the last penny of his fortune.

As Lord Lindley puts it, each individual partner constitutes the other his agent for the purpose of entering into all contracts for him within the scope of the partnership concern and consequently is liable for the performance of all such contracts in the same manner as if they had been entered into personally by him. Therefore, if once the relation of partners is established between one who actively carries on a business and another who passively participates in the profits, the latter will become equally liable with the former for the debts and liabilities of the firm. Consequently the immense importance of the question whether or not persons are partners is obvious.

There is a well-known definition of an archdeacon as a person who performs archidiaconal functions; and an analogous definition must be given to the word 'partner'. Lord Lindley quotes 19 definitions without venturing to suggest one of his own[10], and the Partnership Act 1890 carefully abstains from giving one. It would appear that the only safe definition is that a 'partner' is a person who has entered into the relation of partnership, ie 'the relation which subsists between persons carrying on a business in common with a view of profit.'

Whether a person has done so is a question of fact and often a very difficult one, depending in each case on the substance of the agreement between the parties to be ascertained from the contents of documents, if any, and also from their conduct.

From the definition given above it will be seen that there must be

(1) a business;
(2) carried on in common;
(3) with a view of profit.

---

7 In *Van Grutten v Foxwell* [1897] AC 658 at 671, referring to *Shelley's Case, Wolfe v Shelley* (1581) 1 Co Rep 93b.

8 Ie a partnership registered under the Limited Partnerships Act 1907. See pp 115–123, below.

9 Persons who have entered into partnership with one another are for the purposes of the Partnership Act 1890 called collectively a 'firm' and the name under which their business is carried on is called the 'firm name': Partnership Act 1890, s 4(1).

10 *Lindley on Partnership* (15th edn, 1984), pp 16–18.

1 Business

The Partnership Act 1890, s 45, defines 'business' as including 'every trade, occupation or profession'.

It is not every occupation which can be called a 'business', eg a landowner does not carry on a business although the management of his estate and the collection of his rents may be his only serious occupation and may cause him to be an extremely busy man.

Co-ownership does not imply a business or partnership[11]. Thus owners of an estate or even a chattel, eg a ship, are not, as such, partners, although they may use their best endeavours to develop the land and use the chattel for their mutual profit, unless they go further and carry on business with respect to it.

On similar principles the members of a society formed to purchase investments for their common benefit are not partners because as James LJ said[12], there is nothing to be done by such societies that

comes within the ordinary meaning of business, any more than what is done by the trustees of a marriage settlement who have large properties vested in them, and who have very extensive powers of disposing of the investments, changing the investments, and selling them and reinvesting in other investments, according to their discretion and judgment.

If, however, the owners of a ship use her in the business of carriers of goods and/or passengers, they become partners, at all events quoad that business.

Similarly, if a society were formed to *speculate* in investments with a view to make profits by selling and buying again securities whenever, in the opinion of the management, the turn of the market should make it advisable to do so, then no doubt a partnership would exist because that would be a business, ie a buying and selling of property with a view of profit as distinguished from joint or common ownership[13].

Again, mutual insurance associations[14] or mutual loan societies may constitute partnerships if their object is one which is recognised in commercial life as 'business' notwithstanding the fact that their dealings are limited to their own members[15].

Accordingly, the term 'business' is restricted to what are regarded by business men as commercial or professional businesses, ie callings in which men hold themselves out as willing to sell goods or to provide skilled assistance or other service.

11 See Partnership Act 1890, s 2(1). See p 6, below.
12 In *Smith v Anderson* (1880) 15 Ch D 247 at 276.
13 Ibid at 281 (per Cotton LJ).
14 See Ivamy *Marine Insurance* (4th edn 1985) pp 215–224, 475–479.
15 See generally *Re Padstow Total Loss and Collision Assurance Association* (1882) 20 Ch D 137, CA; *Jennings v Hammond* (1882) 9 QBD 225; *Re Thomas, ex p Poppleton* (1884) 14 QBD 379.

An association of persons to carry out one deal only may constitute a 'business'[16].

There is no partnership when it is merely shown that the persons concerned were preparing to carry on business as a company as soon as they could.

Thus, in *Keith Spicer Ltd v Mansell*[17]:

The defendant and a Mr Bishop decided to go into business together and to form a limited company which was going to carry on the business of the defendant's restaurant. Mr Bishop ordered goods from the plaintiffs so that they could be used by the company after it had been formed, which it eventually was. The goods were not paid for, so the plaintiffs sued the defendant for the price on the ground that he was liable because a partnership existed between Mr Bishop and the defendant.

Held, by the Court of Appeal, that the action failed, because there was no evidence that the defendant and Mr Bishop were carrying on 'a business in common with a view of profit' within the meaning of s 1(1) of the Partnership Act 1890. The evidence merely showed that they were preparing to carry on business as a company as soon as they could[18].

Again, where an inspector and a committee of inspection in relation to a partnership are appointed under a deed of arrangement and the property of the partners is transferred to them, the inspector and the committee of inspection do not themselves become partners.

Thus, in *Marconi's Wireless Telegraph Co Ltd v Newman*[19]:

The plaintiffs owned some patents relating to wireless apparatus, and granted a licence to Langham Radio to use them. Langham Radio assigned the licence to Newman and Baynes, who were partners. Newman and Baynes were unable to meet their obligations, and entered into a deed of arrangement with their creditors, and assigned their property to a Mr Cork as inspector and to a committee of inspection. Newman and Baynes were allowed 'to manage and carry on their business' subject to the terms of the deed. A large sum in respect of royalties was owed to the plaintiffs by Newman and Baynes, and the plaintiffs claimed against Cork and the committee of inspection on the ground that they were liable to them as partners of Newman and Baynes.

Held, by the King's Bench Division, that no partnership existed

---

16 See eg *Mann v D'Arcy* [1968] 2 All ER 172, [1968] 1 WLR 893 where there was a joint venture for the purchase and resale of potatoes on one occasion only.
17 [1970] 1 All ER 462, [1970] 1WLR 333, CA.
18 See the judgment of Harman LJ, ibid, at 463. See further Ivamy *Casebook on Partnership* (2nd edn 1982) pp 1–2.
19 [1930] 2 KB 292, 143 LT 471.

between Cork and the committee of inspection and Newman and Baynes, and that the action failed[20].

2 In common

It is essential for the business to be carried on in common.

Where a business is being carried on with a view of profit and two or more persons share the profit, it does not necessarily follow that they are partners unless the business is carried on by or on behalf of both or all of them.

3 View of profit

The business must be one which is carried on 'with a view of profit'[1].

The fact that two or more persons carry on business jointly with a view of profit is not enough to make them partners. Regard must also be had to the destination of the profits when earned.

Thus, when the owner of a business dies and his executors, if there are more than one, carry on his business in accordance with the provisions of his will, the executors are not partners, but they might be if the business was given by the will to the same persons as were named as executors[2].

Whether a salaried partner is to be regarded as a partner in relation to the other members of the firm depends on the circumstances of each case[3].

Rules for determining the existence of a partnership

Where it is not clear whether a person is a partner, various rules for determining the existence of a partnership, which are set out in the Partnership Act 1890, have to be regarded. These rules concern:

(1) joint tenancy and tenancy in common;
(2) the sharing of gross returns; and
(3) the receipt by a person of a share of the profits.

20 See the judgment of Branson J, ibid, at 296 and 473, respectively. See further Ivamy *Casebook on Partnership* (2nd edn 1982) p 2.

1 For an analysis of the meaning of the word 'profits', see *Re Spanish Prospecting Co Ltd* [1911] 1 Ch 92 at 98–101 (per Fletcher Moulton LJ); *Naval Colliery Co Ltd v IRC* (1928) 138 LT 593.

2 See eg *Re Fisher & Sons* [1912] 2 KB 491. Cf *Holme v Hammond* (1872) LR 7 Exch 218, where it was held that the executors of a deceased partner who claimed a share of the profits earned by the firm after his death, but who never interfered in the business, were not liable as partners.

3 *Stekel v Ellice* [1973] 1 All ER 465, [1973] 1 WLR 191 (See the judgment of Megarry J, ibid, at 473 and 199 respectively.) See further Ivamy *Casebook on Partnership* (2nd edn 1982) pp 3–5.

1 Joint tenancy and tenancy in common

Joint tenancy, tenancy in common, joint property, common property or part ownership does not of itself create a partnership as to anything so held or owned, whether the tenants or owners do or do not share any profits by the use thereof[4].

Thus, in *Davis v Davis*[5]:

A father left his two sons his business and three freehold houses in equal shares as tenants in common. They let one of them and employed the rent in enlarging the workshops attached to the two houses. They continued to carry on the business. They each drew out from it a weekly sum, but no accounts were kept. The rent of the third house was divided between them.

Held, by the Chancery Division, that there was a partnership as to the business, but not as to the freehold houses[6].

2 Sharing of gross returns

The sharing of gross returns does not of itself create a partnership whether the persons sharing such returns have or have not a joint interest in any property from which or from the use of which the returns are derived[7].

Thus, where a publisher agrees to pay to an author a royalty on the value of the number of copies of his book which have been sold, this does not of itself create a partnership between them.

Similarly, the letting of a theatre to a producer of a play on the terms of the theatre owner receiving part of the sums paid by the audience for their seats does not of itself make the theatre owner and the producer partners.

Thus, in *Cox v Coulson*[8]:

The defendant was the manager of a theatre and agreed with a Mr Mill to provide the theatre, and pay for the lighting and for the playbills. He was to receive 60 per cent of the gross takings, whilst Mr Mill was to provide and pay for a theatrical company and provide the scenery and receive the remaining 40 per cent. The plaintiff was injured by a shot fired by an actor during the performance of a play at the theatre. She sought inter alia to make the defendant liable on the ground that he was a partner of Mr Mill.

---

4 Partnership Act 1890, s 2(1).
5 [1894] 1 Ch 393, 70 LT 265.
6 See the judgment of North J, ibid, at 396 and 267, respectively. See further Ivamy *Casebook on Partnership* (2nd edn 1982) pp 5–8.
7 Partnership Act 1890, s 2(2).
8 [1916] 2 KB 177, 114 LT 599, CA. For a similar case decided before the Partnership Act 1890, see *Lyon v Knowles* (1893) 3 B & S 556.

Held, by the Court of Appeal, that the defendant could not be made liable on this ground because he was not a partner, for by s 2(2) of the Partnership Act 1890 the sharing of gross returns did not of itself create a partnership[9].

3 Receipt of share of profits

The receipt by a person of a share of the profits is prima facie evidence that he is a partner in the business but the receipt of such a share, or of a payment contingent on or varying with the profits of a business does not of itself make him a partner in the business[10].

There appears to be somewhat of a contradiction for how can a fact be prima facie evidence of partnership and yet be insufficient of itself to prove a partnership?

The position was explained by North J, in the following way[11]:

Adopting then the rule of law which was laid down before the [Partnership Act 1890], and which seems to be precisely what is intended by s 2(3) of the Act, the receipt by a person of a share of the profits of a business is prima facie evidence that he is a partner in it, and if the matter stops there, it is evidence upon which the Court must act. But if there are other circumstances to be considered, they ought to be considered fairly together; not holding that a partnership is proved by the receipt of a share of profits unless it is rebutted by something else; but taking all the circumstances together, not attaching undue weight to any of them but drawing an inference from the whole.

It appears therefore that the effect of s 2(3) is merely to declare the pre-existing law viz. that the sharing of profits without any other facts being proved implies partnership but if it is one of several facts, then all the facts must be considered together, and no particular weight should be given to the fact of profit sharing[12].

Some other cases of receipt of a share of the profits occur also in the case of

  (i) a payment of a debt by instalments;
 (ii) a contract for the remuneration of a servant or agent;
(iii) a widow or child of a deceased partner;
(iv) a loan to a partnership; and
 (v) the sale of the goodwill of a business.

---

9 See the judgment of Swinfen Eady LJ: [1916] 2 KB 177 at 180, 114 LT 599 at 600. See further Ivamy *Casebook on Partnership* (2nd edn 1982) p 8.

10 Partnership Act 1890, s 2(3).

11 In *Davis v Davis* [1894] 1 Ch 393 at 399, 70 LT 265 at 268.

12 See generally *Cox v Hickman* (1860) 8 HL Cas 268; *Syers v Syers* (1876) 1 App Cas 174; *Pooley v Driver* (1876) 5 Ch D 458, 36 LT 79; *Re Howard, ex p Tennant* (1877) 6 Ch D 303; *Re Megevand, ex p Delhasse* (1878) 7 Ch D 511, 38 LT 106, CA; *Badeley v Consolidated Bank* (1888) 38 Ch D 238, 59 LT 419, CA.

(i) *Payment by instalments*

The receipt by a person of a debt or other liquidated amount by instalments or otherwise out of the accruing profits of a business does not of itself make him a partner in the business or liable as such[13].

Thus, if A lends the partnership £5,000 and receives payment of the debt by instalments of £1,000 for each of 5 years out of the profits of the business, this does not of itself make him liable as a partner.

(ii) *Remuneration of servant or agent*

A contract for the remuneration of a servant or agent of a person engaged in a business by a share of the profits of the business does not of itself make the servant or agent a partner in the business or liable as such[14].

Thus, the fact that a sales representative is employed by a partnership on a salary plus a share of the profits does not of itself make him liable as a partner.

(iii) *Widow or child of deceased partner*

A person being the widow or child of a deceased partner and receiving by way of annuity a portion of the profits made in the business in which the deceased person was a partner, is not by reason only of such receipt a partner in the business or liable as such[15].

It is a common clause in a partnership deed that when a partner dies, his widow or child is to be paid an annuity out of the firm's profits. It could scarcely be envisaged that the receipt of a share in these circumstances could be intended to make the recipient liable as a partner.

(iv) *Loan to partnership*

The advance by way of loan to a person engaged or about to engage in any business on a contract with that person that the lender shall receive a rate of interest varying with the profits, or shall receive a share of the profits arising from carrying on the business, does not of itself make the lender a partner with the person or persons carrying on the business or liable as such, provided that the contract is in writing and signed by or on behalf of all the parties thereto[16].

In *Re Young, ex p Jones*[17]:

---

13 Partnership Act 1890, s 2(3).
14 Ibid, s 2(3).
15 Ibid, s 2(3).
16 Ibid, s 2(3). As to the postponement of the rights of the lender in the event of any person to whom the money has been advanced being adjudged a bankrupt, entering into an arrangement to pay his creditors less than the full sum due to them or dying insolvent, see Partnership Act 1890, s 3 and p 109, below.
17 [1896] 2 QB 484, 75 LT 278.

A Mr Lloyd Jones and a Mr Young entered into an agreement by which it was provided that Lloyd Jones should lend £500 to Young in consideration of the payment to Lloyd Jones of £3 per week out of the profits. Lloyd Jones was also to assist in the office, to have control over the money advanced and to be empowered to draw bills of exchange. He also had the right to enter into a partnership within a period of 7 months. A question arose as to whether Lloyd Jones was a partner.

Held, by the Queen's Bench Division, that he was not a partner[18].

Effect of requirement as to writing Here one comes to a difficulty. Did the draftsman of the Act of 1890 intend by the proviso 'provided that the contract is in writing and signed by or on behalf of all parties thereto' to enact or imply that where there is no written and signed contract, a lender who lends on the terms of receiving a rate of interest varying with the profits or of receiving a share of the profits, is prima facie to be deemed a partner?

Smith LJ in *Re Fort, ex p Schofield*[19] seemed to assume that that was the result of s 2(3), saying[20] that 'if the benefit of the section is desired by the lender, then, under the proviso, the contract must be in writing.'

That observation, however, was only a dictum because the court was considering the meaning of s 3 and the absence of a written contract was irrelevant, and with great respect to the learned Lord Justice, it is submitted, cannot be supported. No doubt it is difficult to give any meaning to the proviso unless its effect is such as that indicated by the learned Lord Justice, but, if he is correct, it would follow that a person, who was never a partner, but only a creditor, and with regard to whom the only scintilla of evidence of a partnership is participation in the profits, is, in the absence of a written and signed contract, to be deemed a partner notwithstanding the express words of s 2 that receipt of profits is not of itself sufficient. That, it is conceived, is not the correct interpretation.

What is the correct meaning to be given to the proviso as to the necessity of a written and signed contract still remains obscure. It may not amount to more than that a lender who receives a rate of interest varying with the profits of the borrower's business or a share of those profits, the contract not being in writing, is called on to explain the absence of a written agreement.

But an arrangement whereby in consideration of the payment of a share of the profits to a third person a creditor agrees not to call in a debt is not within s 2(3)(d) of the Act[1].

---

18 See the judgment of Williams J, ibid, at 487 and 279, respectively. See further Ivamy *Casebook on Partnership* (2nd edn 1982) p 9.
19 [1897] 2 QB 495, 77 LT 274.
20 Ibid, at 501. See further Ivamy *Casebook on Partnership* (2nd edn 1982) pp 11–12.
 1 *Re Pinto Leite & Nephews ex p Nisconde des Olivaes* [1929] 1 Ch 221, 140 LT 587.

Provisions to be avoided   One can deduce from the Act and the reported cases some practical rules for advising persons who desire to finance a business and to receive a share of the profits without thereby becoming liable for the debts. Such rules are that

(a) the advance must really be a loan;
(b) the lender should not take a share of the capital;
(c) a provision that the loan should not be used as part of the capital should be avoided;
(d) words usual in partnership agreements should not be referred to; and
(e) clauses should not be taken from partnership precedents.

By bearing them in mind the practitioner will avoid finding himself in the mortifying position of having landed a client, whose intention was to be merely a bona fide lender, in the position of an apparently mala fide partner with all its consequent litigation, worry and possible ruin.

(*a*) *A true loan*   In the first place it is quite clear that one must put to oneself the question: 'Do these persons honestly mean that this advance is to be a true loan or do they mean that it is to be a contribution to a joint adventure?'

To such a question honestly put the answer will generally not be in doubt. For although the courts decline to bind themselves to any authoritative definition of what will render two or more persons partners, the broad distinction between a loan and a contribution to a joint speculation is sufficiently marked.

In the one case the lender is like a debenture holder in that he has no voice in the management of the business. No doubt he is interested in the well-being of the business just as a debenture holder is interested in the well-being of the company whose debentures he holds because its prosperity is his security. But his interest is the interest of a mortgagee, and not of a joint owner, and he is entitled to claim repayment from the borrower whether or not the assets of the business are sufficient for that purpose.

In the other case a contributor to a joint speculation is like a shareholder in a company in that even though he may have no direct control over the details of management, he has a right to prevent misuse of the business assets.

In considering whether there is a bona fide loan the practitioner must remember that a necessary consequence of a loan is a personal liability on the borrower's part to repay it. An arrangement by which a lender is only to be repaid out of the business can therefore never be a loan but must be a partnership[2].

A provision for the return by the lender of a proportion of the profits

2 See eg *Re Megevand, ex p Delhasse* (1878) 7 Ch D 511, 38 LT 106; *Stewart v Buchanan* 1904 6 F (Ct of Sess) 15.

received by him in one year in case of subsequent losses would be almost certainly a mark of partnership for no bona fide lender would ever assent to such a provision.

(*b*) *Share of capital* The lender must not take an interest in or share of the capital because he thereby becomes jointly interested in capital and profits, ie he becomes part owner and a partner in the business itself. Nor must his share of the profits be in the proportion which his loan shall from time to time bear to the rest of the capital in the business, for that shows that he is not lending his money on the security of a share of the profits but is contributing it to a joint speculation in which he and any other speculators are to take the profits pari passu.

(*c*) *Loan not to be used as part of capital* A provision that the borrower shall not be bound to employ the loan as part of the capital of the business is a dangerous one for although it will not of itself constitute the transaction a partnership, it is a somewhat cogent circumstance which might, when taken along with other circumstances, lead the court to conclude that a partnership was intended.

(*d*) *Reference to words usual in partnership agreements* One cannot by any amount of dexterity prevent a transaction which is in substance a partnership having the consequences which are incident to the partnership relation for as Lord Halsbury said[3]:

> If a partnership in fact exists, a community of interest in the adventure being carried on in fact, no verbal equivalent for the ordinary phrases of profit and loss, no indirect expedient for enforcing control over the adventure will prevent the substance and reality being adjudged a partnership . . . and no phrasing of it by dexterous draftsmen will avail to avert the legal consequences of the contract.

But it must not be forgotten that through want of dexterity a draftsman may make a transaction, which is really and bona fide a loan, appear on the face of the document to be a partnership. Care must be taken therefore in drafting such a document to avoid any reference to words usual in partnership agreements, eg 'capital', 'concern', 'partnership' or the like.

(*e*) *Clauses taken from partnership precedents* The draftsman should not be too technical and introduce clauses taken from partnership

---

3 In *Adam v Newbigging* (1888) 13 App Cas 308 at 315. See further *Bullen v Sharp* (1865) LR 1 CP 86; *Holme v Hammond* (1872) LR 7 Ex Ch 218; *Ross v Parkyns* (1875) LR 20 Eq 331; *Kilshaw v Jukes* (1863) 3 B & S 847.

precedents which the partners themselves would never dream of but which he may think desirable, eg arbitration clauses[4].

(v) Sale of goodwill

A person receiving by way of annuity or otherwise a portion of the profits of a business in consideration of the sale by him of the good-will[5] of the business is not by reason only of such receipt a partner in the business or liable as such[6].

Partnership contrasted with limited company

When a person decides to carry on business with help of another, he will have to decide whether it is more advantageous to form a partnership or a limited company.

Some of the considerations[7] which may guide him relate to the differences between partnerships and limited companies. Such differences concern:

(1) formation;
(2) accounts;
(3) debts;
(4) objects;
(5) property;
(6) transfer;
(7) agency;
(8) capital; and
(9) death or bankruptcy.

1 Formation

The principal advantage is that it is relatively easy to form a partnership and to keep it in being whereas in the case of a limited company expenses

---

4 But in *Re Beard & Co, ex p Trustee* [1915] HBR 191 Horridge J said (ibid, at 197): 'people put arbitration clauses in almost every agreement now', and declined to draw an inference from the fact that the agreement in question had an arbitration clause at the end of it.

5 For the meaning of 'goodwill', see p 93, below.

6 Partnership Act 1890, s 2(3). For the postponement of the rights of the seller of the goodwill in consideration of a share of the profits in the event of the buyer being adjudged bankrupt, entering into an arrangement to pay his creditors less than the full sum due to them or dying in insolvent circumstances, see Partnership Act 1890, s 3, and p 109, below.

7 The question of possible tax advantages is outside the scope of this book, and the reader is referred to the standard books on tax law, eg *Simon's Taxes*, vol E.

are incurred in its registration with the Registrar of Companies, and in seeing that the various forms, eg the annual return, are sent to him[8].

2 Accounts

No disclosure of a partnership's accounts is necessary whereas in the case of a limited company they are made public by the requirement that a copy of them must be sent to the Registrar of Companies[9].

3 Debts

A partner is liable for the debts of the firm whereas in the case of a limited company the general rule is that once his shares are fully paid up, a shareholder is under no liability in respect of debts owed by the company[10].

4 Objects

A partnership has power to engage in any business which it likes whereas the 'objects' clause in its memorandum of association restricts the powers of a limited company[11].

5 Property

The property of the partnership belongs to all the partners in common, whereas a limited company has a separate corporate personality[12] and its property belongs to the company alone.

6 Transfer

Subject to any agreement, express or implied, between the partners a partner cannot transfer his share to a person so as to make him a partner without the consent of the other partners[13]. In the case of public companies shares are freely transferable.

7 Agency

A partner is an agent for the firm to make contracts[14]. But, in general, a shareholder is not an agent for the company.

---

 8 Companies Act 1985, s 363.
 9 Ibid, s 241(3)(a).
10 Ibid, s 502(2)(d).
11 Ibid, s 2(1)(c).
12 *Salomon v A Salomon & Co Ltd* [1897] AC 22, 75 LT 426, HL.
13 Partnership Act 1890, s 24(7). See p 42, below.
14 *Ibid*, s 5. See p 56, below.

8 Capital

The capital of the partnership is freely alterable but the capital of a company can be increased or reduced only in accordance with the provisions of the Companies Act 1985[15].

9 Death or bankruptcy

Unless there is an agreement to the contrary, the death or bankruptcy of a partner dissolves the partnership[16]. A company, however, continues in being irrespective of the death or bankruptcy of its shareholders.

---

15 Companies Act 1985, ss 121, 135.
16 Partnership Act 1890, s 33(1). See p 80, below.

Chapter 2

Formation of partnership

A person must have the necessary capacity to enter into a partnership[1], but there are no requirements as to the form of the agreement which have to be fulfilled[2]. Some partnerships are prohibited by law[3]. There are a number of clauses which are to be found in most types of agreements[4]. Discrimination on the ground of sex is not allowed in respect of a woman in the arrangements for a partnership[5].

Capacity to form a partnership

Broadly speaking everyone unless he is an enemy alien is capable of being a partner. A limited company can be a partner if so authorised by its memorandum of association[6]. The capacity of a married woman to enter into a partnership is the same as that of anyone else[7].

But there are certain classes of persons who are exceptions to the general rule, viz.

(1) minors; and
(2) persons of unsound mind.

1 Minors

A person attains full age on reaching the age of 18[8].

Minors who carry on businesses may be dangerous people to trust, and can be made bankrupt only in respect of debts which are legally enforceable against them[9]. But they can still enter into a partnership.

1 See infra.
2 See p 17 below.
3 See p 17 below.
4 See p 19 below.
5 See p 27 below.
6 See eg *Newstead (Inspector of Taxes) v Frost* [1980] 1 All ER 363 [1980] 1 WLR 135, HL.
7 Law Reform (Married Women and Tortfeasors) Act 1935, s 1.
8 Family Law Reform Act 1969, s 1.
9 *Re A and M* [1926] Ch 274, 134 LT 539 (trade debts); *Re A Debtor (No 564 of 1949), ex p Customs and Excise Comrs v Debtor* [1950] Ch 282, [1950] 1 All ER 308 (purchase tax).

In considering the effect of a partnership between an adult and a minor on the rights of third parties Lord Ashbourne observed that[10] 'if the adult members of a partnership could evade liability because one of the partners was a minor, minors would be found in many partnerships'; in fact, there would be a premium on minors if such a new career of usefulness were thrown open to them. This, however, is not so, and Lord Herschell said[11]:

> I think it clear that there is nothing to prevent [a minor] trading, or becoming a partner with a trader, and that until his contract of partnership be disaffirmed he is a member of the trading firm. But it is equally clear that he cannot contract debts by such trading; although goods may be ordered for the firm, he does not become a debtor in respect of them. The adult partner is, however, entitled to insist that the partnership assets shall be applied in payment of the liabilities of the partnership, and that until these are provided for no part of them shall be received by the [minor] partner, and if the proper steps are taken, this right of the adult partner can be made available for the benefit of the creditors. It is also clear that even if there are circumstances under which [a minor] may be adjudicated bankrupt, or a receiving order may lawfully be obtained as a step towards such adjudication, he cannot be made subject to the bankrupt laws in respect of any debt contracted by the firm of which he is a partner.

His Lordship then proceeded to point out that in such cases the judgment should be either against the adult partner alone or preferably against the firm excepting the minor partner, and that under a judgment in either of those forms a receiving order might be obtained against the adult partner, and in the proceedings in bankruptcy the partnership assets might be available for those who might have given credit to the firm.

If, on attaining the age of 18, a minor partner wishes to free himself from the liability for future debts of the firm, he must determine the partnership at once. If he does not do so, the shield of minority is lost, and his position as a de facto partner will make him equally liable with his co-partners.

Failure to repudiate the contract will not, however, render him liable for debts contracted during his minority[12].

If the minor effectively avoids the contract of partnership on attaining his majority, he can recover any money paid by him under it provided that he can show a total failure of consideration[13].

But he may not avoid the contract and at the same time claim benefits under it, and where he is unable or unwilling to place his partners in the

---

10 *Lovell and Christmas v Beauchamp* [1894] AC 607 at 614.
11 Ibid, at 611.
12 *Goode v Harrison* (1821) 5 B & Ald 147.
13 *Steinberg v Scala (Leeds) Ltd* [1923] 2 Ch 452, 129 LT 624, CA; *Pearce v Brain* [1929] 2 KB 310, 141 LT 264.

position they would be in if he had never agreed to join them, he cannot recover money contributed by him to the joint venture.

2 Persons of unsound mind

If a person enters into a contract of partnership and afterwards alleges that he was of unsound mind at the time and did not know what he was doing, the contract, whether executory or executed, is binding on him in every respect as if he had been sane when he made it unless he can also prove that the other partner knew him to be incapable of understanding what he was about[14].

Form of partnership agreement

There is no statute which requires a partnership agreement to be in writing. It is one of the many anomalies of the law that whereas a contract for the sale of a cottage is not enforceable unless it is in writing or unless there is a sufficient note or memorandum of its terms signed by the person against whom the contract is to be enforced or by his duly authorised agent, a partnership agreement relating to a business employing, eg 1,000 people and having a capital of £1,000,000, may be merely verbal.

Of course, in practice, where the business is a large one, such agreements are reduced to writing and generally the terms are embodied in a deed. The law, however, requires nothing of the kind and the terms of a partnership may be proved by parol evidence or even inferred from the course of dealing of the parties, even though the partnership property consists of land or the object of the partnership is to buy and sell land.

But whatever latitude the law may allow, no business-like person should be content with a mere verbal agreement, the burden of proving which would lie on him.

Illegal partnerships

A partnership must not be one with an illegal purpose nor must the number of partners in it exceed that allowed by law.

1 Illegal purpose

A partnership may be illegal if formed for a purpose forbidden by law or which is against public policy.

14 *Imperial Loan Co v Stone* [1892] 1 QB 599, 66 LT 556.

Thus, an unqualified person is forbidden to carry on practice as a solicitor[15], and consequently a partnership between a solicitor and a person who is not qualified is illegal[16].

So, too, a partnership formed for the purpose of sharing the profits of a brothel would clearly be illegal.

In all such cases the court simply refuses to recognise that the partners have any rights against each other, eg it will not direct accounts[17] to be taken, nor will it order one partner to contribute to the losses suffered by the other[18].

This, however, does not prevent innocent creditors of the illegal firm bringing an action against the members to recover a debt which is not to their knowledge tainted with illegality, eg a yacht builder would be entitled to claim from the firm the price of a yacht which was intended to be used for the carriage of illegal immigrants to this country as long as he was not aware of the illegal object.

2 Number of partners allowed

The general rule is that a partnership must not consist of more than twenty persons[19].

But this does not prohibit the formation of [20] –

(1) a partnership carrying on practice as solicitors and consisting of persons each of whom is a solicitor;

(2) a partnership carrying on practice as accountants and consisting of persons each of whom falls within paragraph (a)[1] or paragraph (b)[2] of the Companies Act 1985, s 389(1);

(3) a partnership carrying on business as members of a recognised stock exchange[3] and consisting of persons each of whom is a member of that stock exchange; and

(4) a partnership carrying on business of a description specified in regulations made by the Secretary of State by statutory instrument.

15 Solicitors Act 1974, s 20.
16 *Williams v Jones* (1826) 5 B & C 108.
17 As to the taking of an account, see pp 97–100, below.
18 *Scott v Brown, Doering, McNab & Co* [1892] 2 QB 724, 67 LT 782.
19 Companies Act 1985, s 716(1).
20 Ibid, s 716(2), (3).
 1 Ie a member of a body of accountants established in the United Kingdom and for the time being recognised by the Secretary of State.
 2 Ie a person for the time being authorised by the Secretary of State to be appointed as an auditor either as having similar qualifications obtained outside the United Kingdom or as having obtained adequate knowledge and experience in the course of his employment by a member of a body of accountants recognised for the purpose of paragraph (a) or as having before 6 August 1947, practised in Great Britain as an accountant.
 3 A 'recognised stock exchange' means any body of persons which is for the time being a recognised stock exchange for the purpose of the Prevention of Fraud (Investments) Act 1958: Companies Act 1985, s 744.

Statutory instruments have been passed relating to partnerships consisting of—

(1) patent agents, surveyors, auctioneers, valuers, estate agents, land agents[4] and those engaged in estate management;
(2) actuaries[5];
(3) consulting engineers[6];
(4) building designers[7]; and
(5) loss adjusters[8].

Some usual clauses

The clauses to be found in partnership agreements will naturally vary in accordance with the type of profession or business concerned, eg there will be different clauses for solicitors engaged in a partnership, for medical practitioners, for estate agents and for shopkeepers.

But, in general, the following matters are dealt with in almost all types of partnership:

(1) the nature and place of business;
(2) the firm name;
(3) the duration of the partnership;
(4) the provision of the capital;
(5) the ascertainment and division of profits;
(6) the firm's bank account and the drawing of cheques;
(7) the management of the business;
(8) the accounts;
(9) the death or retirement of a partner;
(10) the restrictions on a partner carrying on a competing business; and
(11) the reference of disputes to arbitration.

Although some of the above matters might be left to be dealt with by the law instead of being made the subject of express stipulation between the parties, the latter is the better course to adopt, even where the express agreement merely states that which the law would imply. As Lord Lindley says[9]:

4 Partnerships (Unrestricted Size) No. 1 Regulations 1968 (SI 1968/1222). See Appendix B, p 191 below.
5 Partnerships (Unrestricted Size) No. 2 Regulations 1970 (SI 1970/835). See Appendix B, p 192, below.
6 Partnerships (Unrestricted Size) No. 3 Regulations 1970 (SI 1970/992). See Appendix B, p 193, below.
7 Partnerships (Unrestricted Size) No. 4 Regulations 1970 (SI 1970/1319). See Appendix B, p 193, below.
8 Partnerships (Unrestricted Size) No. 5 Regulations 1982 (SI 1982/530). See Appendix B, p 198, below.
9 Op cit, p 188.

In framing articles of partnership it should always be remembered that they are intended for the guidance of persons who are not lawyers; and that it is not always wise to insert only such provisions as are necessary to exclude the operation of rules which apply where nothing to the contrary is said. The articles should be so drawn as to be a code of directions to which the partners may refer as a guide in all their transactions, and upon which they may settle among themselves differences which may arise without having recourse to courts of justice.

1 Nature and place of business

The nature of the partnership business should be stated because it is *that* business, and that business only, which the partners agree to carry on, and with regard to which each partner is the agent of the firm, and can bind his partners[10]. It is, therefore, in the highest degree desirable that there should be no possibility of dispute as to what constitutes the real business of the firm.

The place of business should also be defined and an arrangement made for the vesting of the property in the firm or in one or more partners as trustees for the firm[11].

2 Firm name

In general, with regard to the name under which the business is to be carried on and which is usually called the 'firm name', partners may trade under any name they please whether it be a combination of their own several names or the names of others or a name descriptive merely of their business as long as

(i) they comply with the requirements of the Business Names Act 1985; and

(ii) the name chosen does not cause confusion in the minds of the public.

(i) Business Names Act 1985

Compliance with the provisions of the Business Names Act 1985 is necessary where a partnership carries on a business under a name which does not consist of the surnames of all partners who are individuals and the corporate names of all partners who are bodies corporate without any addition other than an addition permitted by the Act[12].

---

10 Partnership Act 1890, s 5. See p 56, below.
11 Not more than four.
12 Business Names Act 1985, s 1(1). See generally Chapter 13, post. The Act is set out in Appendix A, pp 178–182, below.

(ii) Possibility of confusion

Any person can use his own name for the purpose of trade. The mere fact of somebody else having the same name, and carrying on trade under the same name does not prevent another person from doing the same. Accordingly, if John Brown sells coal, another John Brown may sell potatoes, and there is no law to prevent him from doing so.

Again, nothing can be plainer than that if the first John Brown carried on the business under the name not of John Brown but of John Brown & Co, so might the second[13].

Further, Brown may, if he is so disposed, carry on business under a name not his own, borne or used by some other person so long as his doing so is not calculated to deceive the customers of the other person. Thus, James LJ said[14]:

> It should never be forgotten in these cases that the sole right to restrain anybody from using any name that he likes in the course of any business that he chooses to carry on is a right in the nature of a trade mark, that is to say, a man has a right to say 'you must not use a name, whether fictitious or real, you must not use a description, whether true or not, which is *intended to represent*, or is *calculated* to represent to the world that your business is my business, and so by a fraudulent misstatement deprive me of the profits of the business which would otherwise come to me'. That is the principle, and the sole principle, on which this court interferes. The court interferes solely for the purpose of protecting the owner of a trade or business from a wrongful invasion of that business by somebody else. It does not interfere to prevent the *world outside* from being misled into anything.

The name used must not be calculated to deceive either (a) by diverting customers from the other person to himself, or (b) by causing confusion between the two businesses, eg by suggesting that the new business is an extension, branch or agency or otherwise connected with the old[15].

Where such intention is apparent, the court will interfere to prevent persons trading even under their own names.

Thus, in *Croft v Day*[16]

The plaintiffs carried on the business of Day & Martin, the well-known makers of blacking in Holborn, in which there was no longer either a Day or a Martin, both being long since dead. A real 'Day' and a real 'Martin' commenced trading under the name of 'Day & Martin' as makers of blacking. The plaintiffs applied for an injunction to prevent them from doing so.

Held, by Lord Langdale MR , that an injunction would be granted for the name of 'Day & Martin' had been adopted for the fraudulent

13 *Merchant Banking Co of London v Merchants' Joint Stock Bank* (1878) 9 Ch D 560 at 563 (per Jessel MR).
14 In *Levy v Walker* (1879) 10 Ch D 436 at 447.
15 *Ewing v Buttercup Margarine Co Ltd* [1917] 2 Ch 1, 117 LT 67, CA.
16 (1843) 7 Beav 84.

purpose of representing and holding out to the public that the defendants were the old and well-known firm of that name.

The fact of a new trader carrying on business in the name of an old trader of a different name in the same line is not, therefore, of itself illegal unless he is doing it for the fraudulent purpose of passing off his goods as those of his rival, or unless in the absence of fraudulent intention it is evident that the effect will probably be that his goods will be purchased in mistake for those of his rival[17]. The fact that the newcomer is not using his own name speaks for itself and goes a long way to proving that he is acting mala fide. But mala fides is not essential in such a case if there is a high probability of the two firms being confused.

Where, however, a person is trading under his own name, and it happens that the old trader has a similar name, the question becomes more difficult. In any case where the evidence shows that the newcomer is deliberately making a false suggestion or that his name cannot be used in connection with particular goods without representing that they are the goods of his better known rival[18], an injunction will be granted[19].

But where the evidence shows that there was no intention to deceive, although the effect will be in all probability to mistake the new man for the old, it seems questionable whether the newcomer would be prevented from trading under his own name.

A person may not sell the use of his own name to a firm in circumstances which could lead to the same type of confusion[20].

3 Duration of the partnership

It is usual to provide for the date on which the partnership is to commence and for its duration.

Unless a definite term is stated, the general rule is that the partnership lasts only during the will of the partners[21].

The partnership may, however, be continued after the expiration of the agreed term[1].

17 *North Cheshire and Manchester Brewery Co v Manchester Brewery Co* [1899] AC 83, 79 LT 645, HL.
18 *Valentine Meat Juice Co v Valentine Extract Co Ltd* (1900) 83 LT 259.
19 *Burgess v Burgess* (1853) 3 De GM & G 896 at 905 (per Turner LJ); *Levy v Walker* (1879) 10 Ch D 436, 39 LT 654, CA; *Turton v Turton* (1889) 42 Ch D 128, 61 LT 571; *Teofani & Co Ltd v Teofani, Teofani & Co's Trade Mark* [1913] 2 Ch 545; *Crystalate Gramophone Record Manufacturing Co Ltd v British Crystalite Co Ltd* (1934) 51 RPC 315. Cf *Tussaud v Tussaud* (1890) 44 Ch D 678, 62 LT 633.
20 *Kingston, Miller & Co Ltd v Thomas Kingston & Co Ltd* [1912] 1 Ch 575, 106 LT 586; *WH Dorman & Co Ltd v Henry Meadows Ltd* [1922] 2 Ch 332, 127 LT 655.
21 See p 46, below.
 1 See p 48, below.

4 Provision of the capital

The proportion in which the capital is to be subscribed by the partners should be stated in the agreement, and if it is not subscribed equally, provision ought to be made for the payment of interest on capital before the net profits are divided. In the absence of such a stipulation interest on capital is not allowed for the Partnership Act 1890, s 24(1) states:

> Subject to any agreement express or implied between the partners ... a partner is not entitled, before the ascertainment of profits, to interest on the capital subscribed by him.

The necessity of bearing in mind the question of interest on capital is obvious when one considers that there is no necessary inference that partners share profits in proportion to their respective amounts of capital[2].

Suppose, for instance, that A and B agree to enter into partnership and that A is a clever and experienced buyer of goods but has little capital, whereas B, although he lacks technical experience, has money. In these circumstances it may be quite fair and proper that although A brings in only £10,000 of capital and B subscribes £50,000, the profits should be divided equally. Nevertheless it is also just that before those profits are ascertained, each partner should receive interest on his capital, ie it should be regarded as a loan to the firm. Accordingly, provision to this effect should be made in the articles.

5 Ascertainment and division of profits

Profits (ie net profits which are alone divisible) are the moneys received minus the expenses or outgoings[3].

The Partnership Act 1890, s 24(1) states:

> Subject to any agreement express or implied between the partners .... all the partners are entitled to share equally in the .... profits of the business ....

The inference of law is that the net profits of each year must be ascertained on the footing of the moneys actually received less those actually paid in that year without reference to when the work was done in respect of which the moneys were received[4]. Where, therefore, this inference is not in accordance with the intention of the parties, it is necessary to specify that intention with regard to what is to constitute profit.

---

2 See below.

3 As to the meaning of 'profits', see *Re Spanish Prospecting Co Ltd* [1911] 1 Ch 92 at 99–101 (per Fletcher Moulton LJ); *Vulcan Motor and Engineering Co v Hampson* [1921] 3 KB 597, 125 LT 717, CA; *Naval Colliery Co (1897) Ltd v IRC* (1928) 138 LT 593.

4 *Maclaren v Stainton* (1861) 3 De GF & J 202 at 214 (per Turner LJ); *Badham v Williams* (1902) 86 LT 191; *JP Hall & Co Ltd v IRC* [1921] 3 KB 152, 125 LT 720, CA.

Moreover, the inference of law is so contrary to general practice that the question should always be brought to the notice of intending partners. The system of credit which prevails in all businesses prevents the possibility of large cash returns in the first year of a partnership. Yet at the end of the year the book debts representing work done may be large. It is, therefore, usual to provide that book debts are to be taken into consideration in ascertaining profits subject to a deduction of ten per cent for bad or doubtful debts.

This enables the partners to draw these as profits of the first year as and when they are paid instead of waiting until the expiration of the year in which they are actually paid. It must be understood, however, that where a new partnership is formed to carry on an old business, the new partners do not share in the existing book debts unless there is an express stipulation to that effect[5].

Further, in ascertaining profits an increase in the value of the goodwill[6] is considered as an accretion to capital, and is not to be taken into account in calculating profits[7]. It is usual to provide that in taking the annual accounts goodwill is to be disregarded or put in at book value.

As profits are generally divided only once a year or at the most every six months, some provision should be made enabling the partners to draw out monthly sums for their current private expenses on account of future profits.

Consideration should also be given to the payment of salaries, particularly where not all the partners are required to give their full time and attention to the business.

6 Bank account and drawing of cheques

The articles usually specify the bank and also state that all cheques and moneys received by the firm should forthwith be paid into the bank account.

They also may make some provision as to who is to sign cheques. In the absence of agreement each partner can sign cheques on behalf of the partnership. Where, however, an elderly man takes a young partner or, as sometimes happens, promotes a clerk or employee to a share in the business, it is quite usual to stipulate that all cheques are to be signed by the senior partner.

7 Management of the business

It is usual to specify whether all or some only of the partners are to take

5 *Badham v Williams*, above at 192 (per Kekewich J).
6 As to goodwill, see pp 93–96, below.
7 *Steuart v Gladstone* (1878) 10 Ch D 626, 38 LT 557.

part in the management of the business, and also that the partner or partners who do so are to give their whole time to it. In the absence of such a stipulation each partner is entitled to participate in the management.

It is also desirable in order to prevent disputes to specify what holidays each partner is to be entitled to, and how each partner is to choose the date of them.

It is also usual to insert a stipulation that no partner is to enter into any contract exceeding a specified amount, and that he is not to give credit to a debtor beyond a certain sum. Another clause may state the extent of a partner's power to engage or dismiss an employee.

8 Accounts

Partnership articles should always provide for the keeping of accounts, and for an annual or sometimes half yearly balance sheet. As to such provisions, Lord Lindley says: 'The object of taking partnership accounts is twofold, viz. (1) to show how the firm stands as regards strangers, and (2) to show how each partner stands towards the firm. The accounts, therefore, which the articles should require to be taken, should be such as will accomplish this twofold object. The articles should consequently provide, not only for the keeping of proper books of account, and for the due entry therein of all receipts and payments, but also for the making up yearly of a general account, showing the then assets and liabilities of the firm, and what is due to each partner in respect of his capital and share of profits, or what is due from him to the firm, as the case may be'[8].

9 Death or retirement of a partner

The Partnership Act 1890, s 33(1) states:

> Subject to any agreement between the partners, every partnership is dissolved as regards all the partners by the death . . . of any partner.

A moment's thought, however, will make it clear that this is very undesirable in most businesses, and absolutely ruinous in many cases where a firm has got together a large and valuable connection, and in which that intangible but very valuable asset called 'goodwill'[9] could vanish into air if the firm were dissolved by the death of a partner.

It is usual and desirable therefore to make provision for continuing the firm notwithstanding the death of one or more of the partners, by stating that the business is not to be wound up, but that instead the surviving partner or partners is to continue to carry it on.

8 Op cit, p 201.
9 As to goodwill, see pp 93–96, below.

Provisions are also inserted for the method of ascertainment of the deceased partner's share of the assets and of the amount to be paid to his personal representatives[10]. By this means the continuity of the business is not disturbed while the interests of the personal representatives of the deceased partner are safeguarded.

In framing such clauses it is usual and convenient to provide that the last balance sheet, if it has been made up at the date stated in the articles, is to be conclusive as to the amount of the deceased partner's share of the assets. The appropriate clause may also state that if from any cause the balance sheet has not been so made up, then the omission is to be remedied, the personal representatives of the deceased partner joining with the surviving partners in taking the necessary account.

It is also a convenient plan to provide that the personal representatives of the deceased partner are to be entitled to a fixed allowance or rate of interest on capital in lieu of current profits since the last balance sheet. If this is not done, it will be necessary to take an account of profits from the date of the last balance sheet down to the date of the deceased partner's death.

The above is merely an outline of the simplest form of arrangement in relation to the death of a partner. There are, however, many other forms. Sometimes the personal representatives succeed to the deceased partner's share as sleeping partners. Sometimes an annuity is made payable out of the profits to the deceased partner's widow[11]. Sometimes there are provisions enabling a partner to nominate his successor by his will, but in that case the articles should provide that such a successor must execute a deed agreeing to be bound by the articles.

What is said above in relation to provisions relating to a partner's death applies equally to the case of a partner who desires to retire from the partnership.

10 Restrictions on retiring partner

A restriction intended to prevent a retiring partner from carrying on a competing business is often inserted especially in medical partnerships.

Such a restriction is legally enforceable only if it is a reasonable one. What is reasonable depends on the circumstances of each case[12].

---

10 See eg *Watson v Haggitt* [1928] AC 127, 138 LT 306, PC.
11 A widow of a deceased partner, who receives by way of annuity a portion of the profits of the business in which the deceased person was a partner, is not by reason only of such receipt a partner in the business or liable as such: Partnership Act 1890, s 2 (3).
12 See eg *McFarlane v Kent* [1965] 2 All ER 376, [1965] 1 WLR 1019 (medical partnership); *Lyne-Pirkis v Jones* [1969] 3 All ER 738, [1969] 1 WLR 1293, CA (medical partnership); *Peyton v Mindham* [1971] 3 All ER 1215, [1972] 1 WLR 8 (medical partnership); *Oswald Hickson, Collier & Co v Carter-Ruck* [1984] AC 720n, [1984] 2 All ER 15, CA (solicitors' partnership); *Bridge v Deacons* (a firm) [1984] AC 705, [1984] 2 All ER 19, PC (solicitors' partnership).

Thus, in *Whitehill v Bradford*[13]:

Four doctors carried on a partnership as general medical practitioners in Atherstone in Warwickshire. The partnership deed was dated 9 February 1945 and stated by clause 21 that a retiring partner should be for 21 years prohibited 'from directly or indirectly carrying on or being interested or concerned in carrying on the profession of medicine, surgery, midwifery, or pharmacy or any branch thereof anywhere within a radius of 10 miles of the parish church of Atherstone . . . but the above prohibition shall only apply to a retiring . . . partner carrying on or being interested in the profession of a general medical practitioner'. In 1951 99 per cent of the partnership's patients lived within a radius of 5 miles. In that year Bradford retired and continued to practise in the district. The other partners applied for an injunction to restrain him from doing so.

Held, by the Court of Appeal, that the injunction would be granted. The restraint was reasonable in regard to its extent and its radius[14].

11 Arbitration

There is almost always an arbitration clause. The reason for such a clause is the proverbial one that it is better to wash dirty linen at home. Nothing injures a business as much as the knowledge that the partners are in a state of litigation, and it is consequently well recognised that to resort to private arbitration rather than to the court is much wiser in the interests of all parties[15].

If it is intended to bind persons claiming under the partners, eg the mortgagee of a partner's share, by an arbitration clause, this should be made clear in the clause itself[16].

Sex discrimination

It is unlawful for a firm consisting of six or more partners, in relation to a position as partner in the firm, to discriminate against a woman—

13 [1952] Ch 236, [1952] 1 All ER 115, CA.
14 See the judgment of Sir Raymond Evershed MR: ibid, at 245 and 117 respectively. See further Ivamy *Casebook on Partnership* (2nd edn 1982) pp 83–85.
15 See eg *Stekel v Ellice* [1973] 1 All ER 465, [1973] 1 WLR 191, where a deed relating to a partnership of accountants stated that doubts and questions were to be decided by an expert to be nominated, in default of agreement, by the President of the Institute of Chartered Accountants with an extensive power to give directions including directions dissolving the partnership; *Phoenix v Pope* [1974] 1 All ER 512, [1974] 1 WLR 719, where a clause in a solicitors' partnership deed stated that any dispute was to be referred to a single arbitrator to be appointed by the partners, or, if they could not agree, by a single arbitrator to be nominated by the President of the Law Society.
16 *Bonnin v Neame* [1910] 1 Ch 732, 102 LT 708.

(1) in the arrangements they make for the purpose of determining who should be offered that position[17], or

(2) in the terms on which they offer her that position[18], or

(3) by refusing or deliberately omitting to offer her that position[19].

The above provisions apply to persons proposing to form themselves into a partnership as well as they apply in relation to a firm[20].

---

17 Sex Discrimination Act 1975, s 11(1)(a). This subsection does not apply to a position as partner where, if it were employment, being a man would be a genuine occupational qualification for the job: ibid, s 11(3).

18 Ibid, s 11(1)(b). This subsection does not apply to a provision made in relation to death or retirement: ibid, s 11(4).

19 Ibid, s 11(1)(c). This subsection does not apply to a position as partner, where if it were employment, being a man would be a genuine occupational qualification for the job: ibid, s 11(3).

20 Ibid, s 11(2).

Chapter 3

The relation of partners to one another

The relation of partners to one another may, of course, be wholly governed by the terms of the partnership agreement[1]. One may agree to do all the work in consideration of the other finding the capital. One may reserve to himself the sole right of signing cheques or even of expelling a partner if he thinks fit. One may take a fixed sum out of the profits leaving the remainder, if any, to be divided among the other partners. Further, the business may be ostensibly carried on by one partner only, the other taking no active part in its administration. In such a case the passive partner is called a 'sleeping partner'. But as far as the creditors are concerned he is as much a partner and as responsible as such as if he took an equally active part in the administration of the firm with the partner who ostensibly carries it on[2].

The terms of the partnership agreement may be varied with the consent of all the partners[3].

Property originally brought into the firm or subsequently acquired with money belonging to it is 'partnership property'[4]. A writ of execution cannot be issued against such property except on a judgment against the firm [5], but a charging order may be made in respect of a partner's share in the partnership property for the amount of a judgment debt owed by him to a judgment creditor[6].

In the absence of agreement between them there are certain rights given to a partner, eg as to capital and profits, and as to a right to take part in the management of the partnership business[7].

No majority of the partners may expel any partner[8].

A partnership for an undefined time may be determined by a partner on giving notice of termination[9].

1 See pp 19–27, above.
2 See pp 55–56, below.
3 See p 30, below.
4 See pp 31–35, below.
5 See p 35, below.
6 See pp 35–36, below.
7 See pp 36–45, below.
8 See pp 45–46, below.
9 See pp 46–47, below.

The partners' rights and duties may remain the same even though the original term of the partnership has expired[10].

Certain duties are imposed on partners, eg to render true accounts and full information to each other[11].

An assignee of a partner's share in the firm has only limited rights in respect of its business[12].

Sex discrimination against a woman partner in a firm over a certain size is unlawful[13].

Variation of terms of partnership

The mutual rights and duties of partners, whether ascertained by agreement or defined by the Partnership Act 1890, may be varied by the consent of all the partners, and such consent may be either express or inferred from a course of dealing[14].

Thus, in *Cruikshank v Sutherland*[15]:

Clause 13 of a partnership deed stated that on 30 April a full and general account was to be made of the partnership dealings for the preceding year. By clause 16 the amount of the share of a deceased partner was to be ascertained by reference to the account made on 30 April next after his death. The partnership was for four years from 1 May 1914, and was a renewal of partnership relations which had subsisted between the parties. In forming the partnership of 1914 the assets of the previous firm were taken over at the value appearing in the partnership books. The accounts of 30 April 1915, and 30 April 1916, were prepared on the footing of bringing in the assets at their book values. Mr Cruikshank, who was one of the partners, was a party to the 1915 accounts but not to the 1916 accounts. He died on 27 October 1916. An issue arose as to whether his share of the partnership profits had to be calculated on the fair value of the property or on its book value. The other partners contended that by the course of dealing the value of the property was to be ascertained by looking at its book value.

Held, by the House of Lords, that the value of the property should be taken as its fair value to the firm, and that no course of dealing had been proved to show that the value should be the book value[16].

10 See p 48, below.
11 See pp 48–51, below.
12 See pp 51–53, below.
13 See p 53, below.
14 Partnership Act 1890, s 19.
15 (1923) 128 LT 449, HL.
16 See the judgment of Lord Wrenbury, ibid, at 451. See further Ivamy *Casebook on Partnership* (2nd edn 1982) pp 24–26.

Partnership property

1 Importance and meaning of 'partnership property'

The point as to whether property is partnership property is often of great importance

(1) *as between the partners themselves* because an increase in the value of partnership property belongs to the firm, whereas if the property is the property of an individual partner, the increased value belongs to him alone[17];

(2) *as between the creditors of the firm and the creditors of the individual partners* in the event of the firm becoming insolvent[18]; and

(3) *as between the persons who take a deceased's partner's real estate and those who take his personal estate* because his interest in partnership land is personalty and not realty[19].

All property and rights and interests in property originally brought into the partnership stock or acquired, whether by purchase or otherwise, on account of the firm, or for the purposes and in the course of the partnership business, are called in the Partnership Act 1890 'partnership property', and must be held and applied by the partners exclusively for the purposes of the partnership and in accordance with the partnership agreement[20].

Difficult questions frequently arise as to whether property is the property of the firm or of individual partners, for property may be used for the purposes of the partnership and yet may not be part of the partnership property.

The first principle in relation to the question whether property is partnership property depends on the agreement, express or implied, between the partners.

Where there is an express and unambiguous agreement between them in relation to any item of property, no difficulty arises. Thus, although the 'goodwill' of the business is prima facie partnership property, it is open to one of the partners to prove that the goodwill was his before the partnership was formed, and that it was agreed that, although the firm should have the benefit of it during the partnership, it should revert to him on a dissolution[1]. Again, office furniture or tools may be used by the firm and yet, by agreement, remain the property of one partner.

In the absence of express agreement, however, one must fall back on an implied one, ie both partners being given credit for common sense and

---

17 *Robinson v Ashton* (1875) LR 20 Eq 25.
18 See p 103, below.
19 See p 34, below.
20 Partnership Act 1890, s 20(1).
 1 As to goodwill, see pp 93–96, below

business capacity, a reasonable inference as to what was the exact understanding between them must be drawn.

The question whether property is or is not partnership property is always one of fact, and one must endeavour to ascertain whether the property has been treated as part of the common stock, or merely used, either at a rent or by gratuitous licence, as ancillary to the carrying on of the business.

Thus, in *Miles v Clarke*[2]:

Clarke carried on business as a photographer at premises of which he owned the lease for seven years from 1948. In 1950 he and Miles, who was a freelance photographer, entered into partnership by which all the profits were to be shared equally. Miles brought with him his personal connection. The partners quarrelled, and a dispute arose as to whether the following items constituted partnership property: (i) the consumable stock-in-trade; (ii) the personal connection brought in by each partner; (iii) the lease of the premises; and (iv) the furniture, fittings and equipment of the studios.

Held, by the Chancery Division, that no more agreement between the parties should be supposed than was absolutely necessary to give business efficacy to the relationship between the parties. Accordingly, since the only agreement was as to the share of the profits, only the consumable stock-in-trade should be regarded as partnership property[3].

2 Co-owners of estate in land

Where co-owners of an estate or interest in any land, not being itself partnership property, are partners as to profits made by the use of that land, and purchase other land or estate out of the profits to be used in like manner, the land or estate so purchased belongs to them, in the absence of an agreement to the contrary, not as partners, but as co-owners for the same respective estates and interests as are held by them in the land or estate at the date of the purchase[4].

Thus, in *Davis v Davis*[5]:

Partners in a business borrowed money on the security of some property of which they were tenants in common. They expended the money partly in erecting some workshops on the property as an addition to works in which they carried on the partnership business, and which also belonged to them as co-owners.

2 [1953] 1 All ER 779, [1953] 1 WLR 537.
3 See the judgment of Harman J, ibid, at 781 and 540 respectively. See further Ivamy *Casebook on Partnership* (2nd edn 1982) pp 26–28.
4 Partnership Act 1890, s 20(3).
5 [1894] 1 Ch 393, 70 LT 265.

Held, by the Chancery Division, that the workshops did not become partnership property, for there was no evidence that the parties had such àn intention[6].

But, in *Waterer v Waterer*[7]:

A nurseryman carried on business on a piece of freehold land belonging to him in fee simple. On his death he devised all his property to his three sons as tenants in common. They continued the nursery business in partnership, and out of money belonging to the father's estate completed the purchase of adjacent land which he had agreed to buy. The land was also used in the business. Two of the sons then purchased the third son's share in the land and the business, and continued the business. One of the two sons died and the question arose as to whether the land was partnership property.

Held, by James LJ, that it was partnership property[8].

3 Property bought with partnership money

Unless the contrary intention appears, property bought with money belonging to the firm is deemed to have been bought on account of the firm[9].

Thus, in *Wray v Wray*[10]:

William Wray carried on business under his own name. He took into partnership his sons Henry Wray and William James Wray, and also Joseph Turnbull. The business was still carried on in the name of 'William Wray'. William Wray died in 1885, and his widow, Eliza Wray, became a partner. In 1890 the partners bought North Hill House, Highgate, and the purchase price was paid out of the partnership assets. The property was conveyed to 'William Wray', this name being signed by Henry Wray with the concurrence of the other partners. Henry Wray retired and received the full value of his share of the partnership assets. He died in 1902. The three continuing partners sought a declaration that the conveyance of North Hill House to 'William Wray' passed to the persons carrying on business under the style of 'William Wray' ie the continuing partners and the late Henry Wray as part of the partnership property, because it had been purchased out of the partnership assets.

Held, by the Chancery Division, that the declaration would be granted[11].

6 See the judgment of North J, ibid, at 396 and 267, respectively.
7 (1873) LR 15 Eq 402.
8 See the judgment of James LJ, ibid, at 406.
9 Partnership Act 1890, s 21.
10 [1905] 2 Ch 349, 93 LT 304.
11 See the judgment of Warrington J, ibid, at 351 and 305, respectively. See further Ivamy *Casebook on Partnership* (2nd edn 1982) pp 28–29.

Further, if the property which has been bought with partnership money is brought into the common stock and credited in the books as part of the capital of one of the partners[12], or otherwise treated by the partners as part of the partnership property[13], the inference is that it is partnership property; and none the less so because the property happens to have been conveyed to or taken in the name of only one of the partners[14], or that it was originally devised to the partners as co-owners[15].

4 Devolution of partnership property

Where land has become partnership property, it is to be treated, unless the contrary intention appears, as between the partners (including the representatives of a deceased partner), as personal and not real estate[16].

The principle is that prima facie (ie in the absence of agreement to the contrary) all the property of the firm, real and personal, has to be sold on the dissolution of the partnership[17]. Consequently, in Equity, it is deemed to have been already converted into personal estate and therefore devolves as such.

If, however, on the true construction of the partnership articles, it appears to have been the intention that the real estate of the firm should not be sold on dissolution, but should continue to be held in joint tenancy or tenancy in common, the presumption is rebutted, and it will devolve as real estate[18].

Anyhow, the conversion, even where it exists, is only a tenure in Equity, and the legal estate or interest devolves according to the nature and tenure of the land, but in trust for the persons beneficially interested in the land[19].

Consequently if several partners are joint owners of land in fee simple or for a term of years, the legal estate will devolve, on the death of one of them, on the survivors subject to the equitable rights of the deceased partner's personal representatives[20].

Again, if the legal estate in the land is vested in one partner alone, it will vest, on his death, in his personal representatives in trust for the

---

12 *Robinson v Ashton* (1875) LR 20 Eq 25.
13 *Waterer v Waterer* (1873) LR 15 Eq 402. See p 33, above.
14 *Smith v Smith* (1800) 5 Ves 189 at 193.
15 *Waterer v Waterer* (above).
16 Partnership Act 1890, s 22.
17 As to the dissolution of partnership, see pp 79–85, below.
18 See *Re Wilson, Wilson v Holloway* [1893] 2 Ch 340, 68 LT 785; *Steward v Blakeway* (1869) 4 Ch App 603.
19 Partnership Act 1890, s 20(2).
20 *Wray v Wray* [1905] 2 Ch 349, 93 LT 304.

other partners and the persons entitled to the deceased partner's estate according to the partnership agreement[1].

Procedure against partnership property

Writ of execution

A writ of execution cannot be issued against any partnership property[2] except on a judgment against the firm[3].

Thus, in *Peake v Carter*[4]:

Peake and Bellamy were partners, and by an agreement dated 14 July 1914, bought a china clay mine including its machinery. The purchase price in respect of the machinery was paid by Peake. Carter obtained judgment against Bellamy in respect of a debt, and the machinery was seized by the sheriff. Peake contended that the goods were his own property, but the trial Judge held that he had not established his claim to them, and without calling on the execution creditor to give evidence, gave judgment for him. Peake appealed and applied for a new trial.

Held, by the Court of Appeal, that a new trial would be ordered for although Peake had failed to prove that the machinery was his own property, he was not thereby precluded from relying on the fact that it had been found to be partnership property, and accordingly under s 23(1) of the Partnership Act 1890 execution could not issue against the machinery except on a judgment against the firm[5].

Charging order

The High Court, or a judge thereof, or a county court, may on the application by summons of any judgment creditor of a partner, make an order charging the partner's interest in the partnership property with payment of the amount of the judgment debt and interest[6].

The High Court, or a judge thereof, or a county court, may by the same or a subsequent order appoint a receiver of that partner's share of

1 Administration of Estates Act 1925, s 1; *Re Somerville and Turner's Contract* [1903] 2 Ch 583, 89 LT 405.
2 See p 31, above.
3 Partnership Act 1890, s 23(1).
4 [1916] 1 KB 652, 114 LT 273, CA.
5 See the judgment of Swinfen Eady LJ, ibid, at 274. See further Ivamy *Casebook on Partnership* (2nd edn 1982) pp 29–30.
6 Partnership Act 1890, s 23(2). A master or the Admiralty Registrar or a district registrar may exercise the powers conferred on a judge by this subsection: RSC Ord 81, r 10(2).

the profits (whether already declared or accruing), and of any other money which may be coming to him in respect of the partnership, and direct all accounts and inquiries, and give all other orders and directions which might have been directed or given if the charge had been made in favour of the judgment creditor by the partner, or which the circumstances of the case may require[7].

But the power to order accounts to be taken will be exercised only in special circumstances.

Thus, in *Brown, Janson & Co v A Hutchinson & Co (No 2)*[8]:

The plaintiffs applied for an order under s 23(2) of the Partnership Act 1890 charging the interest of a partner in the partnership business with the amount of a judgment debt. The order was made, and they now applied for an order for accounts and inquiries under the same subsection.

Held, by the Court of Appeal, that the order would not be made except in exceptional circumstances, and no such circumstances were proved to exist in the present case[9].

The other partner or partners are at liberty at any time to redeem the interest charged, or, in the case of a sale being directed, to purchase it[10].

The detailed procedure to be followed in the case of an application for an order charging a partner's interest in partnership property is set out in RSC Order 81, rule 10[11].

A partnership may at the option of the other partners be dissolved if any partner suffers his share of the partnership property to be charged for his separate debt[12].

But there is no similar provision with regard to voluntary assignments or mortgages of a share although partners might reasonably object to one of their number depriving himself of all beneficial interest in the business, and, therefore, of all incentive to exertion for the common good[13].

Rights of partners

The Partnership Act 1890, s 24 gives certain rights to partners, subject to any agreement express or implied between them. These rights relate to:

7 Partnership Act 1890, s 23(2).
8 [1895] 2 QB 126, 73 LT 8, CA.
9 See the judgment of Rigby LJ, ibid, at 131 and 10, respectively. See further Ivamy
   Casebook on Partnership (2nd edn 1982) pp 31–32.
10 Partnership Act 1890, s 23(3).
11 See Appendix C, p 205, below.
12 Partnership Act 1890, s 33(2). See p 80, below.
13 As to the rights of an assignee, see p 51, below.

(1) capital and profits[14];
(2) indemnity against liability in the firm's business[15];
(3) advances to the firm made by a partner[16];
(4) interest on capital[17];
(5) management of the partnership business[18];
(6) remuneration[19];
(7) introduction of a new partner[20];
(8) differences as to ordinary matters[1]; and
(9) the partnership books[2].

1 Capital and profits

Subject to any agreement express or implied between the partners, all the partners are entitled to share equally in the capital and profits of the business, and must contribute equally towards the losses of capital or otherwise sustained by the firm[3].

There are many partnerships, perhaps the majority, in which the capital is not contributed equally, and indeed, is perhaps all contributed by one partner. For although every partner must contribute either money or goods or industry to the undertaking, 'capital' in the legal sense only embraces property and not mere skill or industry.

Consequently s 24(1) of the Partnership Act 1890 does not mean that where of two partners one contributes, eg £10,000 as capital, and the other contributes no money, but merely great technical skill and knowledge, the assets into which the £10,000 has been converted are, on the dissolution of the firm, to be divided equally as one common fund, for the facts negative the idea that the capital was equal, and s 24(1) only applies in the absence of a contrary agreement, express or implied.

What s 24(1) means is that in such a case the *profits* would be divided equally because in the absence of express agreement the inference is that the £10,000 of the moneyed partner was considered to be the equivalent of the skill or knowledge of the other partner.

But if they divide the profits equally, they must likewise equally divide the losses, and losses include not only the liabilities of the firm to third parties but also losses of capital. Therefore, assuming that the £10,000 were lost, the partner who brought no capital into the firm would

14 See pp 37–39, below.
15 See pp 39–40, below.
16 See p 40, below.
17 See pp 40–41, below.
18 See p 41, below.
19 See pp 41–42, below.
20 See pp 42–43, below.
 1 See pp 43–44, below.
 2 See pp 44–45, below.
 3 Partnership Act 1890, s 24(1).

nevertheless have to bear half that loss in favour of the moneyed partner.

Suppose, therefore, that A, B and C enter into partnership on the terms of A finding £10,000 capital, B £5,000 and C contributing only skill and knowledge, and that the profits are to be shared equally. Suppose further that on a dissolution of the partnership, the surplus assets amount to £6,000 only. This means a loss of £9,000 capital which must be borne equally, each partner contributing £3,000. The £6,000 surplus plus the £9,000 contributed will then be used to repay to A and B the £10,000 and £5,000 respectively. Each partner will then be £3,000 out of pocket.

If any partner is insolvent and unable to contribute his share of lost capital, the solvent partners are not liable to contribute it for him, but the amount available after the solvent partners have made their proper contributions is divided rateably according to the amount of capital standing to the credit of each partner (not including, of course, an insolvent partner who has failed to bear his share of the loss).

Thus, in *Garner v Murray*[4]:

A partnership had been formed upon the terms that the capital should be contributed by the three partners in unequal shares, but that they should receive equal shares of the net profits. After all the liabilities of the firm had been paid and all advances made by the partners had been repaid the assets were insufficient to repay the capital. The deficit arose by reason of the default of the third partner to contribute his share of the deficiency. The question was how this deficiency was to be borne.

Held, by the Chancery Division, each partner was liable to contribute one-third of the deficiency, because this was the proportion in which the profits were divisible. There was nothing in the Partnership Act 1890, s 44[5] to make a solvent partner liable to contribute for an insolvent partner, who failed to pay his share[6].

Suppose therefore that A, B and C enter into partnership on the same terms as those in the earlier example, but that C is insolvent. In this case A and B do not contribute £4,500 each so as to make up C's share, but only their proper shares of £3,000 each. The total of £6,000 surplus and the £6,000 contributed ie £12,000 thus made available for division will go as to £8,000 to A, and as to £4,000 to B. A will be £5,000 out of pocket and B £4,000.

In short, all that s 24(1) means is that there is no necessary connection between the proportion in which the capital is contributed and that of profit and loss, and that therefore prima facie partners share profits and bear losses equally, notwithstanding that the capital contributed by each

---

4 [1904] 1 Ch 57, 89 LT 665.
5 See p 100, below.
6 See the judgment of Joyce J: [1904] 1 Ch 57 at 59 and 89 LT 665 at 666. See further Ivamy *Casebook on Partnership* (2nd edn 1982) p 74.

may not be equal. In other words profit and loss are not shared in proportion to the *capital* contributed by each partner.

On the other hand, there is an inference that *losses* are to be borne in the same proportion as *profits* are shared. Therefore an agreement to share profits in certain proportions is by the Partnership Act 1890, s 44[7] made prima facie evidence that it was intended that losses should be borne in the same proportions and not equally.

2 Indemnity against liability in firm's business

Subject to any agreement express or implied between the partners, the firm must indemnify every partner in respect of payments made and personal liabilities incurred by him in the ordinary and proper conduct of the business of the firm[8].

Thus, in *Matthews v Ruggles-Brice*[9]:

Leasehold premises were let to Mr Coope and Mr Matthews for 42 years from 12 February 1879. They took up the lease as trustees for themselves and 8 other partners in Ind Coope & Co. In 1886 Ind Coope & Co Ltd was incorporated to take over the partnership undertaking and assets, and the company agreed to take over all the debts and liabilities of the partnership. Coope died in 1886. In 1887 Matthews assigned the lease to the company. Matthews died in 1891, and the plaintiffs were his executors. In 1909 the lessor sued the plaintiffs for arrears of rent and breaches of covenants in the lease. The company was insolvent, and the action was settled by the surrender of the lease and a payment of £5,750. The plaintiffs claimed a contribution from the defendants, who were Coope's executors in respect of the money so paid.

Held, by the Chancery Division, that the action succeeded[10].

As a general rule the right to indemnity is not lost by reason of the partner who incurred the liability being more at fault than the other members of the firm unless he has been guilty of fraud or gross negligence[11].

Further, subject to any agreement express or implied between the partners, the firm must indemnify every partner in respect of payments made and personal liabilities incurred by him in or about anything

7 See p 100, below.
8 Partnership Act 1890, s 24(2)(a).
9 [1911] 1 Ch 194, 103 LT 491.
10 See the judgment of Swinfen Eady J, ibid, at 202 and 492, respectively. See further Ivamy *Casebook on Partnership* (2nd edn 1982) pp 32–33.
11 Cf *Re Protestant Assurance Association, ex p Letts and Steer* (1857) 26 LJ Ch 455 and *Thomas v Atherton* (1877) 10 Ch D 185, 40 LT 77.

necessarily done for the preservation of the business or property of the firm[12].

The right to indemnity lies in respect of necessary acts and does not extend to mere voluntary ones which the partner, who undertakes the liability, thinks may be advantageous[13].

3 Advances to firm made by partner

Subject to any agreement express or implied between the partners, a partner making, for the purpose of the partnership, any actual payment or advance beyond the amount of capital which he has agreed to subscribe, is entitled to interest at the rate of five per cent per annum from the date of the payment or advance[14].

The reason for this is stated by Lord Lindley to be that such an advance is not treated as an increase of capital but rather as a loan on which interest ought to be paid and by commercial usage is payable[15].

The rate of interest may be different if an agreement can be inferred from the custom of the particular trade[16] or from the course of dealing between the partners[17].

Although the firm pays interest to a partner on his advances, the converse does not hold good, and in the absence of fraud or express agreement a partner who is indebted to the firm is not liable to pay interest on the debt[18].

4 Interest on capital

Subject to any agreement express or implied between the partners, a partner is not entitled, before the ascertainment of profits, to interest on the capital subscribed by him[19].

If a partner is unwilling to find the necessary capital without receiving interest, he should make the payment of interest on capital an express condition of his bargain with his partner whose skill has prima facie been accepted by the moneyed partner as an equivalent for the latter's capital.

It is usual for the partnership deed to provide that, before the profits are ascertained, each partner is to be entitled to receive interest at a specified rate per annum on the amount of capital from time to time standing to his credit, and that such interest is to be treated as an outgoing, and paid in priority to any division of profits.

12 Partnership Act 1890, s 24(2)(b).
13 See the judgment of Turner LJ in *Burdon v Barkus* (1862) 4 De GF & J 42 at 51.
14 Partnership Act 1890, s 24(3).
15 Op cit, p 199.
16 *Bate v Robbins* (1863) 32 Beav 73.
17 *Re Magdalena Steam Navigation Co* (1860) John 690.
18 *Cooke v Benbow* (1865) 3 De GJ & Sm 1; *Meymott v Meymott* (1862) 31 Beav 445.
19 Partnership Act 1890, s 24(4).

Indeed, in the majority of cases, the omission of a clause providing for interest would be most unreasonable. For instance, where the old and experienced members of a firm take in the son of a partner, who brings in little or no capital, and a minimum of skill and experience, there is no reason why he should have the benefit of the senior partners' capital for nothing.

Even where there is a provision for interest on capital, such interest ceases to be payable directly the partnership is dissolved[20], although months or years may elapse before the assets are completely realised and the capital repaid[1].

5 Management of the partnership business

Subject to any agreement express or implied between the partners, every partner may take part in the management of the partnership business[2].

The Partnership Act 1890 does not state, but the law implies, that each partner shall attend to and work in the business. If he fails to do so, it is a ground for dissolution[3], and the court may order him to make compensation to the industrious partner for the extra trouble caused by his own idleness[4].

Although the law infers that the partners must attend to business, the rule is often negatived by a term in the partnership articles that whereas a junior partner is expressly bound to attend diligently and exclusively to the business, a senior partner merely reserves the right, but not conceding any obligation, to attend to business.

A clause in the partnership deed may authorise each working partner to take a salary as manager of his department in addition to his share of the profits. Such salary is paid before the net profits are computed, and is treated as an outgoing of the firm with the result that the working partners receive more than those who are not obliged to devote their whole time to the firm's business.

6 Remuneration

Subject to any agreement express or implied between the partners, no partner is entitled to remuneration for acting in the partnership business[5].

The rule as to the gratuitous nature of a partner's services does not apply during a winding-up where one of the partners is dead or retires or

20 As to the dissolution of partnership, see pp 79–85, below.
1 *Barfield v Loughborough* (1872) 8 Ch App 1, 27 LT 499.
2 Partnership Act 1890, s 24(5).
3 As to the dissolution of partnership, see pp 79–85, below.
4 *Airey v Borham* (1861) 29 Beav 620.
5 Partnership Act 1890, s 24(6).

becomes of unsound mind. In such cases, all the work being thrown on the other partner or partners, he or they are entitled to some compensation for their trouble out of the profits, if any, but not otherwise[6]. A partner, who has been appointed receiver and manager in a dissolution action[7] may also be awarded compensation, where he has voluntarily and with benefit to the assets done work outside his duties as receiver and manager[8].

No remuneration will, however, be allowed to partners after the death of a co-partner where they are also his executors, as it is their duty *qua* executors to work gratuitously[9].

7 Introduction of new partner

Subject to any agreement express or implied between the partners, no person may be introduced as a partner without the consent of all existing partners[10].

But if the partnership deed provides that one or more of the partners shall have the option of introducing a new partner, either as his successor or otherwise, the other partners will be bound to accept his nominee, for the consent required by the law may be given in advance and without reference to any particular individual[11].

Where a person has been duly nominated as a partner under a clause in a partnership deed and the other partners refuse to admit him as a partner, he is entitled to such relief as a Court of Equity is in the habit of granting to persons who stand in the relation of partners.

Thus, in *Byrne v Reid*[12]:

Under cl 29 of a partnership deed a father had power to nominate his son as a partner. He did so, but the other partners refused to admit him into the firm. Later a consent order was made by which they gave an undertaking to execute all such deeds as might be necessary for him to be admitted. They did not comply with the undertaking, so the son applied to the court to compel them to do so.

Held, by the Court of Appeal, that they must do so. Even if there had been no such undertaking, the court would have given relief to the

---

6 *Re Aldridge, Aldridge v Aldridge* [1894] 2 Ch 97, 70 LT 724; *Mellersh v Keen* (1859) 27 Beav 236; *Yates v Finn* (1880) 13 Ch D 839.

7 As to the dissolution of partnership, see pp 79–85, below.

8 *Harris v Sleep* [1897] 2 Ch 80, 76 LT 458. As to the right of a partner who is appointed receiver to be paid his remuneration and costs as receiver although as a partner he is indebted to the firm and unable to pay what he owes, see *Davy v Scarth* [1906] 1 Ch 55. See p 89, below.

9 *Burden v Burden* (1813) 1 Ves & B 170; *Stocken v Dawson* (1843) 6 Beav 371 at 376 (per Langdale MR).

10 Partnership Act 1890, s 24(7).

11 *Byrne v Reid* [1902] 2 Ch 735, 87 LT 507, CA.

12 [1902] 2 Ch 735, 87 LT 507, CA.

son, for, on his accepting the nomination, he became in the eye of a
Court of Equity a partner and entitled to such relief as the court was in
the habit of granting to persons who stood in the relation of
partners[13].

Where a partnership deed states that a partner can nominate another
person as a partner and the other partners are deemed to have consented
to such admission, provided always that their consent is not to be
unreasonably withheld, and states that a rejected nominee can refer the
matter to arbitration, such a nominee has no right to arbitration because
he is not a party to the submission to arbitration contained in the deed.
Thus, in *Re Franklin and Swathling's Arbitration*[14]:

By cl 31 of a partnership deed any general partner was entitled to
introduce a qualified person as a new general partner, and it went on
to say that: 'The general partners shall have consented to the
admission as a new general partner of such qualified person, provided
always that such consent shall not be unreasonably withheld;
provided further that if any general partner entitled to vote or such
qualified persons so nominated shall be of opinion that such consent
shall have been unreasonably withheld, the matter shall upon his
application be referred to arbitration . . .' Franklin was one of the
general partners, and nominated his son as the new partner, but the
other partners refused to admit him as a partner. The son claimed that
their consent had been unreasonably withheld, and that the matter
should be referred to arbitration.

Held, by the Chancery Division, that he was not entitled to
arbitration, for he was not, within the Arbitration Act 1889[15], a party
to the submission to arbitration which was contained in the
partnership deed[16].

8 Difference as to ordinary matters

Subject to any agreement express or implied between the partners, any
difference arising as to ordinary matters connected with the partnership
business may be decided by a majority of the partners, but no change
may be made in the nature of the partnership business without the
consent of all existing partners[17].

13 See the judgment of Stirling LJ, ibid, at 741 and 509, respectively. See further Ivamy
   Casebook on Partnership (2nd edn 1982) pp 36–38.
14 [1929] 1 Ch 238, 140 LT 403.
15 Now Arbitration Act 1950.
16 See the judgment of Maugham J: [1929] 1 Ch 238 at 240 and 140 LT 403 at 404. See
   further Ivamy *Casebook on Partnership* (2nd edn 1982) pp 38–39.
17 Partnership Act 1890, s 24(8).

Thus, in *Highley v Walker*[18]:

The business of a partnership of three partners was that of worsted spinning, and was a very considerable and important one. The plaintiff, who was one of the partners, applied for an injunction to prevent the other two partners, who had resolved to introduce into the partnership a son of one of them with a view to learning the business, from doing so.

Held, by the Chancery Division, that the injunction would not be granted, for the difference between the partners was as to 'an ordinary matter connected with the partnership business', and should be decided by a majority of them[19].

Where the voting is equal, it would seem that those partners who voted against a proposed course of action would be entitled to have their view respected, in accordance with the general principle applicable to all voting, ie, that the onus lies on those who affirm a proposition, and not on those who oppose it.

The statutory power of a majority to bind a dissentient minority in ordinary matters must be exercised subject to the overriding principle that every partner must act with the utmost good faith. A majority, therefore, cannot bind a minority without notice to them and without giving them the opportunity of discussion. If this were not so, it would practically put the entire management in the hands of a high-handed majority, and would be in conflict with the rule that every partner is entitled to take part in the management of the business[20].

Occasionally the partnership deed provides that differences of opinion on matters of importance are to be referred to arbitration but this is not usual, and there are obvious objections to the calling in of a third party to pronounce on a private difference of opinion[1].

9 Partnership books

Subject to any agreement express or implied between the partners, the partnership books are to be kept at the place of business (or the principal place, if there is more than one), and every partner may, when he thinks fit, have access to and inspect and copy any of them[2].

This right may be exercised by a partner in person and also through an

---

18 (1910) 26 TLR 685.

19 See the judgment of Warrington J, ibid, at 685. See further Ivamy *Casebook on Partnership* (2nd edn 1982) pp 33–34.

20 See p 41, above.

1 See eg *Re Franklin and Swathling's Arbitration* [1929] 1 Ch 238, 140 LT 403, where there was provision for arbitration on the question of admission of a new partner nominated by any partner.

2 Partnership Act 1890, s 24(9).

agent, provided that he is a person to whom the other partners can have no reasonable objection.

Thus, in *Bevan v Webb*[3]:

The sleeping partners in a brewery business were about to enter into a contract to sell their interests to the managing partners. They, therefore, employed a valuer to inspect the books for them, but the managing partners refused to allow him to do so, claiming that the right of inspection could only be exercised by a partner personally. So the sleeping partners applied for an injunction to compel the managing partners to allow the valuer to have access to the books.

Held, by the Court of Appeal, that the injunction would be granted. The right of inspection could be delegated to an agent, assuming that he was a person to whom no reasonable objection could be taken, and that he was willing to undertake not to use for any other purpose the information he acquired during the inspection of the books[4].

Expulsion of partner

No majority of the partners can expel any partner unless a power to do so has been conferred by express agreement between the parties[5].

Where a partnership deed states that 'if a partner is guilty of misconduct, the others may expel him,' one partner acting alone cannot exercise the power of expulsion, even though the Law of Property Act 1925, s 61 states that 'the singular includes the plural and vice versa.'

Thus, in *re A Solicitors' Arbitration*[6]:

Clause 31 of a partnership deed relating to a partnership consisting of three solicitors named Egerton, Nicholas and Smeaton, stated that 'If any partner shall commit or be guilty of any act of professional misconduct . . . the other partners may by notice in writing given to him . . . expel him from the partnership . . .' Egerton served on the other two partners a notice to expel them from the partnership on the ground of their alleged misconduct. He claimed that the clause gave him this power because s 61 of the Law of Property Act 1925 stated that 'in all deeds . . . unless the context otherwise requires . . . (c) the singular includes the plural and vice versa'.

Held, by the Chancery Division, that Egerton had no power to

---

3 [1901] 2 Ch 59, 84 LT 609, CA.
4 See the judgment of Henn Collins LJ, ibid, at 66 and 609, respectively. See further Ivamy *Casebook on Partnership* (2nd edn 1982) pp 34–36.
5 Partnership Act 1890, s 25.
6 [1962] 1 All ER 772, [1962] 1 WLR 353.

expel Nicholas or Smeaton except as a joint action with Smeaton or Nicholas [7].

Even where a partnership agreement provides that a partner may be expelled for breach of certain specified articles, the other partners are not entitled to use this provision otherwise than in good faith. It will not justify an expulsion the motive of which is really to get an undue advantage over the partner who is to be expelled by purchasing his interest on terms unfavourable to him [8].

But where there has been a flagrant breach of the partnership articles, such a provision will justify the service of a notice of expulsion on the partner committing a breach without giving him preliminary warning of the cause of complaint, or an opportunity of meeting the case alleged against him.

Thus, in *Green v Howell* [9]:

A clause in a partnership agreement stated that a partner, who was guilty of a flagrant breach of his duties, could be expelled by the other partner subject to an appeal to an arbitrator. The other partner concerned, acting in good faith, served on him a notice of expulsion without giving him an opportunity of explanation. The question was whether this constituted a valid notice.

Held, by the Court of Appeal, that it did [10].

Determination of partnership at will

Where no fixed term has been agreed on for the duration of the partnership, any partner may determine the partnership at any time on giving notice of his intention to do so to all the other partners [11].

But a provision that the partnership is to be terminated 'by mutual arrangement only' will prevent termination at the instance of a single partner.

Thus, in *Moss v Elphick* [12]:

Moss and Elphick were partners in a partnership for an undefined

---

7 See the judgment of Russell J, ibid, at 774 and 357 respectively, where he said that any other construction of cl 31 would mean, incidentally, that it operated to enable a minority to expel a majority which would be strange in view of the Partnership Act 1890, s 25. See further Ivamy *Casebook on Partnership* (2nd edn 1982) pp 41–42.
8 *Green v Howell* [1910] 1 Ch 495 at 504, 102 LT 347 at 350, CA (per Cozens-Hardy MR).
9 [1910] 1 Ch 495, 102 LT 347, CA.
10 See the judgment of Cozens-Hardy MR, ibid, at 504 and 352, respectively. See further Ivamy *Casebook on Partnership* (2nd edn 1982) p 40.
11 Partnership Act 1890, s 26(1).
12 [1910] 1 KB 846, 102 LT 639, CA.

time. A clause in the partnership deed stated that it could be terminated 'by mutual arrangement only.' Moss gave notice to Elphick of his intention to dissolve the partnership.

Held, by the Court of Appeal, that the notice was invalid. Since the clause stated that the partnership could be terminated 'by mutual arrangement only', the Partnership Act 1890, s 26(1) was inapplicable. Further, the partnership was not dissolved by notice under s 32 because the words of that section stated 'subject to the agreement between the partners', and there was such an agreement in the present case [13].

Whether a 'fixed term' has been agreed is a matter of construction in each case.

Thus, in *Abbott v Abbott* [14]:

A father and his five sons went into partnership as from 11 October 1923. The partnership deed stated by cl 2: 'The death or retirement of any partner shall not terminate the partnership.' Clause 10 provided that: 'If any partner shall . . . do or suffer any act which would be a ground for the dissolution of the partnership by the court, he shall be considered to have retired.' One of the sons gave notice of dissolution, and brought an action for a declaration that the partnership had been dissolved. He contended that he was entitled to give notice as no term had been fixed for the duration of the partnership within the meaning of s 26(1) of the Partnership Act 1890.

Held, by the Chancery Division, that the declaration would not be made. The partnership was not a partnership at will, and was one to continue unless dissolved by the court or some other event, so long as two of the partners were still living and had not retired. Consequently the notice of dissolution given by the son was ineffective[15].

Again, in the case of a syndicate, ie a partnership formed to carry out a special financial or commercial project, eg to purchase, develop and sell a particular estate or to erect and sell a particular building, the court, in the absence of an express stipulation, will consider such a partnership as intended to last until the project has been completed[16].

Where a partnership has originally been constituted by deed, a notice in writing, signed by the partner giving it, is sufficient for the purpose of determining the partnership[17].

---

13 See the judgment of Vaughan Williams LJ, ibid, at 847 and 639, respectively. See further Ivamy *Casebook on Partnership* (2nd edn 1982) pp 43–45.
14 [1936] 3 All ER 823.
15 See the judgment of Clauson J, ibid, at 826. See further Ivamy *Casebook on Partnership* (2nd edn 1982) pp 42–43.
16 See Partnership Act 1890, s 32(b) and *Oppenheimer v Frazer and Wyatt* [1907] 2 KB 50 at 68 (per Fletcher Moulton LJ) and at 75–76 (per Kennedy LJ).
17 Partnership Act 1890, s 26(2). Cf s 32(c). See p 79 below.

Continuance of partnership after expiration of agreed term

Where a partnership entered into for a fixed term is continued after the term has expired, and without any express new agreement, the rights and duties of the partners remain the same as they were at the expiration of the term, so far as is consistent with the incidents of a partnership at will [18].

Thus, in *Brooks v Brooks* [19]:

A partnership was entered into between the plaintiff and the defendant for 10 years from 1 January 1889. Clause 25 of the partnership agreement stated that the plaintiff was to be at liberty to determine the partnership 'by giving the defendant six months' notice, and whether so determined or by effluxion of time' she should have the right to purchase the defendant's share at a valuation. The partnership was continued after the date of its expiry. The plaintiff claimed that she was entitled to exercise her right to purchase the defendant's share. But the defendant contended that cl 25 was inapplicable because it was inconsistent with the incidents of a partnership at will.

Held, by the Chancery Division, that the action succeeded, for the clause was consistent with the incidents of a partnership at will within the meaning of s 27(1) of the Partnership Act 1890 [20].

Whether a salaried partnership amounts to a 'partnership' for the purpose of s 27 depends on the circumstances of each case [1].

A continuance of the business by the partners or such of them as habitually acted in it during the term, without any settlement or liquidation of the partnership affairs, is presumed to be a continuance of the partnership [2].

Duties of partners

The Partnership Act 1890, ss 28 and 30, imposes certain duties on partners. These relate:

(1) the duty to render true accounts and full information [3];

---

18 Partnership Act 1890, s 27(1).
19 (1901) 85 LT 453.
20 See the judgment of Farwell J, ibid, at 454. See further Ivamy *Casebook on Partnership* (2nd edn 1982) pp 45–46.
1 *Stekel v Ellice* [1973] 1 All ER 465, [1973] 1 WLR 191. (See the judgment of Megarry J, ibid, at 471.)
2 Partnership Act 1890, s 27(2).
3 See p 48, below.

(2) the duty to account for any benefit derived from any transaction concerning the partnership[4]; and

(3) the duty to account for profits derived from a competing business[5].

1 Rendering true accounts and full information

Partners are bound to render true accounts and full information of all things affecting the partnership to any partner or his legal representatives[6].

In a transaction between the partners for the sale by one to the other of a share in the partnership business, there is a duty resting on the purchaser who knows, and is aware that he knows, more about the partnership accounts than the vendor, to put the vendor in possession of all material facts with reference to the partnership assets, and not to conceal what he alone knows. Unless such information has been furnished, the sale is voidable and may be set aside at the instance of the vendor.

Thus, in *Law v Law*[7]:

A partner sold his share in the partnership to another partner for £21,000, but later found that the partnership assets consisted of mortgages and other securities, the existence of which had not been disclosed to him by the other partner, who knew all about them. So the partner, who had sold his share, asked for the agreement to be set aside.

Held, by the Court of Appeal, that an order to this effect would have been made, but, on the facts, a settlement of the claim had been made, and the partner had elected to be bound by it. So the transaction would not, in the circumstances, be set aside[8].

2 Accountability of partners for private profits

Every partner must account to the firm for any benefit derived by him without the consent of the other partners from any transaction concerning the partnership, or from any use by him of the partnership property[9], name or business connection[10].

4 See below.
5 See p 50, below.
6 Partnership Act 1890, s 28.
7 [1905] 1 Ch 140, 92 LT 1, CA.
8 See the judgment of Cozens-Hardy LJ, ibid, at 156 and 5, respectively. See further Ivamy *Casebook on Partnership* (2nd edn 1982) p 47.
9 See pp 31–35, above.
10 Partnership Act 1890, s 29(1). This section applies also to transactions undertaken after a partnership has been dissolved by the death of a partner and before the affairs of the partnership have been completely wound up, either by any surviving partner or by the representatives of the deceased partner: ibid, s 29(2). As to dissolution of a partnership by the death of a partner, see p 80, below.

Thus, a partner must account to the firm for all commissions on sales or purchases of the firm's property. He must not, without full disclosure to the other partners, take an interest as purchaser or part purchaser in a sale of the partnership property[11], nor as vendor or part vendor may he make a profit by the sale of property to the firm[12]. Where a partner uses his position so as to get a private agreement with a customer of the firm, in relation to goods dealt in by the firm, beneficial to himself only, he will have to share the profits with the other partners for he is abusing his position for his own ends and to the detriment of the business[13].

A partner cannot retain the benefit of the renewal to himself of a lease of property leased to the firm[14], whether he obtains the renewal secretly or openly if the lease is renewable by the firm as of right[15].

Again, in *Pathirana v Pathirana*[16]:

R W Pathirana and A Pathirana were partners in the business of selling Caltex petrol from a service station belonging to Caltex (Ceylon) Ltd; and had been appointed by Caltex as their agents. Differences arose between them and on 10 September 1948, A Pathirana gave three months' notice of dissolution of the partnership. On 21 September R W Pathirana wrote to Caltex without his partner's knowledge or consent, and enclosed a copy of the notice of dissolution of the partnership. He asked for the name and style of the agency to be altered from 1 October to 'R W Pathirana' instead of the present style of 'R W & A Pathirana'. R W Pathirana then carried on the business on the premises in his own name and did not account to his partner for his share of the profits. A Pathirana claimed that a share was due to him by reason of s 29(1) of the Partnership Act 1890.

Held, by the Judicial Committee of the Privy Council (on appeal from the Supreme Court of Ceylon), that he was so entitled[17].

3 Accountability of partners for profits from competing business

If a partner, without the consent of the other partners, carries on any business of the same nature as and competing with that of the firm, he

---

11 *Dunne v English* (1874) LR 18 Eq 524; *Re Olympia Ltd* [1898] 2 Ch 153, 78 LT 629.
12 *Bentley v Craven* (1853) 18 Beav 75.
13 *Russell v Austwick* (1826) 1 Sim 52.
14 *Clegg v Fishwick* (1849) 1 Mac & G 294; *Clements v Hall* (1857) 2 De G & J 173 at 186 (per Lord Cranworth LC); *Bevan v Webb* [1905] 1 Ch 620, 93 LT 298, CA, where the lease was not renewable and a partner was held entitled to purchase the reversion; *Thompson's Trustee in Bankruptcy v Heaton* [1974] 1 All ER 1239, [1974] 1 WLR 605, where one of the former partners had acquired a freehold reversion, and the question was whether he was accountable after the dissolution of the partnership.
15 *Re Biss, Biss v Biss* [1903] 2 Ch 40, 88 LT 403, CA; *Clegg v Edmondson* (1857) 8 De GM & G 787.
16 [1967] 1 AC 233, [1966] 3 WLR 666, PC.
17 See the judgment of Lord Upjohn, ibid, at 240.

must account for and pay over to the firm all profits made by him in that business [18].

Thus, in *Trimble v Goldberg* [19]:

> In 1902 Goldberg, Trimble and Bennett entered into a partnership for the purpose of buying and then re-selling certain properties belonging to a Mr Hollard. They consisted of 5,500 shares in a company called Sigma Syndicate, and of stands or plots of land in Johannesburg and elsewhere in South Africa. Trimble went out to Johannesburg to see Hollard, and bought on behalf of the partnership all the property belonging to Hollard and the 5,500 shares. Whilst he was there, Trimble bought for himself and Bennett some plots of land belonging to Sigma Syndicate. Goldberg learnt of this purchase some time afterwards, and now brought an action against Trimble claiming the benefit of the purchase.
>
> *Held*, by the Judicial Committee of the Privy Council (allowing an appeal from the decision of the Supreme Court of the Transvaal), that the action failed. The purchase of the plots was not within the scope of the partnership, nor was it in rivalry with the partnership [20].

Rights of assignee of share in partnership

An assignment by any partner of his share in the partnership, either absolute or by way of mortgage or redeemable charge, does not, as against the other partners, entitle the assignee, during the continuance of the partnership, to interfere in the management or administration of the partnership business or affairs, or to require any accounts of the partnership transactions, or to inspect the partnership books [1].

The assignee is entitled only to receive the share of the profits to which the assigning partner would otherwise be entitled, and the assignee must accept the account of profits agreed to by the partners [2].

The assignee, therefore, cannot object to salaries bona fide paid by the firm to individual partners for managing departments of the business, although his share of the profits may be considerably reduced in consequence.

18 Partnership Act 1890, s 30.
19 [1906] AC 494, 95 LT 163, PC.
20 See the judgment of Lord MacNaghten, ibid, at 496 and 163, respectively. See further Ivamy *Casebook on Partnership* (2nd edn 1982) pp 48–50. See also *Aas v Benham* [1891] 2 Ch 244, 65 LT 25, CA.
 1 Partnership Act 1890, s 31(1).
 2 Ibid, s 31(1).

Thus, in *Re Garwood's Trusts, Garwood v Paynter* [3]:

Garwood, Paynter and Dunn carried on business as colliery owners. None of them received a salary. In 1889 Garwood charged his share of the partnership with the payment of £10,000 to two trustees, of whom Paynter was one, and subsequently agreed to pay them the rest of his share of the profits. In 1893 arrangements were made for each of the partners to receive a salary of £150 per annum, but Garwood received nothing by way of salary after 1895. These arrangements were made bona fide. Mrs Garwood, who was one of the beneficiaries of the trust, objected to the payment of the salaries to Paynter and Dunn.

Held, by the Chancery Division, that the payment of the salaries was binding on the trustees, for the payment was an act 'in the management or administration of the partnership business' within the meaning of s 31(1) of the Partnership Act 1890, and the trustees could not interfere [4].

In the case of a dissolution of the partnership [5], whether as respects all the partners or as respects the assigning partner, the assignee is entitled to receive the share of the partnership assets to which the assigning partner is entitled as between himself and the other partners, and, for the purpose of ascertaining that share, to an account as from the date of the dissolution [6].

Where a partnership deed contains an arbitration clause and a partner has mortgaged his share in the partnership, the mortgagee is entitled to an account if the partnership is dissolved, and cannot be compelled to submit to arbitration any dispute which arises.

Thus, in *Bonnin v Neame* [7]:

A partnership deed contained a clause stating that if any difference arose between the partners, it should be submitted to arbitration. One of the three partners in the firm mortgaged his share to a mortgagee. The other two partners dissolved the partnership, and a dispute arose as to the manner in which the interests of the partners should be ascertained. They appointed an arbitrator, and the partner who had mortgaged his share also appointed an arbitrator. The mortgagee claimed an account against the three partners under s 31 of the Partnership Act 1890, but the two partners applied for the action to be stayed and referred to arbitration.

Held, by the Chancery Division, that the action would not be

3 [1903] 1 Ch 236.
4 See the judgment of Buckley J, ibid, at 238. See further Ivamy *Casebook on Partnership* (2nd edn 1982) pp 50–52.
5 See pp 79–85, below.
6 Partnership Act 1890, s 31(2).
7 [1910] 1 Ch 732, 102 LT 708.

stayed. The mortgagee was not a party to the partnership deed, and could not be compelled to submit to arbitration[8].

If a partner purports to sell his share to a third party without the assignee's consent, such an arrangement is not binding on the assignee. Thus, in *Watts v Driscoll*[9]:

A son setting up in partnership was lent £1,900 for this purpose by his father. The sum advanced was secured by an assignment to the father of the son's share in the partnership. Disputes arose between the partners, and the son sold his share to the other partner for £500. The father then claimed that he was entitled to an account to ascertain the value of the share in the partnership.

Held, by the Court of Appeal, that he was entitled to one. The sale to the other partner could not affect the assignee's rights, since the sale had taken place without his consent[10].

Sex discrimination

It is unlawful for a firm consisting of six or more partners, in relation to a position as a partner, to discriminate against a woman in a case where she already holds that position

(1) in the way they afford her access to any benefits, facilities or services, or by refusing her or deliberately omitting to afford her access to them; or

(2) by expelling her from that position or subjecting her to any other detriment[11].

---

8 See judgment of Swinfen Eady J, ibid, at 737 and 710, respectively. See further Ivamy *Casebook on Partnership* (2nd edn 1982) pp 53–54.

9 [1901] 1 Ch 294, 84 LT 97, CA.

10 See the judgment of Lord Alverstone CJ, ibid, at 306 and 98, respectively. See further Ivamy *Casebook on Partnership* (2nd edn 1982) pp 52–53.

11 Sex Discrimination Act 1975, s 11(1)(d). This subsection does not apply to provision made in relation to death or retirement.

Chapter 4

The relation of partners to persons dealing with them

It is only in certain circumstances that a partner has power to bind the firm or the other partners in respect of the contracts or engagements entered into by him with third parties[1]. The firm is liable for the torts of a partner committed in the ordinary course of its business[2]. There are special rules where the property or money of a third person or trust property is misapplied[3]. Sometimes the liability of a partner is joint whilst at other times it is joint and several[4]. Finally, the liabilities of incoming and outgoing partners need to be considered[5].

Power of a partner to bind the firm

It must not be inferred that a partner can bind the firm to any engagement into which he may purport to enter on its behalf any more than any other agent can bind the firm to an extent greater than his actual or usual authority, as the case may be.

1 Distinction between actual and usual authority

Actual authority does not necessarily mean express authority. It no doubt includes all express authorities in cases where there are any, but in every case, except as regards persons having notice to the contrary, it includes that usual authority with which in the absence of express prohibition, the law clothes every partner for the purpose of doing all acts necessary or proper for carrying on the firm's business in the way usual in businesses of a similar nature.

In many firms none of these acts are prohibited, and in such cases the actual authority of each partner is at least as great as his usual authority; and, of course, it may be even greater by express agreement.

But it is common to find provisions in partnership agreements

1 See pp 54–60, below.
2 See pp 60–65, below.
3 See p 65, below.
4 See pp 65–67, below.
5 See pp 67–70, below.

expressly prohibiting individual partners or some of them (eg junior partners) from doing certain acts. For instance, there may be a clause prohibiting a partner from buying, ordering or contracting for any goods or articles for the use of the firm exceeding a certain value without the consent in writing of the other partners.

In such cases the actual authority is less than the usual authority, and if a partner exceeds his actual authority in fact by doing a prohibited act, the question at once arises as to whether what he has done was within his usual authority. If it was, then although it was expressly forbidden by the partnership agreement, the firm will be bound unless the person who dealt with the partner knew of the prohibition. If he knew of the prohibition, the firm will not be bound for in that case, so far from the partner having a usual authority, it would be clear that he had none.

Indeed the Partnership Act 1890, s 8 states:

> If it has been agreed between the partners that any restriction shall be placed on the power of any one or more of them to bind the firm, no act done in contravention of the agreement is binding on the firm with respect to persons having notice of the agreement.

2 Principle on which usual authority rests

The principle on which usual authority rests is that of estoppel by conduct, ie that if a man so conducts his business as to mislead others, he must bear the consequences.

Accordingly, if one employs another to transact a particular class of business for him, he is estopped from denying that the agent had authority to do any acts which are usually ancillary to the transaction of that class of business. He must not blow hot and cold and mislead third parties by holding out another as his agent in relation to the conduct of a business, and then, when a particular transaction does not suit him, repudiate the agency on the ground that the agent had exceeded or disobeyed his instructions.

Thus, where a man employs an agent to sell goods, he cannot repudiate a sale made within the agent's usual authority on the ground that the agent has sold for less than a minimum price in disobedience to his orders or on the ground that the agent gave credit to the other party to the sale contrary to express instructions to sell for cash only.

3 Liability of undisclosed partner

If, as is submitted, the principle of the doctrine of usual authority depends on the third party having been misled, it follows that where he is not misled, eg as in the case of sleeping partnerships where the third party thinks that the person with whom he deals is, in fact, the sole principal, and therefore does not give any credit to the undisclosed principal, the sleeping partner will not be liable if the partner contracting has exceeded his actual authority.

But this view is inconsistent with the decision in *Watteau v Fenwick*[6] where Wills J, said[7] that in the case of a sleeping partner no limitation of authority as between the sleeping and the active partner would avail the sleeping partner as to acts within the ordinary authority of a partner. His Lordship's attention does not seem to have been called to the Partnership Act 1890, s 5[8], which states that an act is binding on the other partners unless (inter alia) the person with whom the partner in question is dealing 'does not know or believe him to be a partner'. The decision is doubted by Lord Lindley[9], and it is felt that it is erroneous.

4 Requirements to be fulfilled

The power of a partner to bind the firm being limited to his actual or usual authority, the practical result is that whenever a dispute takes place as to whether the firm is bound by the act of a partner, the question at once arises: 'Was the act one which, in the absence of notice to the contrary, a third persons would be justified in regarding as being within the usual authority of each of the partners?'

If the answer to the question is 'Yes', the question of actual authority is immaterial.

The Partnership Act 1890, s 5 states:

> Every partner is an agent of the firm and his other partners for the purpose of the business of the partnership; and the acts of every partner who does any act for carrying on in the usual way business of the kind carried on by the firm of which he is a member, bind the firm and his partners, unless the partner so acting has in fact no authority to act for the firm in the particular matter, and the person with whom he is dealing either knows that he has no authority, or does not know or believe him to be a partner.

Accordingly, for a third person to be able to hold the firm or the other partners liable, the following requirements must be fulfilled:

  (i) the act must be done in relation to the partnership business;
 (ii) the act must be an act for carrying on business in the usual way; and
(iii) the act must be done as a partner and not as an individual.

---

6 [1893] 1 QB 346, DC.
7 Ibid, at 349.
8 See below.
9 Op cit p 286, note 9, and p 353, note 2. *Watteau v Fenwick* (above) was followed in *Kinahan & Co Ltd v Parry* [1910] 2 KB 389, 102 LT 826, but that decision was reversed on a question of fact: [1911] 1 KB 459, 103 LT 867, CA. See further 9 LQR 111.

(i) Act in relation to partnership business
In order to bind the firm the act must be one which is done in relation to the partnership business. If A and B carry on business as butchers, a contract signed by A in the firm name to supply furniture would not be binding on B unless it was made with B's express authority.

By the mere fact of taking him as a partner, B never made A his agent for such a purpose either actually or ostensibly, for the business is that of a butcher and not that of a furniture supplier, and a third party cannot reasonably assume that in such a case a partner has authority to bind the firm to a transaction which is altogether foreign to its usual type of business.

The Partnership Act 1890, s 7, sums up the position as follows:

> Where one partner pledges the credit of the firm for a purpose apparently not connected with the firm's ordinary course of business, the firm is not bound, unless he is in fact specially authorised by the other partners; but this section does not affect any personal liability incurred by an individual partner.

The last proviso is intended to preserve the personal liability of the partner who actually makes the contract or to meet the case of A, who is one of several partners A, B, C and D, having so acted as to mislead the third party into the belief that B had the authority of the firm to enter into a contract on their behalf, or that A had given B actual authority to bind him (A).

(ii) Act for carrying on business in usual way
The matter is fairly simple where the act in question is obviously one foreign to the usual business of the firm. The difficulty arises when the act, although clearly done in relation to the partnership business (eg referring a dispute between the firm and the third party to arbitration) is alleged by the firm to be one which was not within the usual authority of a single partner.

The Partnership Act 1890, s 5[10], does not provide much assistance, for it merely describes the acts which a partner has usual authority to do as acts 'for carrying on in the usual way business of the kind carried on by the firm'.

Whether the act is one for carrying on business in the usual way will depend on whether the partnership is a trading partnership, ie one whose principal operations are buying and selling[11], or a non-trading partnership. Some acts, however, are never within the usual authority of a partner of any kind of partnership.

---

10 See p 56 above.
11 *Wheatley v Smithers* [1906] 2 KB 321, 95 LT 96; *Higgins v Beauchamp* [1914] 3 KB 1192, 111 LT 1103.

(a) Trading partnership   In the absence of express prohibition the usual authority of a partner in a trading partnership[12] enables him to

(1) pledge the partnership goods[13];
(2) sell the partnership goods[14];
(3) buy goods on account of the firm[15];
(4) borrow money on account of the firm[16];
(5) contract debts on behalf of the firm;
(6) pay debts on its account;
(7) draw, make, sign, endorse, accept, transfer, negotiate and procure the discounting of negotiable instruments;
(8) engage employees for the firm[17];
(9) receive, and give receipts for, debts due to the firm[18];
(10) create an equitable mortgage of the firm's land or buildings by a deposit of title deeds[19];
(11) retain a solicitor to conduct an action for recovering debts due to the firm[20]; and
(12) employ a solicitor to defend an action against the firm[1].

Again, in *Mercantile Credit Co Ltd v Garrod* [2]

Parkin was a partner in a firm carrying on a garage business mainly concerned with letting lock-up garages and repairing cars. Garrod was a sleeping partner. A clause in the partnership deed excluded the buying and selling of cars. Parkin, without Garrod's authority, sold a car, to which he had no title, to the Mercantile Credit Co Ltd so that it could let it on hire-purchase to a customer. The company paid Parkin £700. When the company found that Parkin had no title to it, it claimed the £700 from Garrod.

Held, by the Queen's Bench Division, that the action succeeded. The sale of the car to the company so that it could be let out on hire-purchase was 'an act for carrying on in the usual way business of the kind carried on by the firm' within the meaning of the Partnership Act 1890, s 5, and the firm was accordingly bound[3].

12 See generally, *Bank of Australasia v Breillat* (1847) 6 Moo PCC 152 at 193 (per Mr Pemberton Leigh (later Lord Kingsdown)).
13 *Ex p Bonbonus* (1803) 8 Ves 540; *Butchart v Dresser* (1853) 4 De GM & G 542.
14 *Dore v Wilkinson and Spurvey* (1817) 2 Stark 287; *Butchart v Dresser* (above).
15 *Bond v Gibson* (1808) 1 Camp 185.
16 *Lane v Williams* (1692) 2 Vern 277.
17 *Drake v Beckham* (1843) 11 M & W 315.
18 *Porter v Taylor* (1817) 6 M & S 156.
19 *Re Clough, Bradford Commercial Banking Co v Cure* (1885) 31 Ch D 324, 53 LT 716; *Re Bourne, Bourne v Bourne* [1906] 2 Ch 427, 95 LT 131, CA.
20 *Court v Berlin* [1897] 2 QB 396, 77 LT 293, CA.
1 *Tomlinson v Broadsmith* [1896] 1 QB 386.
2 [1962] 3 All ER 1103.
3 See the judgment of Mocatta J: ibid, at 1105. See further Ivamy *Casebook on Partnership* (2nd edn 1982) pp 13–14.

(b) Non-trading partnership Non-trading partnerships include firms of solicitors[4], quarry workers[5], auctioneers[6], and cinema proprietors[7].

In the case of such partnerships a partner cannot accept, make or issue negotiable instruments other than ordinary cheques[8] nor borrow or pledge the partnership property.

Thus, in *Higgins v Beauchamp*[9]

Beauchamp was a sleeping partner in a business of cinema proprietors carried on by another partner named Milles. The partnership deed provided that no partner should contract any debt on account of the partnership without the consent of the other partners except in the usual and regular course of business. Milles borrowed money from Higgins, stating that it was for his own use. Higgins then sued Beauchamp to recover the sum lent.

Held, by the Divisional Court of the King's Bench Division, that the action failed. The business was not a trading business (for this term meant a business involved in the buying and selling of goods), and therefore Milles had no implied authority to bind the firm in respect of the debt[10].

(c) Acts never within usual authority In no case, whether the partnership is a trading partnership or a non-trading partnership, has a partner usual authority to –

(1) execute a deed[11], unless his authority is expressly conferred by deed[12];
(2) give a guarantee in the firm name unless a trade custom to that effect is proved[13];
(3) submit a dispute to arbitration[14];
(4) accept property, eg fully paid-up shares in a company in lieu of money in satisfaction of a debt due to the firm[15];

4 *Hedley v Bainbridge* (1842) 3 QB 316.
5 Cf *Thicknesse v Bromilow* (1832) 2 Cr & J 425.
6 *Wheatley v Smithers* [1906] 2 KB 321, 95 LT 96; reversed on another point [1907] 2 KB 684, 97 LT 418, CA.
7 *Higgins v Beauchamp* [1914] 3 KB 1192, 111 LT 1103.
8 *Backhouse v Charlton* (1878) 8 Ch D 444. A post-dated cheque is on the same footing as a bill of exchange: *Forster v MacKreth* (1867) LR 2 Exch 163.
9 [1914] 3 KB 1192, 111 LT 1103.
10 See the judgment of Lush J, ibid, at 1194 and 1104, respectively. See further Ivamy *Casebook on Partnership* (2nd edn 1982) p 15.
11 *Harrison v Jackson* (1797) 7 Term Rep 207.
12 *Berkeley v Hardy* (1826) 5 B & C 355; *Harrison v Jackson* (above). But in transactions where a deed is not necessary a sealed writing executed by one partner will bind the firm: *Marchant v Morton, Down & Co* [1901] 2 KB 829, 85 LT 169; *Re Briggs & Co, ex p Wright* [1906] 2 KB 209, 95 LT 61.
13 *Brettel v Williams* (1849) 4 Exch 623.
14 *Adams v Bankart* (1835) 1 Cr M & R 681.
15 *Niemann v Niemann* (1899) 43 Ch D 198.

(5) make his partners into partners with other persons in another business [16]; or

(6) authorise a third person to make use of the firm's name in legal or other proceedings[17].

(d) Act to be done as a partner   Where a partner has not entered into a transaction in his character of a partner, he cannot bind the firm even though the transaction relates to a matter which is within the scope of the partnership business and within that of his actual or usual authority.

But if he enters into the transaction in the firm's name or in relation to the firm's business, no doubt can be entertained that he contracted as agent for the firm. Indeed, the Partnership Act 1890, s 6, states that:

> An act or instrument relating to the business of the firm and done and executed in the firm name, or in any other manner showing an intention to bind the firm, by any person thereto authorised, whether a partner or not, is binding on the firm, and all the partners. Provided that this section shall not affect any general rule of law relating to the execution of deeds or negotiable instruments.

Thus, in *Re Briggs & Co, ex p Wright* [18]:

> The firm of Briggs and Co had two partners – a father and son. The firm was being pressed by a creditor, and there was no money to meet the claim. So in consideration of the creditor giving time to pay it was agreed that an assignment of the book debts to the creditor should be made. The son consented to this, but did not inform his father. The deed of assignment purported to made was between 'R. B. Briggs and H. R. Briggs, trading under the style or firm of Briggs & Co'. In fact, the father's name had been forged by the son. Later the firm became bankrupt, and the trustee in bankruptcy sought to set aside the deed on the ground that it had been executed by one partner only.

> *Held*, by the King's Bench Division, that the deed was binding under s 6 of the Partnership Act 1890, for it was an instrument relating to the business of the firm done or executed in a manner showing an intention to bind the firm and executed by a partner[19].

Torts other than misapplication of third party's property and of trust property

With regard to torts of this nature, there is a rule applicable generally. A

16 *Hawksley v Outram* [1892] 3 Ch 359, 67 LT 804, CA. But see *Mann v D'Arcy* [1968] 2 All ER 172, [1968] 1 WLR 893.

17 *Marsh v Joseph* [1897] 1 Ch 213, 75 LT 558, CA.

18 [1906] 2 KB 209, 95 LT 61.

19 See the judgment of Bigham J: ibid, at 211 and 61, respectively.

special rule operates in the case of fraudulent representations as to a third person's character or solvency.

1 General rule

The general rule is that (except in the case of misapplication of a third party's property[20] or of trust property[1]) where by any wrongful act or omission of any partner acting in the ordinary course of the business of the firm or with the authority of his co-partners, loss or injury is caused to any person not being a partner in the firm, or any penalty is incurred, the firm is liable for it to the same extent as the partner so acting or omitting to act[2].

If, therefore, the tort is committed without the actual authority of the partners and outside the scope of the partner's usual authority, the firm will not be liable any more than it would be for a contract entered into in similar circumstances.

Although a firm cannot be assumed to have given one of its members authority to commit a wrong, yet where it has given him authority to do a class of acts on its behalf, it is liable for his tort either in the manner of doing such acts or in doing them in circumstances in which they ought not to have been done at all.

Thus, a firm of solicitors is liable for the negligence of one of the partners[3]. A medical partnership would be liable for the negligent treatment of a patient by one of its members. A firm of building contractors would be liable for the negligence of a partner in the design or construction of works. Similarly, a firm of newspaper proprietors would be liable for a libel inserted in one of its papers by an editor who was a partner, and a firm of company promoters would be liable for a fraudulent prospectus issued in the course of business by an individual partner.

Again, a partner who unlawfully induces the clerk of a competing trader to divulge the latter's trade secrets would render the firm liable as well as himself.

Thus, in *Hamlyn v John Houston & Co*[4]:

A partner in Houston & Co bribed a clerk in a rival firm to disclose to him confidential information relating to it. The rival firm suffered a loss in consequence, and sued Houston & Co for damages.

Held, by the Court of Appeal, that the action succeeded. Houston & Co were liable for the partner's wrongful act as he had been acting in the ordinary course of business of the firm. It was in the ordinary

20 See p 62, below.
1 See p 65, below.
2 Partnership Act 1890, s 10.
3 *Blyth v Fladgate* [1891] 1 Ch 337, 63 LT 546; *Marsh v Joseph* [1897] 1 Ch 213, 75 LT 558, CA.
4 [1903] 1 KB 81, 87 LT 500, CA.

course of business to obtain information about a trade rival. Whether the partner did so by legitimate or illegitimate means was immaterial[5].

On the other hand, a firm will not be liable for a tort committed by a partner outside the scope of his authority[6], eg where he wrongfully commences a malicious prosecution for an alleged theft of partnership property, for such a proceeding is not within the scope of his authority as it has nothing to do with carrying on the business of the firm in the usual way[7]. Indeed, it is difficult to imagine a case in which a firm would be liable for the violent acts of a member against the person or property of a third party unless the partner was expressly authorised to commit such an act or the firm subsequently ratified it.

The question whether the act was committed for the benefit of the particular partner is material only in so far as it tends to show whether or not the act was within his authority as a partner[8].

2 Fraudulent representations as to third person's character or solvency

A firm is not liable for a fraudulent representation as to the character or solvency of any person unless the representation is in writing signed by all the partners[9]. The signature of the firm name is insufficient even if all the partners are privy to the representation[10].

Misapplication of money or property of a third person

The liability for the misapplication of the money or the property of a third person arises in two cases:

(1) where the money or property is received by a partner; and
(2) where the money or property is received by the firm.

1 Receipt by partner

Where one partner acting within the scope of his apparent authority receives the money or property of a third person and misapplies it, the firm is liable to make good the loss[11].

---

5 See the judgment of Collins MR: ibid, at 84 and 502 respectively. See further Ivamy *Casebook on Partnership* (2nd edn 1982) pp 17–18.
6 *Mara v Browne* [1896] 1 Ch 199 at 208 (per Lord Herschell).
7 *Arbuckle v Taylor* (1815) 3 Dow 160.
8 *Lloyd v Grace, Smith & Co* [1912] AC 716, 107 LT 531, HL.
9 Statute of Frauds Amendment Act 1828, s 6. The section applies to fraudulent representations only: *Banbury v Bank of Montreal* [1918] AC 626, 119 LT 446, HL.
10 *Swift v Jewsbury* (1874) LR 9 QB 301.
11 Partnership Act 1890, s 11(a).

Such misapplications mostly occur in the case of solicitors, and the question almost always resolves itself into this: 'Was the acceptance of the money or property by the defaulting partner within the scope of his apparent authority or not?'

Some of the cases have laid down certain definite rules of law as to what acceptances are, and what acceptances are not, within the ordinary scope of a solicitor's apparent authority. But others really turn on the evidence of partnership usage tending to prove actual, as distinguished from apparent, authority and, therefore, decide no general principles of law at all.

Thus, the receipt of money by a partner in a firm of solicitors from a client for the purpose of investing it as soon as he could find a good security has been held not to be an act within the scope of his apparent authority so as to render his partners liable to account for the money so deposited, for such a transaction was not the business of a solicitor[12].

On the other hand, money received by a partner in a firm of solicitors in the course of the management and settlement of the affairs of a client of the firm was held to be money paid to the firm in the course of its professional business, and the other partners were liable to make good any loss occasioned by the negligence or dishonesty of the partner receiving the money, for it was received by him in the performance of the duties for which the firm was employed[13].

In order to render the firm liable it must be shown that the third person dealt with the partner as such, and not in his capacity of an individual.

Thus, in *British Homes Assurance Corpn Ltd v Patterson*[14]:

In 1899, the British Homes Corporation Ltd appointed Atkinson, a solicitor in the firm of 'Atkinson & Atkinson', to act for it in mortgage transactions. On 5 February 1901, Atkinson gave notice to the company that he had taken Patterson into partnership, and that the name of the firm was thenceforth 'Atkinson & Patterson'. On 28 February the company sent Atkinson a cheque payable to 'Atkinson & Atkinson' for the purposes of completing a mortgage. The cheque was misappropriated, so the company sued Patterson in respect of the loss under s 11 of the Partnership Act 1890.

Held, by the Chancery Division, that Patterson was not liable because the company had dealt with Atkinson in his personal capacity, and not in that of a partner in the firm[15].

---

12 *Harman v Johnson* (1853) 2 E & B 61.
13 *Earl of Dundonald v Masterman* (1869) LR 7 Eq 504.
14 [1902] 2 Ch 404, 86 LT 826.
15 See the judgment of Farwell J, ibid, at 408 and 828, respectively. See further Ivamy *Casebook on Partnership* (2nd edn 1982) pp 18–19.

2 Receipt by firm

Where a firm in the course of its business receives money or property of a third person, and the money or property so received is misapplied by one or more of the partners while it is in the custody of the firm, the firm is liable to make good the loss[16].

In such cases no question of the partnership's authority to receive the money or property arises. The question is whether the receipt is in the ordinary course of the firm's business.

Thus, in *Rhodes v Moules*[17]:

Rhodes wished to obtain a loan, so he mortgaged his property. He was told by Rew, who was a partner in the solicitors' firm of Messrs Hughes and Masterman, that the mortgagees wanted additional security, so he handed him some share warrants payable to bearer. Rew misappropriated them, so Rhodes sued the firm in respect of the loss under s 11 of the Partnership Act 1890.

Held, by the Court of Appeal, that the action succeeded, for the warrants had been received by the firm in the ordinary course of business[18].

To render the firm liable the misapplication must be made while the money or property was in the firm's custody.

Thus, where a firm of solicitors accepts from a client money to be invested in a specific mortgage and it is so invested, the subsequent fraud of one of the partners who induces the mortgagor to repay the money to him and not to the client will not render the firm liable, for the misapplication is not made while the money is in the custody of the firm[19].

Again, in *Tendring Hundred Waterworks Co v Jones*[20]:

The plaintiffs wished to purchase an estate called the Lawford Estate. They employed Jones and Garrard, who were solicitors in partnership, to negotiate the purchase for them. For their own convenience the plaintiffs arranged for the property to be conveyed into Garrard's name and not their own. The vendors handed the title deeds to him. Later Garrard raised £500 by the deposit of the deeds with a Mr Nunn, and afterwards executed a legal mortgage to Nunn. The partnership was dissolved. The plaintiffs brought an action against Jones claiming that he was liable under s 11(b) of the Partnership Act 1890 for the fraud of his partner.

16 Partnership Act 1890, s 11(b).
17 [1895] 1 Ch 236, 71 LT 599, CA.
18 See judgment of Lindley LJ, ibid, at 248 and 603, respectively. See further Ivamy *Casebook on Partnership* (2nd edn 1982) p 19.
19 *Sims, Abernethie's Executors v Brutton and Clipperton* (1850) 5 Exch 802.
20 [1903] 2 Ch 615.

Held, by the Chancery Division, that the action failed, for by their own acts and conduct the plaintiffs had given Garrard the legal title to the deeds, and by virtue of such title he had withdrawn the deeds. Consequently they were not 'in the custody of the firm' within s 11(b) of the Act of 1890 when he handed them over to Nunn[1].

Improper employment of trust property for partnership purposes

If a partner, being a trustee, improperly employs trust property in the business or on the account of the partnership, no other partner is liable for the trust property to the persons beneficially interested in it[2].

But this does not affect any liability incurred by any partner by reason of his having notice of a breach of trust[3], and does not prevent trust money from being followed and recovered from the firm if still in its possession or under its control[4].

No one could contend that it is within the scope of a partner's authority to bring trust funds into the business as part of his capital or otherwise.

Joint and/or several liability

Sometimes a partner is liable jointly with the other partners whilst in some cases he is liable severally.

Contract

Every partner is liable jointly with the other partners for all debts and obligations of the firm incurred while he is a partner[5].

Thus, in *Bagel v Miller*[6]:

Bagel supplied goods to a partnership of which Miller was a member. Some were ordered and delivered before Miller died, but others were delivered after his death. Bagel brought an action to recover the price from Miller's executors.

1 See the judgment of Farwell J, ibid, at 621. See further Ivamy *Casebook on Partnership* (2nd edn 1982) pp 19–21.
2 Partnership Act 1890, s 13.
3 Ibid, s 13 proviso (1).
4 Ibid, s 13 proviso (2).
5 Ibid, s 9.
6 [1903] 2 KB 212, 88 LT 769.

Held, by the Divisional Court of the King's Bench Division, that the action succeeded in respect of the goods delivered before Miller's death, but failed in respect of those delivered afterwards, since the obligation to pay did not arise whilst Miller was a partner[7].

After his death his estate is also severally liable in a due course of administration for such debts and obligations, so far as they remain unsatisfied, but subject to the prior payment of his separate debts[8].

Tort

Every partner is liable jointly with his co-partners and also severally for everything for which the firm is liable while he is a partner in it under ss 10[9] and 11[10] of the Partnership Act 1890[11].

Effect of distinction between liability in contract and liability in tort

With regard to debts and contractual obligations the plaintiff can only bring one action and not several actions against members of the firm. He is not, however, bound to join all the members of the firm. But if he chooses not to do so, he loses his rights against those whom he has omitted.

With regard to torts, on the other hand, the plaintiff may issue separate writs against each partner either contemporaneously or successively. If the first one sued becomes bankrupt, the fact of his having sued him alone would not be a bar to a second action against another partner.

Effect of judgment

Judgment recovered against any person liable in respect of any debt or damage is not a bar to an action or the continuance of an action against any other person who is jointly liable with him in respect of the same debt or damage[12].

7 See the judgment of Lord Alverstone CJ: ibid, at 214 and 769, respectively. See further Ivamy *Casebook on Partnership* (2nd edn 1982) pp 16–17.
8 Partnership Act 1890, s 9.
9 See p 61, above.
10 See p 62, above.
11 Partnership Act 1890, s 12.
12 Civil Liability (Contribution) Act 1978, s 3. A person is liable in respect of any damage for the purposes of this Act if the person who suffered it (or anyone representing his estate or dependants) is entitled to recover compensation in respect of that damage (whatever the legal basis of his liability whether tort, breach of contract, breach of trust or otherwise): ibid, s 6(1). An action brought by or on behalf of a person who suffered any damage includes an action brought for the benefit of his estate or dependants: ibid, s 6(2). 'Dependants' has the same meaning as in the Fatal Accidents Act 1976: ibid, s 6(3).

If more than one action is brought in respect of any damage by or on behalf of the person by whom it was suffered against persons liable in respect of the damage (whether jointly or otherwise), the plaintiff is not entitled to costs in any of those actions other than that in which judgment is first given unless the court is of the opinion that there was reasonable ground for bringing the action[13].

Suing in the firm name

Any difficulty arising from the above provisions can be avoided by suing in the firm name and then using the procedure laid down by RSC Order 81[14].

Liabilities of incoming and outgoing partners

Incoming partner

A person who is admitted as a partner into an existing firm does not thereby become liable to the creditors of the firm for anything done before he became a partner[15].

But by novation[16] he may take over the liabilities of the existing firm and make himself liable to the creditors. Novation implies an agreement with the creditors either expressed or inferred from conduct[17].

Outgoing partner

(i) *Existing debts and obligations*

A partner who retires from a firm does not thereby cease to be liable for partnership debts or obligations incurred before his retirement[18].

Thus, in *Court v Berlin*[19]:

The plaintiff was a solicitor who was employed by a partnership, which carried on business under the name of 'I. Berlin', to recover a debt due to the firm. The partnership consisted of Berlin, who was the managing partner, and two dormant partners. While the action

---

13 Ibid, s 4.
14 See pp 73–78, below.
15 Partnership Act 1890, s 17(1).
16 See p 68, below.
17 *British Homes Assurance Corpn Ltd v Patterson* [1902] 2 Ch 404 at 409 (per Farwell J).
   In this case a solicitor entering a partnership was held not to be liable for defalcations of his partner at the suit of persons who had no dealings with the partnership as such.
18 Partnership Act 1890, s 17(2).
19 [1897] 2 B 396, 77 LT 293, CA.

brought by the solicitor to recover the debt was proceeding, the two dormant partners retired from the partnership. The plaintiff continued the proceedings, and then sued Berlin and the dormant partners for his costs, but the dormant partners refused to pay the costs incurred after their retirement.

Held, by the Court of Appeal, that the dormant partners were liable for the costs incurred subsequent to their retirement. The solicitor's retainer was one entire contract to conduct the proceedings to the end. Their liability for costs did not arise from day to day as they were incurred. The plaintiff did not have to obtain fresh instructions at each step in the proceedings[20].

Similarly, where a partner dies, his personal representatives continue to be liable for executory engagements made in his lifetime by the firm unless they were made dependent on the personal conduct or capacity of the deceased and have therefore become incapable of performance by reason of his death[1].

But a retiring partner may be discharged from any existing liabilities by an agreement to that effect between himself and the members of the firm as newly constituted and the creditors[2].

Such a tripartite agreement is known as a 'novation'. It may be either expressed or inferred as a fact from the course of dealing between the creditors and the firm as newly constituted[3].

The question is always one of fact, and, in the absence of express novation, the court is slow to infer a novation from the course of dealing. The mere adoption by the creditors of the new firm as their debtor does not of itself discharge the retiring partner.

On the other hand, a novation is not void because it cannot be shown that the creditors benefited in any way[4]. Where a creditor knows of the change in the constitution of the firm and continues to deal with the new firm, making no claim on the retiring partner for a long period, a novation may be inferred[5]. Further, the acceptance of a bill of exchange or other security for the debt from the new firm in some, although not conclusive, evidence of novation[6].

---

20 See the judgment of Lord Esher MR, ibid, at 398 and 294, respectively. See further Ivamy *Casebook on Partnership* (2nd edn 1982) pp 22–23.
1 *Phillips v Hull Alhambra Palace Co* [1901] 1 KB 59.
2 Partnership Act 1890, s 17(3).
3 Ibid, s 17(3).
4 *Thompson v Percival* (1834) 5 B & Ad 925 at 932–933 (per Denman CJ).
5 *Rolfe and Bank of Australasia v Flower, Salting & Co* (1865) LR 1 PC 27; *Bilborough v Holmes* (1876) 5 Ch D 255 35 LT 759.
6 *Swire v Redman* (1876) 1 QBD 536, 35 LT 470; *Re Head, Head v Head* [1893] 3 Ch 426, 69 LT 753.

(*ii*) *Guarantees*

A continuing guarantee given either to a firm or to a third person in respect of the transactions of a firm, is, in the absence of agreement to the contrary, revoked as to future transactions by any change in the constitution of the firm to which, or of the firm in respect of the transactions of which, the guarantee was given[7].

(*iii*) *Future dealings*

Where a person deals with a firm after a change in its constitution, he is entitled to treat all apparent members of the old firm as still being members of the firm until he has notice of the change[8].

The word 'apparent' means 'appeared to be members to persons dealing with the firm'.

Thus, in *Tower Cabinet Co Ltd v Ingram*[9]:

Christmas and Ingram carried on a business of household furnishers under the name 'Merry's'. The partnership was dissolved in April 1947, but Christmas carried on the business under the same name. In 1948 Tower Cabinet Co Ltd, which had not previously dealt with Merry's, received an order to supply them with six suites of furniture. The price was never paid, and the company obtained judgment against Merry's, and sought to enforce it against Ingram. The only knowledge which the company had of Ingram was that his name appeared on some old headed notepaper, which had been used by Christmas without Ingram's authority in confirming the order for the purchase of the furniture, and which Ingram had failed to destroy before he left the firm.

Held, by the King's Bench Division, that Ingram was not liable because the company had no knowledge of his connection with Merry's except for the name on the notepaper. 'Apparent' in section 36 meant 'appeared to be members to persons dealing with the firm'[10].

An advertisement in the 'London Gazette' is notice to persons who had no dealings with the firm before the date of dissolution or change so advertised[11].

The estate of a partner who dies, or who becomes bankrupt, or of a partner who, not having been known to the person dealing with the firm to be a partner, retires from the firm, is not liable for partnership debts contracted after the date of the death, bankruptcy or retirement respectively[12].

7 Partnership Act 1890, s 18.
8 Ibid, s 36(1).
9 [1949] 2 KB 397, [1949] 1 All ER 1033.
10 See the judgment of Lynskey J, ibid, at 1037. See further Ivamy *Casebook on Partnership* (2nd edn 1982) pp 68–70.
11 Partnership Act 1890, s 36(2).
12 Ibid, s 36(3).

Thus, a partner ceases to be liable for the future liabilities of the new firm because, by retiring, he cancels the agency.

Actual notice of retirement should be given to all customers of the old firm.

To persons who had no dealings with the firm before the retirement notice in the 'London Gazette' is sufficient, and in the case of persons dealing with the firm to whom the retiring partner was not known as a partner no notice is necessary[13]. The justice of this requirement is obvious, for a person who deals with a firm is entitled in common fairness to treat all apparent members of the old firm as still being members until he has notice of the change or until any partner dies.

(iv) Liability for holding out as partner

The outgoing partner, in spite of his retirement, may be liable for holding himself out as a partner or knowingly suffering himself to be represented as a partner[14].

---

13 *Graham v Hope* (1792) Peake 208. But it would seem that a due compliance by the continuing partners with the Business Names Act 1985, s 4(1) would fix all customers with notice. As to the requirements of this section, see p 179, below.
14 See pp 71–72, below.

Chapter 5
Persons liable by 'holding out'

Everyone who by words spoken or written or by conduct represents himself, or who knowingly suffers himself to be represented, as a partner in a particular firm, is liable as a partner to any one who has on the faith of any such representation given credit to the firm, whether the representation has or has not been made or communicated to the person so giving credit by or with the knowledge of the apparent partner making the representation or suffering it to be made[1].

Doctrine based on estoppel

The doctrine of holding out is a branch of the doctrine of estoppel. If a person holds himself out as a partner in a firm, and thereby induces another person to act upon that representation, he is estopped as regards that person from saying that he is not a partner. The representation may be made either by acts or by words, but the estoppel can be relied on only by the person to whom the representation has been made in either way, and who has acted on the faith of it[2].

It is immaterial that the representation was not communicated directly to the creditor by the person holding himself out as a partner. It is sufficient if the representation is communicated to the creditor by a third party[3].

Retiring partner

It is really on the ground of holding out that a retiring partner, who does not give notice that the partnership has been dissolved[4], may be liable for the future debts of the firm.

It is obvious that questions of 'holding out' may occur where a partner retires and still permits his former partners to retain his name as part of the firm name. It would seem, however, that where proper notices of the

---

1 Partnership Act 1890, s 14(1).
2 *Re Fraser, ex p Central Bank of London* [1892] 2 QB 633 at 637 (per Lord Esher).
3 *Martyn v Gray* (1863) 14 CBNS 824, where the third party was not aware of the name of the person who was spoken of to him as 'a gentleman down from London, a man of capital'.
4 See p 87, below.

dissolution are given, the mere fact that the retiring partner allows the continuing partner to carry on business in the old firm name, is not such a holding out of the former as a partner as will render him liable for a debt of the firm contracted after the dissolution, even with a person who had not dealt with the old firm, and who had, therefore, no express notice of the dissolution[5]. This appears to be so, although the retiring partner actually authorises the use of his name[6].

The word 'knowingly' in the Partnership Act 1890, s 14(1), does not mean mere carelessness in allowing himself to be represented as a partner.

Thus, in *Tower Cabinet Co Ltd v Ingram*[7]:

Christmas and Ingram carried on a business of household furnishers under the name 'Merry's'. The partnership was dissolved in April 1947, but Christmas carried on business under the same name. In 1948 Tower Cabinet Co Ltd, which had not previously dealt with Merry's, received an order to supply them with six suites of furniture. The price was never paid, and the company obtained judgment against Merry's and sought to enforce it against Ingram. The only knowledge which the company had of Ingram was that his name had appeared on some old headed notepaper, which had been used by Christmas without Ingram's authority in confirming the order for the purchase of the furniture, and which Ingram had failed to destroy before he left the firm.

Held, by the King's Bench Division, that Ingram was not liable under s 14(1) of the Partnership Act 1890 because he had not 'knowingly' suffered himself to be represented as a partner[8].

Death of partner

Where after a partner's death the partnership business is continued in the old firm name, the continued use of that name, or of the deceased partner's name as part thereof, does not of itself make his executors or administrators, estate or effects liable for any partnership debts contracted after his death[9].

---

5 *Re Fraser, ex p Central Bank of London*, above.
6 *Newsome v Coles* (1811) 2 Camp 617.
7 [1949] 2 KB 397, [1949] 1 All ER 1033.
8 See the judgment of Lynskey J, ibid, at 401 and 1036, respectively. See further Ivamy *Casebook on Partnership* (2nd edn 1982) pp 21–22.
9 Partnership Act 1890, s 14(2).

Chapter 6

Procedure in an action by or against partners

The procedure for actions by or against partners in the High Court is laid down by RSC Order 81[1]. Similar rules apply in the county court[2].

Actions by and against firms

Any two or more persons claiming to be entitled, or alleged to be liable, as partners in respect of a cause of action and carrying on business within the jurisdiction may sue, or be sued, in the name of the firm (if any) of which they were partners at the time when the cause of action accrued[3].

Disclosure of partners' names

Any defendant to an action brought by partners in the name of a firm may serve on the plaintiffs or their solicitor a notice requiring them or him to furnish the defendant with a written statement of the names and places of residence of all the persons who were partners in the firm at the time when the cause of action accrued[4]. If the notice is not complied with, the court may order the plaintiffs or their solicitor to furnish the defendant with such a statement and to verify it on oath or otherwise as may be specified in the order, or may order that further proceedings in the action be stayed on such terms as the court may direct[5].

Any plaintiff in an action brought against partners in the name of the firm may serve on the defendants or their solicitor a notice requiring them or him to furnish the plaintiff with a written statement of the names and places of residence of all the persons who were partners in the firm at the time when the cause of action accrued[6]. If the notice is not complied with, the court may order the defendants or their solicitor to furnish the plaintiff with such a statement and to verify it on oath or otherwise as may be specified in the order[7].

---

1 Ord 81 is set out in Appendix C, p 201, below.
2 See CCR Ord 5, r 21.
3 RSC Ord 81, r 1.
4 Ibid, r 2(1).
5 Ibid, r 2(1).
6 Ibid, r 2(1), (3).
7 Ibid, r 2(1), (3).

When the names of the partners have been declared in compliance with a notice or order, the proceedings are to continue in the name of the firm but with the same consequences as would have ensued if the persons whose names have been declared had been named as plaintiffs in the writ[8].

Service of writ

Where partners are sued in the name of a firm, the writ may be served

(1) on any one or more of the partners; or
(2) at the principal place of business of the partnership within the jurisdiction, on any person having at the time of service the control or management of the partnership business there; or
(3) by sending a copy of the writ by ordinary first-class post to the firm at the principal place of business of the partnership within the jurisdiction[9].

Where service of the writ is effected in accordance with these provisions, the writ is deemed to have been duly served on the firm, whether or not any member of the firm is out of the jurisdiction[10].

Where a partnership has, to the knowledge of the plaintiff, been dissolved[11] before an action against the firm is begun, the writ by which the action is begun must be served on every person within the jurisdiction sought to be made liable in the action[12].

Every person on whom a writ is served must at the time of service be given a written notice stating whether he is served as a partner or as a person having the control or management of the partnership business or both as a partner and as such a person[13]. Any person on whom a writ is so served but to whom no such notice is given is deemed to be served as a partner[14].

Acknowledgment of service in an action against a firm

Where persons are sued as partners in the name of their firm, service may not be acknowledged in the name of the firm but only by the partners in their own names, but the action is nevertheless to continue in the name of the firm[15].

---

8 Ibid, r 2(2).
9 Ibid, r 3(1).
10 Ibid, r 3(1).
11 As to dissolution of partnership, see pp 79–85, below.
12 RSC Ord 81, r 3(3).
13 Ibid, r 3(4).
14 Ibid, r 3(4).
15 Ibid, r 4(1).

Where, in an action against a firm, the writ by which the action is begun is served on a person as a partner, that person, if he denies that he was a partner or liable as such at any material time, may acknowledge service of the writ in the action and state in his acknowledgment that he does so as a person served as a partner in the defendant firm but who denies that he was a partner at any material time[16]. An acknowledgment of service given in accordance with this provision is to be treated as an acknowledgment by the defendant firm[17].

Where an acknowledgment of service is so given by a defendant,

(1) the plaintiff may either apply to the court to set it aside on the ground that the defendant was a partner or liable as such at a material time or may leave that question to be determined at a later stage of the proceedings;

(2) the defendant may either apply to the court to set aside the service of the writ on him on the ground that he was not a partner or liable as such at a material time or may at a proper time serve a defence on the plaintiff denying in respect of the plaintiff's claim either his liability as a partner or the liability of the defendant firm or both[18].

The court may at any stage of the proceedings in an action in which a defendant has so acknowledged service, on the application of the plaintiff or of that defendant, order that any question of the liability of that defendant or as to the liability of the defendant firm be tried in such manner and at such time as the court directs[19].

Where in an action against a firm the writ by which the action is begun is served on a person as a person having the control or management of the partnership business, that person may not acknowledge service of the writ in the action unless he is a member of the firm sued[20].

Enforcing judgment or order against firm

Where a judgment is given or order made against a firm, execution to enforce the judgment or order may[1] issue against property of the firm within the jurisdiction[2].

Where a judgment is given or order made against a firm, execution to enforce the judgment or order may[3] issue against any person who

(1) acknowledged service of the writ in the action as a partner, or

---

16 Ibid, r 4(2).
17 Ibid, r 4(2).
18 Ibid, r 4(3).
19 Ibid, r 4(4).
20 Ibid, r 4(5).
 1 Subject to r 6. See p 77, below.
 2 RSC Ord 81, r 5(1).
 3 Subject to rr 5(3) (below) and 6 (p 77, below).

(2) having been served as a partner with the writ of summons, failed to acknowledge service of it in the action, or

(3) admitted in his pleading that he is a partner, or

(4) was adjudged to be a partner[4].

Execution to enforce a judgment or order given or made against a firm may not issue against a member of the firm who was out of the jurisdiction when the writ of summons was issued unless he

(1) acknowledged service of the writ in the action as a partner, or

(2) was served within the jurisdiction with the writ as a partner, or

(3) was, with the leave of the court given under RSC Ord 11, served out of the jurisdiction with the writ, or notice of the writ, as a partner[5].

A judgment or order given or made against a firm does not[6] render liable, release or otherwise affect a member of the firm who was out of the jurisdiction when the writ was issued[7].

Where a party who has obtained a judgment or order against a firm claims that a person is liable to satisfy the judgment or order as being a member of the firm, and the foregoing provisions do not apply in relation to that person, that party may apply to the court for leave to issue execution against that person[8].

Where the person against whom such an application is made does not dispute his liability, the court hearing the application may[9] give leave to issue execution against that person[10].

Where that person disputes his liability, the court may order that the liability of that person be tried and determined in any manner in which any issue or question in an action may be tried and determined[11].

Enforcing judgment or order in actions between partners

Execution to enforce a judgment or order given or made in

(1) an action by or against a firm in the name of the firm against or by a member of the firm, or

(2) an action by a firm in the name of the firm against a firm in the name of the firm where those firms have one or more members in common, is not to issue except with the leave of the court[12].

---

4 RSC Ord 81, r 5(2).
5 Ibid, r 5(3).
6 Except as provided by r 5(1) and the foregoing provisions of r 5(3).
7 RSC Ord 81, r 5(3).
8 Ibid, r 5(4). The application is to be made by summons which must be served personally on that person: ibid, r 5(4).
9 Subject to r 5(3).
10 RSC Ord 81, r 5(5).
11 Ibid, r 5(5).
12 Ibid, r 6(1).

The court hearing an application under this provision may give such directions, including directions as to the taking of accounts and the making of inquiries, as may be just[13].

Attachment of debts owed by firm

An order may be made under RSC Order 49, r 1, in relation to debts due or accruing due from a firm carrying on business within the jurisdiction notwithstanding that one or more members of the firm is resident out of the jurisdiction[14].

An order to show cause under RSC Order 49, r 1, relating to such debts must be served on a member of the firm within the jurisdiction or on some other person having the control or management of the partnership business[15].

Where an order made under RSC Order 49, r 1, requires a firm to appear before the court, an appearance by a member of the firm constitutes a sufficient compliance with the order[16].

Person carrying on business in another name

An individual carrying on business within the jurisdiction in a name or style other than his own name may whether or not he is within the jurisdiction be sued in that name or style as if it were the name of his firm[17].

Application for orders charging partner's interest in partnership property

Every application to the court by a judgment creditor of a partner for an order under the Partnership Act 1890, s 23[18], and every application by a partner of the judgment debtor made in consequence of an application made by such a judgment creditor must be made by summons[19].

Every summons issued by a judgment creditor under this provision, and every order made on such a summons, must be served on the judgment debtor and on such of his partners as are within the jurisdiction[20].

---

13 Ibid, r 6(2).
14 Ibid, r 7(1).
15 Ibid, r 7(2).
16 Ibid, r 7(3).
17 Ibid, r 9. RSC Ord 81, rr 2 to 8, so far as applicable apply as if he were a partner and the name in which he carries on business were the name of his firm: ibid, r 9.
18 See p 35, above.
19 RSC Ord 81, r 10(1).
20 Ibid, r 10(3).

Every summons issued by a partner of a judgment debtor under the above provision and every order made on such a summons, must be served

(1) on the judgment creditor; and
(2) on the judgment debtor; and
(3) on such of the other partners of the judgment debtor as do not join in the application and are within the jurisdiction[1].

A summons or order so served on some of the partners only, is deemed to have been served on all the partners[2].

1 Ibid, r 10(4).
2 Ibid, r 10(5).

Chapter 7
Dissolution of partnership

A partnership may be dissolved

(1) by the expiration of the period for which it is to last or by notice of dissolution;
(2) by the death or bankruptcy of a partner or a charge on his share;
(3) under a clause giving a right to claim dissolution if a specified event occurs;
(4) by illegality;
(5) by an order of the court; or
(6) by an order of an arbitrator.

1 Dissolution by expiration or notice

Subject to any agreement between the partners, a partnership is dissolved

(1) if entered into for a fixed term, by the expiration of that term:
(2) if entered into for a single adventure or undertaking, by the termination of the adventure or undertaking:
(3) if entered into for an undefined time, by any partner giving notice to the other or others of his intention to dissolve the partnership[1].

In the last case the partnership is dissolved as from the date mentioned in the notice as the date of dissolution, or, if no date is so mentioned, as from the date of the communication of the notice[2].

Thus, in *McLeod v Dowling*[3]:

A partnership deed was entered into between two solicitors, McLeod and Dowling, and contained a clause which stated that 'if either partner died during the term of the partnership, the surviving partner was to be exclusively entitled to the business and goodwill of the partnership'. The partnership was originally for 7 years from 13 April 1913, but had been carried on after the expiration of this period without any new agreement being entered into. McLeod gave notice to Dowling by a notice dated 23 March 1927, to determine the

1 Partnership Act 1890, s 32.
2 Ibid, s 32.
3 (1927) 43 TLR 655.

partnership as from that date. The notice was posted on 23 March at between 3 pm and 4 pm and was received by Dowling on 24 March at 10 am. In the meanwhile McLeod died on 24 March, at 3.15 am. Dowling claimed that the partnership had been dissolved by McLeod's death as stated by s 33(1) of the Partnership Act 1890 and not by the notice under s 32(c), and therefore he himself was entitled, under the clause in the partnership deed set out above, to the business and goodwill of the partnership.

Held, by the Chancery Division, that he was so entitled, for the dissolution by the notice was not brought about until it had been communicated as required by s 32(c) of the Act[4].

In the case of a partnership at will the notice can be given whether or not the other partner or partners are of sound mind[5].

Where the articles provide that the partnership for an undefined time can be terminated 'by mutual arrangement only', one partner alone cannot terminate it by giving notice[6].

Once the notice has been given, it cannot be withdrawn except with the consent of all the partners[7].

2 Dissolution by death, bankruptcy or charge

Subject to any agreement between the partners, every partnership is dissolved as regards all the partners by the death or bankruptcy of any partner[8].

But the articles frequently provide that on the death of a partner the business may be continued by the survivors either alone or in partnership with the personal representatives of the deceased partner.

A partnership may, at the option of the other partners, be dissolved if any partner suffers his share of the partnership property to be charged for his separate debt[9].

3 Dissolution under express clause

Any circumstance such as unsoundness of mind, physical incapacity, incompatibility of temperament, or dishonesty (even outside the business) may by an express clause in the articles be a ground for

---

4 See the judgment of Russell J, ibid, at 656. See further Ivamy *Casebook on Partnership* (2nd edn 1982) pp 57–58.
5 *Jones v Lloyd* (1874) LR 18 Eq 265.
6 *Moss v Elphick* [1910] 1 KB 846, 102 LT 639, CA. See p 46, above.
7 *Jones v Lloyd*, above.
8 Partnership Act 1890, s 33(1).
9 Ibid, s 33(2).

dissolution of the partnership without the intervention of the court[10]. Thus, in *Carmichael v Evans*[11]:

Carmichael was a partner in a firm of drapers. He was convicted of travelling on a railway without a ticket with intent to avoid payment. A clause in the partnership agreement stated that the partnership could be dissolved by the other partners if one of them were guilty of any flagrant breach of any of his duties. So they gave Carmichael notice that they intended to dissolve the partnership, but he applied for an interlocutory injunction to stop them doing so.

Held, by the Chancery Division, that the injunction would not be granted. Carmichael's conviction, since it involved dishonesty, fell within the expulsion clause. There was ample justification for giving notice of dissolution of the partnership[12].

4 Dissolution by reason of illegality

A partnership is in every case dissolved by the happening of any event which makes it unlawful for the business of the firm to be carried on or for the members of the firm to carry it on in partnership[13].

The fact of a partner becoming an enemy alien would necessarily make the continuance of the partnership illegal since the other partners would be trading with the enemy.

Thus, in *R v Kupfer*[14]:

The defendant was a partner in a firm which consisted of himself and his two brothers. They carried on the business of the firm in Frankfurt whilst he managed the affairs of the firm in London. The Frankfurt office placed an order for goods with a Dutch company in Terborg, Holland, and payment was to be made by the defendant from the

10 See eg *Peyton v Mindham* [1971] 3 All ER 1215, [1972] 1 WLR 8, where a clause in a medical partnership deed stated: 'In the event of either partner being incapacitated from performing his fair share of the work of the practice for more than 9 consecutive months or for a total of more than 300 days during any period of 24 calendar months or if he shall become lunatic or committed any gross or persistent breach of the clause herein contained or shall wilfully neglect the practice or do or suffer anything whereby the interests of the partnership shall be or shall be in danger of being seriously injured or prejudiced or if his name shall be removed from the Medical Register (except under Section XIV of the Medical Act (1858) . . . or if he shall be made bankrupt or enter a composition or arrangement with or for the benefit of his creditors or shall suffer his share to be charged, it shall be lawful for the other by notice to determine the partnership.'

11 [1904] 1 Ch 486, 90 LT 573.

12 See the judgment of Byrne J, ibid, at 490 and 575, respectively. See further Ivamy *Casebook on Partnership* (2nd edn 1982) pp 56–57. An appeal against the decision was brought, but the action was subsequently settled: [1904] WN 47.

13 Partnership Act 1890, s 34.

14 [1915] 2 KB 321, 112 LT 1138.

London office. War broke out on 4 August 1914. The defendant paid the Dutch company the amount due, and he was charged with an offence of trading with the enemy contrary to the Trading with the Enemy Act 1914. One of the issues which arose was whether the partnership had been dissolved by the outbreak of war.

Held, by the Court of Criminal Appeal, that it was so dissolved[15].

Again, where a solicitor's practising certificate lapses, a partnership between himself and the other partners is automatically dissolved[16].

A clause in the articles stating that a partnership was to continue even in the event of illegality supervening would be ineffective.

5 Dissolution by order of court

On application by a partner[17] the court has power to order dissolution of the partnership in cases of –

  (*i*) mental disorder;
 (*ii*) permanent incapacity;
(*iii*) conduct prejudicial to the business;
 (*iv*) persistent breaches of the partnership agreement;
  (*v*) the partnership being carried on at a loss; or
 (*vi*) the dissolution being just and equitable.

In the event of recourse being had to the court to order a dissolution, it is not unusual, directly the action is started for the plaintiff to apply, pending judgment in the case, for the appointment of a receiver, or sometimes of a receiver and manager[18]. On such a motion the judge asks whether, the parties being at arm's length and in a state of litigation, the partnership can possibly go on. If counsel agree that it cannot do so, an immediate order of dissolution, with the usual accounts and inquiries, may by consent be made, a course which may save a considerable sum in costs[19].

(*i*) *Mental disorder*

Where a judge, after considering medical evidence, is satisfied that a person is incapable by reason of mental disorder of managing his property and affairs, the judge may exercise his powers under Part VII of

---

15 See the judgment of Lord Reading, ibid at 333 and 1141, respectively. See further Ivamy *Casebook on Partnership* (2nd edn 1982) pp 58–59.
16 *Hudgell, Yeates & Co v Watson* [1978] QB 451, [1978] 2 All ER 363, CA.
17 A salaried partner, who has no proprietary interest in the partnership, generally has no claim to an order for dissolution: *Stekel v Ellice* [1973] 1 All ER 465, [1973] 1 WLR 191. (See the judgment of Megarry J, ibid, at 475 and 201 respectively.)
18 As to receivers and managers, see p 88, below.
19 For the form of order, see Atkin's *Court Forms* (2nd edn 1968) p 106.

the Mental Health Act 1983[20]. A person as to whom the judge is so satisfied is referred to as a 'patient' in that Part of the Act[1].

One of the powers is to make orders for the dissolution of a partnership of which the patient is a member[2].

When proceedings are pending in the High Court for the dissolution of a partnership, the court can grant an interlocutory injunction to restrain a partner who is mentally incapable from interfering with the conduct of the partnership business.

(ii) Permanent incapacity

On application by a partner the court may decree a dissolution of the partnership when a partner, other than the partner suing, becomes, other than by reason of mental disorder, permanently incapable of performing his part of the partnership contract[3].

(iii) Conduct prejudicial to the business

On application by a partner the court may decree a dissolution of partnership when a partner, other than the partner suing, has been guilty of such conduct as, in the opinion of the court, regard being had to the nature of the business, is calculated prejudicially to affect the carrying on of the business[4].

(iv) Persistent breaches

On application by a partner the court may decree a dissolution of partnership when a partner, other than the partner suing, wilfully or persistently commits a breach of the partnership agreement, or otherwise so conducts himself in matters relating to the partnership business that it is not reasonably practicable for the other partner or partners to carry on the business in partnership with him[5].

(v) Carrying on at a loss

On application by a partner the court may decree a dissolution of the partnership when the business of the partnership can only be carried on at a loss[6].

The words 'can only be carried on at a loss' mean that there must be a practical impossibility of making a profit.

---

20 Mental Health Act 1983, s 94(2). For the 'judge', see ibid, s 94(1). Mental disorder means 'mental illness, arrested or incomplete development of mind, psychopathic disorder and any other disorder or disability of mind': ibid, s 1(2).
1 Ibid, s 94(2).
2 Ibid, s 96(1)(g).
3 Partnership Act 1890, s 35(b).
4 Ibid, s 35(c).
5 Ibid, s 35(d).
6 Ibid, s 35(e).

Thus, in *Handyside v Campbell*[7]:

The plaintiff was a partner in a firm of stevedores and riggers, and applied to the court for a decree of dissolution of partnership. He alleged that the partnership could only be carried on at a loss. The other partners admitted that a loss was being made at present, but alleged that it was owing in part to past mismanagement by the plaintiff, and in part to his long absence from business due to illness, and that his absence still continued. They contended that if proper attention was given, it was quite possible for the business to be carried on at a profit.

Held, by the Chancery Division, that no decree for dissolution of the partnership would be made, for in order to bring the ground mentioned in s 35(e) of the Partnership Act 1890 into operation, the practical impossibility of making a profit must be proved, and no such proof had been given in the present case[8].

(*vi*) *Just and equitable*

On application by a partner the court may decree a dissolution of the partnership whenever in any case circumstances have arisen which, in the opinion of the court, render it just and equitable that the partnership be dissolved[9].

It is impossible to specify all the acts and circumstances which would enable the court to decree a dissolution on the wide ground that it is 'just and equitable'.

But on the analogy of a similar provision in the Companies Act 1985, s 517(1) the words would probably be held not to be limited to circumstances *ejusdem generis* with the other grounds set out in the Partnership Act 1890, s 35, on which the court may order a dissolution[10].

6 Dissolution by order of arbitrator

If the partnership articles contain a clause referring all matters in dispute to arbitration, and the dispute involves a claim for dissolution, the arbitrator is empowered to dissolve the partnership just as the court might[11].

But in such a case, if one partner brings an action for dissolution, the court has a discretion to decide whether the matter shall be tried or referred to arbitration.

7 (1901) 17 TLR 623.
8 See the judgment of Farwell J, ibid, at 624. See further Ivamy *Casebook on Partnership* (2nd edn 1982) pp 60–61.
9 Partnership Act 1890, s 35(f).
10 *Ebrahimi v Westbourne Galleries Ltd* [1973] AC 360, [1972] 2 All ER 492, HL.
11 *Vawdrey v Simpson* [1896] 1 Ch 166.

Thus, in *Olver v Hillier*[12]:

A partnership deed between two partners in a dairy business stated that 'all disputes which shall either during the partnership or afterwards arise between the partners . . . touching this agreement . . . or any account, valuation or division of assets . . . shall be referred to a single arbitrator.' One of the partners brought an action claiming (i) dissolution of the partnership; (ii) the taking of accounts and inquiries; and (iii) the appointment of a receiver and manager on the ground that by reason of the conduct of the other partner it was just and equitable that the partnership should be dissolved under s 35(d) and (f) of the Partnership Act 1890. The other partner applied for the action to be stayed on account of the arbitration clause in the deed.

Held, by the Chancery Division, that the action would not be stayed because the power of ordering dissolution was expressly given to the court under s 35(d) and (f) of the Act, which was the ground for dissolution contended for, and also because the application was for the appointment of a receiver and manager as well as for a dissolution[13].

On the other hand, in *Belfield v Bourne*[14]:

A partnership deed stated that 'if during the continuance of the partnership or at any time afterwards any difference should arise in regard to the construction of any of the articles herein contained, or to any division, act or thing to be made or done in pursuance hereof, or to any other matter or thing relating to the said partnership or the affairs thereof' the difference should be referred to arbitration. One of the partners brought an action for a dissolution of the partnership claiming (inter alia) a return of the sum which he had paid by way of premium. The other partner applied for the action to be stayed and the matter referred to arbitration.

Held, by the Chancery Division, that the application would be granted. By the terms of the partnership deed the arbitrator had power to award a dissolution, and this power included a right to order a return of premium[15].

---

12 [1959] 2 All ER 220, [1959] 1 WLR 551.
13 See the judgment of Roxburgh J, ibid, at 221 and 553 respectively. See further Ivamy *Casebook on Partnership* (2nd edn 1982) pp 62–63.
14 [1894] 1 Ch 521, 69 LT 786.
15 See the judgment of Stirling J, at 523 and 788, respectively. See further Ivamy *Casebook on Partnership* (2nd edn 1982) pp 61–62.

Chapter 8

The consequences of dissolution of partnership

Where a partnership is dissolved for fraud or misrepresentation, the partner defrauded is given certain rights[1].

In cases where a partner has paid a premium to enter into the partnership, part of the premium may sometimes be repayable[2].

A partner is entitled to notify publicly that the partnership has been dissolved [3].

The authority of the partners continues to a limited extent even after dissolution [4].

The court has power to appoint a receiver and manager[5].

An outgoing partner may be entitled to share in the profits of the partnership made after the dissolution[6].

A retiring or deceased's partner's share is a debt accruing at the date of dissolution or death[7].

The assets of the partnership must be realised[8], an account must be taken [9], and the assets distributed[10].

Questions may arise as to the costs involved in the dissolution[11].

Rights where partnership is dissolved for fraud or misrepresentation

Where a partnership contract is rescinded on the ground of the fraud or misrepresentation of one of the parties to it, the party entitled to rescind is, without prejudice to any other right, entitled

1 See below.
2 See p 87, below.
3 See p 87, below.
4 See p 88, below.
5 See p 88, below.
6 See p 91, below.
7 See p 92, below.
8 See p 92, below.
9 See p 97, below.
10 See p 100, below.
11 See p 102, below.

(1) to a lien on the surplus of the partnership assets, after satisfying the partnership liabilities, for any sum of money paid by him for the purchase of a share in the partnership and for any capital contributed by him, and is
(2) to stand in the place of the creditors of the firm for any payments made by him in respect of the partnership liabilities, and
(3) to be indemnified by the person guilty of the fraud or making the representation against all the debts and liabilities of the firm[12].

Apportionment of premium

Where one partner has paid a premium to another on entering into a partnership for a fixed term and the partnership is dissolved before the expiration of that term otherwise than by the death of a partner, the court may order the repayment of the premium or of such part of it as it thinks just, having regard to the terms of the partnership contract and to the length of time during which the partnership has continued[13].

But no repayment will be ordered if

(1) the dissolution is, in the judgment of the court, wholly or chiefly due to the misconduct of the partner who paid the premium; or
(2) the partnership has been dissolved by an agreement containing no provision for a return of any part of the premium[14].

Where the articles contain the usual wide arbitration clause, an arbitrator has power to order the return of part of a premium[15].

Rights of partners to notify dissolution

On the dissolution of a partnership any partner may publicly notify the same, and may require the other partner or partners to concur for that purpose in all necessary or proper acts, if any, which cannot be done without his or their concurrence[16].

---

12 Partnership Act 1890, s 41.
13 Ibid, s 40. For a case decided before the Act, see *Atwood v Maude* (1868) 3 Ch App 369.
14 Partnership Act 1890, s 40.
15 *Belfield v Bourne* [1894] 1 Ch 521, 69 LT 786. See p 85, above.
16 Partnership Act 1890, s 37. This provision was, no doubt, inserted in the Act because the publishers of *The London Gazette* refused to insert such notices unless they were signed by *all* the partners.

Continuing authority of partners

After the dissolution of a partnership the authority of each partner to bind the firm, and the other rights and obligations of the partners, continue notwithstanding the dissolution so far as may be necessary to wind up the affairs of the partnership, and to complete transactions begun but unfinished at the time of the dissolution, but not otherwise[17].

Thus, in *Re Bourne, Bourne v Bourne*[18]:

A partnership was dissolved by the death of one of the partners. The surviving partner carried on the business, and deposited with a bank the title deeds relating to some land owned by the partnership in order to secure an overdraft. The executors of the deceased partner claimed that the surviving partner was not allowed to do this, and that they had a right to the land in preference to the bank's claim.

Held, by the Court of Appeal, that the bank had a prior claim, for the title deeds had been deposited in order to wind up the affairs of the partnership[19].

But the firm is in no case bound by the acts of a partner who has become bankrupt[20].

If the dissolution is caused by the death or bankruptcy of a partner, this authority to wind up the business devolves on the surviving or solvent partners alone, to the exclusion of the bankrupt partner and of the personal representatives, or trustee in bankruptcy, of the deceased or bankrupt[1].

Receivers and managers

The continuing authority of the partners may be taken away by the court if the parties fall out, or if special grounds are shown by the personal representatives of a deceased partner, or the trustee in bankruptcy of a bankrupt partner either by the appointment of

(1) a receiver to get in the outstanding assets; or
(2) a receiver and manager to conduct the entire winding up.

---

17 Partnership Act 1890, s 38.
18 [1906] 2 Ch 427, 95 LT 131.
19 See the judgment of Vaughan Williams LJ, ibid, at 430 and 134, respectively. See further Ivamy *Casebook on Partnership* (2nd edn 1982) p 71.
20 Partnership Act 1890, s 38, proviso. But this proviso does not affect the liability of any person who has after the bankruptcy represented himself or knowingly suffered himself to be represented as a partner of the bankrupt: ibid.
 1 See ibid, s 14(2).

A receiver will generally (but not as a matter of course) be appointed on the application of any partner, even though disputes between the partners are to be referred to arbitration in accordance with a clause to that effect in the partnership deed[2].

The appointment of a manager requires a stronger case than the appointment of a receiver. A receiver takes the income and pays the necessary outgoings. A manager takes over and carries on the entire business. The appointment of a receiver only practically brings the trade to a dead stop. If, therefore, it is desired to continue the trade, it is necessary to appoint a manager. A manager is often given power to employ one or more sub-managers. Any of the partners may be a sub-manager.

The court will not, as a rule, appoint a manager, and so take control out of the hands of the partners except with the view of winding up the concern[3] by carrying into effect existing contracts, and entering into such new ones as are necessary for carrying on business in the ordinary way, but not so as to impose, by speculative dealing or otherwise, onerous liabilities on the partners[4].

Where a partner is appointed as a receiver, he is entitled to remuneration for his services, even though he is unable to pay a debt which he owes to the partnership.

Thus, in *Davy v Scarth*[5]:

Mr Davy and Mr Scarth were partners. The partnership was dissolved by Davy's death, and Scarth was appointed by the court as receiver. At the date of Davy's death, Scarth owed the partnership £1457 19s 5d. Davy's executrix brought an action for an account and claimed that the partnership owed her £1464 5s 10d. as representing Davy's share of the partnership property. The total partnership assets in Scarth's hands were £1392 12s 8d. Scarth contended that although he was unable to pay his debt to the partnership, he was entitled to deduct his remuneration of £280 and his costs of £48 1s 6d. from the assets.

Held, by the Chancery Division, that he was so entitled, for as a receiver he was an officer of the court on the terms that he should do certain work and be paid for it[6].

Where one partner is insolvent, the other partner is usually appointed manager without a salary[7]. But in other cases the court will not, as a

2 *Pini v Roncoroni* [1892] 1 Ch 633, 66 LT 255.
3 *Const v Harris* (1824) T & R 496 at 517 (per Lord Eldon LC); *Sargant v Read* (1876) 1 Ch D 600.
4 *Taylor v Neate* (1888) 39 Ch D 538, 60 LT 179.
5 [1906] 1 Ch 55.
6 See the judgment of Farwell J, ibid, at 56. See further Ivamy *Casebook on Partnership* (2nd edn 1982) p 90.
7 *Collins v Barker* [1893] 1 Ch 578, 68 LT 572.

general rule, appoint any of the partners except by consent, unless the business is a personal one, or other strong grounds exist for appointing one of the partners[8].

In appointing a manager the court may order that he is not to act as such beyond a fixed date without its leave.

He is appointed on the terms that he becomes personally liable on all contracts entered into by him, but is entitled to be indemnified out of the assets of the business in priority to all creditors of the firm[9]. But he is not entitled to an indemnity from the partners personally even where the order appointing him was made with their consent.

Thus, in *Boehm v Goodall*[10]:

A partnership was dissolved, and a person was appointed by the court with the consent of the partners as a receiver and manager. He incurred expenses in carrying on the partnership business and in paying rent due by the firm. He now claimed that the partners were personally liable to indemnify him in respect of the sums which he had paid.

Held, by the Chancery Division, that they were not liable, and he could look only to the assets of the firm for an indemnity, even though the partners consented to his appointment[11].

If necessary, the court will prevent by the issue of an injunction either partner from interfering with the manager to the detriment of the business or the goodwill[12].

Thus, in *Dixon v Dixon*[13].

A partnership of two brothers named Robert Dixon and George Dixon, carrying on business as grocers and merchants under the name of George Dixon & Sons, fell into difficulties, and on 12 February 1903 Robert Dixon issued a writ for the dissolution of the partnership, and on 20 February a receiver and manager was appointed. On 28 April, the court declared that the partnership was dissolved on 12 February. George Dixon was dismissed from the management of the business on 21 February, and managed a rival business under the name of Dixon Brothers. He attempted to induce employees to give proper notice and leave George Dixon & Sons and to enter his service. He also tried to obtain for himself the tenancy of a field used by the partnership business of George Dixon & Sons. Robert Dixon now sought an

8 *Sargant v Read*, above.
9 *Burt, Boulton and Hayward v Bull* [1895] 1 QB 276, 71 LT 810, CA; *Strapp v Bull Sons & Co* [1895] 2 Ch 1, 72 LT 514, CA.
10 [1911] 1 Ch 155, 103 LT 717.
11 See the judgment of Warrington J, ibid, at 159 and 718, respectively. See further Ivamy *Casebook on Partnership* (2nd edn 1982) p 91.
12 As to goodwill, see pp 93–96, below.
13 [1904] 1 Ch 161, 89 LT 272.

injunction to prevent him from so acting on the ground that it was an interference with the management of the receiver and manager.

Held, by the Chancery Division, that the injunction would be granted, for the court was bound to protect its receiver and manager[14].

Right of outgoing partner to share profits made after dissolution

Where any member of a firm has died or otherwise ceased to be a partner, and the surviving or continuing partners carry on the business of the firm with its capital or assets without any final settlement of accounts as between the firm and the outgoing partner or his estate, then, in the absence of any agreement to the contrary, the outgoing partner or his estate is entitled at the option of himself or his representatives

(1) to such share of the profits[15] made since the dissolution as the court may find to be attributable to the use of his share in the partnership assets, or

(2) to interest at the rate of 5% per annum on the amount of his share of the partnership assets[16].

Thus, in *Manley v Sartori*[17]:

One of the partners in a firm died, and the business was carried on by the surviving partners. The personal representatives applied to the court under s 42(1) for it to ascertain what sum was due to the estate.

Held, by the Chancery Division, that the personal representatives were prima facie entitled to a share of the profits proportionate to the deceased's share in the assets of the partnership; but that the surviving partners were entitled to an allowance in respect of the management of the business after the dissolution[18].

But where by the partnership contract an option is given to surviving or continuing partners to purchase the interest of a deceased or outgoing partner, and that option is duly exercised, the estate of the deceased

14 See the judgment of Swinfen Eady J, ibid, at 163. See further Ivamy *Casebook on Partnership* (2nd edn 1982) pp 91–92.

15 The word 'profits' means profits which have accrued in the ordinary course of carrying on the partnership business pending realisation: *Barclays Bank Trust Co Ltd v Bluff* [1981] 3 All ER 232 at 239 (per H E Francis, QC).

16 Partnership Act 1890, s 42(1).

17 [1927] 1 Ch 157, 136 LT 238.

18 See the judgment of Romer J, ibid, at 161 and 239, respectively. See further Ivamy *Casebook on Partnership* (2nd edn 1982) p 72.

partner, or the outgoing partner or his estate, as the case may be, is not entitled to any further or other share of profits[19].

If any partner assuming to act in the exercise of the option does not in all material respects comply with its terms, he is liable to account[20].

Where the continuing partners are carrying out an agreement to purchase an outgoing or deceased partner's share and to indemnify him or his estate against partnership debts, the outgoing partner or the representatives of the deceased partner cannot demand the repayment of a firm overdraft granted to a firm and not yet called in[1].

Retiring or deceased partner's share to be debt

Subject to any agreement between the partners, the amount due from surviving or continuing partners to an outgoing partner or the representatives of a deceased partner in respect of the outgoing or deceased partner's share is a debt accruing at the date of the dissolution or death[2].

For the purposes of the Limitation Act 1980 time begins to run from that date[3].

Realising the assets

Duty to assist in getting in firm's assets

Upon dissolution one partner is entitled by action in the firm's name to get in the firm's assets on giving the other partners an indemnity against the costs of the action. In such a case the other partners must assist him at any rate to the extent of complying with an order for discovery made against the firm.

Thus, in *Seal and Edgelow v Kingston*[4]:

A partnership between two solicitors – Seal and Edgelow – was dissolved in 1905, but Seal continued the business in the firm's name. In 1906 Seal brought an action against Kingston, who had been a client of the firm, for costs alleged to be due to the firm before the dissolution. Seal gave an indemnity to Edgelow, who disclaimed any right to any sum which might be recovered, in respect of the costs to be incurred in the action. An order was made requiring 'the plaintiffs' to

---

19 Partnership Act 1890, s 42(2).
20 Ibid, s 42(2).
1 *Bradford v Gammon* [1925] Ch 132, 132 LT 342.
2 Partnership Act 1890, s 43.
3 *Betjemann v Betjemann* [1895] 2 Ch 474, 73 LT 2.
4 [1908] 2 KB 579, 99 LT 504, CA.

make a further and better affidavit of documents. Edgelow refused to comply with this order, so Seal took out a summons to attack him for failing to obey it. A question arose as to whether the court had jurisdiction to make such an order.

Held, by the Court of Appeal, that the court had jurisdiction[5].

Goodwill

The assets include not only the stock-in-trade and book debts, furniture, tools, machinery etc. but also the 'goodwill' of the business.

Lord Eldon said that 'goodwill' was nothing more than the probability of the old customers resorting to the old place[6]. Other definitions are 'a connection formed by years of work'[7], 'the benefit arising from connection and reputation'[8], 'the whole advantage whatever it may be, of the reputation and connection of the firm, which may have been built up by years of honest work or gained by lavish expenditure of money'[9], and 'the advantage, whatever it may be, which a person gets by continuing to carry on, and being entitled to represent to the outside world that he is carrying on, a business which has been carried on for some time previously'[10].

Generally, and in the absence of agreement[11], the goodwill must be sold[12]. There is said, however, to be an exception in the case of businesses of a very personal nature, eg those of solicitors, and on dissolution each partner (or the survivor in case of dissolution by death) retains whatever benefit may be derived from goodwill[13]. Further, it is unlawful for a medical practitioner providing general medical services under the National Health Service Act 1977 to sell the goodwill or any part of the goodwill of his medical practice[14].

The sale of the goodwill does not prevent the seller from carrying on a

5 See the judgment of Farwell LJ, ibid, at 583 and 506, respectively. See further Ivamy *Casebook on Partnership* (2nd edn 1982) p 75.
6 *Cruttwell v Lye* (1810) 17 Ves 335 at 346.
7 *Ginesi v Cooper & Co* (1880) 14 Ch D 596 at 599 (per Jessel MR).
8 Lindley, op cit, p 247.
9 *Trego v Hunt* [1896] AC 7 at 24 (per Lord MacNaghten).
10 *Hill v Fearis* [1905] 1 Ch 466 at 471 (per Warrington J).
11 The partnership articles may provide that, on the assets being taken over by a surviving partner, the goodwill is to belong to him absolutely: *Hordern v Hordern* [1910] AC 465, 102 LT 867, PC. Such provision may be implied eg where the value of a deceased partner's share is to be ascertained according to the last periodical balance sheet, for in such balance sheets the value of the goodwill should not be included in the absence of a contrary agreement: *Scott v Scott* (1903) 89 LT 582. Whether or not the articles have this effect is a question of construction in each case: *Smith v Nelson* (1905) 92 LT 313.
12 *Pawsey v Armstrong* (1881) 18 Ch D 698; *Page v Ratliffe* (1897) 76 LT 63, CA; *Re David and Matthews* [1899] 1 Ch 378, 80 LT 75; *Hill v Fearis*, above.
13 *Arundell v Bell* (1883) 52 LJ Ch 537. But cf *Burchell v Wilde* [1900] 1 Ch 551.
14 National Health Service Act 1977, s 54(1). 'General medical services' mean personal medical services for all persons in the Area Health Authority's area who wish to take advantage of the arrangements: ibid, s 29(1).

business in competition with that of the purchaser, but the former partners may be restrained from soliciting any person who was a customer of the old firm.

Thus, in *Gillingham v Beddow*[15]:

The plaintiff and the defendant were partners carrying on business as printers. The partnership deed stated that on the expiration of the partnership 'the partner who will give the largest sum for the goodwill and assets of the partnership' was entitled to have them made over to him, and that 'nothing herein contained shall prevent either partner from starting a similar business in the neighbourhood after the expiration of the partnership'. The partnership term expired, and the plaintiff purchased the goodwill and assets. The defendant started a similar business, and claimed that he was entitled to send circulars to the customers of the old firm to solicit orders. The plaintiff applied for an injunction to prevent him from doing so.

Held, by the Chancery Division, that the injunction would be granted, for the partnership deed, in stating that a partner selling the goodwill could start up a similar business, did not mean that he was entitled to solicit the customers of the old firm[16].

Accordingly, where goodwill forms part of the partnership property and one of the partners dies, it should be valued on the basis that the surviving partners can carry on a rival business but cannot use the firm name nor solicit its customers.

Thus, in *Re David and Matthews*[17]:

Article 8 of a partnership deed between M. Letricheux and Edmond David, who carried on business as coal merchants under the name of 'Letricheux and David', stated that 'in case of the death of one of the partners a general account of the position shall be made including all effects and securities of whatsoever nature that they possess, and the value of such effects and securities shall be estimated [by an appraiser] as at the date of such decease'. Edmond David died. The goodwill formed part of the partnership assets, and a question arose as to how it should be valued.

Held, by the Chancery Division, that it should be valued on the basis that if the business were sold, the surviving partner could not use the name of the partnership firm nor solicit its customers[18].

The partners may also be restrained from carrying on a similar business

---

15 [1900] 2 Ch 242, 82 LT 791.
16 See the judgment of Cozens-Hardy J, ibid, at 244 and 792, respectively. See further Ivamy *Casebook on Partnership* (2nd edn 1982) pp 78–79.
17 [1899] 1 Ch 378, 80 LT 75.
18 See the judgment of Romer J, ibid, at 378 and 76, respectively. See further Ivamy *Casebook on Partnership* (2nd edn 1982) pp 79–80.

under the name of the old firm or from representing themselves as carrying on the old business[19]. Further, an executor, who is carrying out his testator's contract to sell the goodwill of a business, is, equally with the testator, under a duty to do nothing to destroy or depreciate the value of the goodwill which he has sold.

Thus, in *Boorne v Wicker*[20]:

> By the terms of a partnership agreement it was provided that, if one of the partners died, the survivor would purchase his share of the goodwill and assets, or the goodwill and assets would be sold to a third party. The deceased partner's executor joined a rival firm, and attempted to solicit the customers of the former partnership. The surviving partner applied for an injunction to prevent him from doing so.
>
> *Held*, by the Chancery Division, that the injunction would be granted[1].

This principle is also applicable to a case where a person has been taken into partnership on terms that, on the expiration of the partnership, the goodwill is to belong exclusively to the other partner.

Thus, in *Trego v Hunt*[2]:

> In 1889 Hunt was taken into the partnership of Tabor, Trego & Co for a term of seven years, and it was agreed that the goodwill should remain the sole property of Mrs Trego, the other partner. In 1894 Mrs Trego found that Hunt had employed a clerk of the firm to copy for him the names and addresses of the firm's customers so that, when the partnership came to an end, he could canvass them and endeavour to obtain their custom for himself. She, therefore, applied for an injunction to restrain him from making such copies for the purpose other than the business of the partnership.
>
> *Held*, by the House of Lords, that the injunction would be granted. Hunt was entitled to set up a competing business, but he had no right to avail himself of his special knowledge of old customers to help him to do so[3].

The same principle applies also to the case where, on the dissolution, one partner purchases the assets from the others[4].

If the goodwill is not sold, each partner may not only canvass old

19 *Boorne v Wicker* [1927] 1 Ch 667, 137 LT 409.
20 [1927] 1 Ch 667, 137 LT 409.
 1 See the judgment of Tomlin J, ibid, at 672 and 412, respectively. See further Ivamy *Casebook on Partnership* (2nd edn 1982) p 79.
 2 [1896] AC 7, 73 LT 514 HL.
 3 See the judgment of Lord Herschell, ibid, at 10 and 515, respectively, and that of Lord MacNaughten ibid, at 22 and 519, respectively. See further Ivamy *Casebook on Partnership* (2nd edn 1982) pp 76–78.
 4 *Jennings v Jennings* [1898] 1 Ch 378, 77 LT 786.

customers, but, subject to any question as to endangering the other partners under the doctrine of 'holding out', may also use the firm name notwithstanding the obvious inconvenience of this course.

Thus, in *Burchell v Wilde*[5]:

A firm of solicitors carried on business as 'Burchell & Co'. It was dissolved by the agreement of the three partners, and the goodwill and business were divided. Two of the partners were called Burchell, and the third was Wilde. There was no arrangement as to the use of the firm name after the dissolution. The Burchells carried on business under the name of 'Burchell & Co' at the same address, whilst Wilde used the same name elsewhere. The Burchells applied for an injunction to restrain Wilde from so doing.

Held, by the Court of Appeal, that the injunction would not be granted. Each partner was entitled to use the firm name as long as it did not involve the other partners in liability, and no such liability had been proved in the present case[6].

Where the accounts, from which the sum to be paid to a deceased partner's estate is to be ascertained, are accounts for the purpose of ascertaining the profits, and the goodwill is not to be included in them, the goodwill is not to be included in the valuation of his share.

Thus, in *Scott v Scott*[7]:

Article 10 of a partnership deed stated that if either of the partners died before the expiration of the partnership, his personal representatives 'shall be entitled to such sum of money as the share of the deceased partner of the capital and property of the partnership shall upon the last general account amount to . . .'. One of the partners died during the continuance of the partnership. His executors claimed that a sum representing goodwill should be included in the valuation of the deceased's share.

Held, by the Chancery Division, that the goodwill was not to be included[8].

Appointments held by partners personally

It would seem that where (as in some professional partnerships) one of the partners holds an appointment or office which is personal to himself, but the emoluments of which have been treated as profits of the firm, he

---

5 [1900] 1 Ch 551, 82 LT 576, CA.
6 See the judgment of Lindley MR, ibid, at 561 and 579, respectively. See further Ivamy *Casebook on Partnership* (2nd edn 1982) pp 81–82. See also *Banks v Gibson* (1865) 34 Beav 566.
7 (1903) 89 LT 582.
8 See the judgment of Joyce J, ibid, at 582. See further Ivamy *Casebook on Partnership* (2nd edn 1982) pp 80–81.

must, on dissolution, in the absence of agreement to the contrary, be debited with its value. For although such an office cannot be sold for the benefit of the firm, yet if one of the partners retains it, he must account for its value[9].

Account

Where by agreement one or more members of the firm continue the business on the terms of paying off the share of the outgoing or deceased partner or partners, ascertained on a certain agreed basis, no final account and distribution are necessary because the agreement is substituted for it[10].

But where there is a true dissolution of the firm, each partner going his own way and the partnership property being sold, then a general account is necessary, and may be claimed not only by living partners and the assignees of the shares of living partners[11] but also by the personal representatives of deceased partners.

The remedy of taking an account is the only one available.

Thus, in *Green v Hertzog*[12]:

A partnership was dissolved and one partner, who had lent money to the firm, sued the former partners for its return. She claimed the sum at common law, and did not use the procedure of taking accounts under s 44 of the Partnership Act 1890.

Held, by the Court of Appeal, that there was no right of action at common law and the claim failed. The money could be recovered only by taking accounts under s 44 of the Act[13].

Mode of taking account

The final account will start from the last settled account, ie in ordinary cases on the footing that the last periodical balance sheet is correct, for the court will not disturb a settled account unless there is proof of fraud or error.

Occasionally, however, there are cases where a partnership has lasted

---

9 *Smith v Mules* (1852) 9 Hare 556; *Ambler v Bolton* (1872) LR 14 Eq 427.
10 Such an agreement demands the greatest good faith and candour, and in the absence of full disclosure of all material facts it may be set aside: *Law v Law* [1905] 1 Ch 140. See p 49, above.
11 Partnership Act 1890, s 31(2).
12 [1954] 1 WLR 1309.
13 See the judgment of Lord Goddard LCJ, ibid, at 1312. See further Ivamy *Casebook on Partnership* (2nd edn 1982) p 73.

for years without any settled accounts. In such cases it is necessary to take the accounts from the beginning.

From whatever date the final account is to begin, it must in every case be continued right down to the date of the dissolution, and then be kept open so as to let in all transactions occurring in the actual winding up.

In taking the accounts the uniform course of practice of the firm with regard to previous accounts must, so far as applicable to the final account, be observed. No doubt in complete dissolutions this is not often of much importance. But where an account is taken to ascertain what is due to a partner who has died or retired on the terms of his receiving the value of his share at the date of death or retirement, it may be of the utmost importance.

Thus, in *Re Barber, ex p Barber*[14]:

Partnership articles provided for a balance sheet being made out up to 31 December in each year, which, after a certain time, was to be binding on the partners, except that manifest errors, when discovered, should be corrected. It was also provided that a like account should be made out on 31 December next after the death of a partner, and that his executors should be entitled to receive, by six instalments, from the surviving partners, the value of his interest as appearing from such balance sheet. The uniform practice of the firm in making out their balance sheets was to treat the loss occasioned by any asset turning out bad, as attributable to the year in which it was discovered to be bad. In the year 1864 one of the partners died; and after the balance sheet had been made out, various assets which had been treated as good were ascertained to be irrecoverable, owing to the failure, since 31 December, of debtors of the firm, and depreciation of consignments which, when the balance sheet was made out, had not been realised.

Held, that the executors of the deceased partner were nevertheless entitled to receive the value of his share as appearing by the balance sheet, without any deduction for the losses subsequently ascertained.

Where there is no different term in the partnership deed to the contrary, the profits of the firm must be ascertained on the basis of the sums actually paid and received in that year. The date when the work, in respect of which the sums have been received, was done is immaterial.

Thus, in *Badham v Williams*[15]:

Badham and Williams were solicitors and entered into partnership on 22 July 1880. By the terms of the partnership deed Williams was to receive £300 per annum up to the end of 1880, and £350 for the following two years. From 1 January 1885, he was to receive one-

---

14 (1870) 5 Ch App 687. See also *Steuart v Gladstone* (1878) 10 Ch D 626, 38 LT 557; *Garwood v Garwood* (1911) 105 LT 231.
15 (1902) 86 LT 191.

fourth of the profits for the next five years, and after that one-third of the profits. The partnership was dissolved in August 1899. No division of profits was ever made. A question arose as to whether the actual receipts and payments for each year were to be taken for the purpose of ascertaining the profits of the firm for that year, or whether money received after 1885 for work done before 1885 should be considered as belonging to Badham alone and not as profits of the firm.

Held, by the Chancery Division, that the actual receipts and payments for the year were to be taken for the purpose of ascertaining the profits of that year. Consequently Williams was entitled to a share of the profits for 1885 and subsequent years although the work had been done before 1885[16].

The words 'net profits' of a partnership do not necessarily have the same meaning in all the clauses of the partnership deed.

Thus, in *Watson v Haggitt* [17]:

A partnership deed between two solicitors – Watson and Haggitt – stated by cl 3 that Watson was to be entitled during the continuance of the partnership term to a salary of £1,500 per annum and half of the net profits, and Haggitt to £1,000 and the other half of the net profits. Clause 21 stated that if either of the partners should die, the surviving partner would, for the next five years, pay to the deceased's estate a sum equivalent to one-third of the 'net annual profits.' Haggitt died and the partnership was dissolved. A question arose as to whether, in calculating the net annual profits for the purpose of cl 21, there should be deducted from the gross takings of the business the salaries provided by the deed as payable to the partners or either of those salaries.

Held, by the Judicial Committee of the Privy Council, that no deductions should be made. The expression 'net profits' did not have the same meaning in all the clauses of the deed[18].

The partnership deed may define profits as 'including a salary derived by a partner from any office which he may hold', and then they must be calculated accordingly.

Thus, in *Carlyon-Britton v Lumb* [19]:

The plaintiff and defendant were solicitors in partnership from 1909 under a partnership deed, which stated that the partnership was to be for 10 years and thenceforeward until determined by notice. Clause 11

16 See the judgment of Kekewich J, ibid, at 192. See further Ivamy *Casebook on Partnership* (2nd edn 1982) pp 63–65.
17 [1928] AC 127, 138 LT 306, PC.
18 See the judgment of Lord Warrington, ibid, at 128 and 307, respectively. See further Ivamy *Casebook on Partnership* (2nd edn 1982) pp 65–67.
19 (1922) 38 TLR 298.

provided that the 'salary or other benefit derived by either partner from any office which he may hold during the continuance of the partnership shall be treated as forming part of the profits'. Clause 13 stated that for five years from July 1909 both partners should devote their whole time to the business, but that after that period the plaintiff should not be obliged to attend to the business any further than he thought proper. In December 1914 the plaintiff joined the Army as a major, and was demobilised in 1918, and during the period of his service received the ordinary pay and allowances of his rank. The partnership was dissolved in 1921 at the defendant's instance, and an account was taken. The question arose as to whether the plaintiff's Army pay and allowances ought to be treated as forming part of the profits of the partnership.

Held, by the Chancery Division, that they should be so treated[20].

Distribution of assets

In settling accounts between the partners after a dissolution there are certain rules, which, subject to any agreement[1], must be observed in relation to the payment of losses. These rules relate to:

(1) the payment of losses; and
(2) the application of the assets.

1 Payment of losses

The rule is that losses, including losses and deficiencies of capital, must be paid out of profits, next out of capital, and lastly, if necessary, by the partners individually in the proportion in which they were entitled to share profits[2].

2 Application of the assets

Here the rule is that the assets of the firm including the sums, if any, contributed by the partners to make up losses or deficiencies of capital, are to be applied in the following manner and order:

(1) in paying the debts and liabilities of the firm to persons who are not partners in it.

---

20 See the judgment of Russell J, ibid, at 298. See further Ivamy *Casebook on Partnership* (2nd edn 1982) pp 67–68.
1 See eg *Wood v Scoles* (1866) 1 Ch App 369, 14 LT 470.
2 Partnership Act 1890, s 44.

(2) in paying to each partner rateably what is due from the firm to him for advances as distinguished from capital.

(3) in paying to each partner rateably what is due from the firm to him in respect of capital.

(4) the ultimate residue, if any, is to be divided among the partners in the proportion in which profits are divisible[3].

Where a partnership is dissolved, and, after the debts to third parties have been paid and advances made by a partner have been repaid, the assets are insufficient to repay each partner his capital in full, any deficiency must be borne by the partners in the same proportion as the profits would have been divided[4].

Partner's rights as to application of partnership property
On the dissolution of a partnership every partner is entitled, as against the other partners in the firm, and all persons claiming through them in respect of their interests as partners, to have the property of the partnership[5] applied in payment of the debts and liabilities of the firm, and to have the surplus assets after such payment applied in payment of what may be due to the partners respectively after deducting what may be due to them as partners to the firm[6].

For that purpose any partner or his representatives may on the termination of the partnership apply to the court to wind up the business and affairs of the firm[7].

This right is said to be in the nature of an equitable lien existing throughout the partnership, although it does not become active until a dissolution, when it immediately attaches to what was partnership property at that date[8].

It is, in fact, a kind of floating lien analagous to a floating charge created by a debenture of a limited company, and is lost by the conversion of the assets into the separate property of one of the partners[9]. The lien is enforceable, in the absence of agreement to the contrary, by a sale of the whole of the assets[10]. But it is subject to a mortgage created by a surviving partner to secure a partnership debt[11].

---

3 Ibid, s 44.
4 *Garner v Murray* [1904] 1 Ch 57, 89 LT 665. For the facts of the case, see p 38, above.
5 As to partnership property, see pp 31–35, above.
6 Partnership Act 1890, s 39.
7 Ibid, s 39.
8 *Payne v Hornby* (1858) 25 Beav 280; *Re White, Ex p Morley* (1873) 8 Ch App 1026.
9 *Re Bourne, Bourne v Bourne* [1906] 2 Ch 427, 95 LT 131, CA.
10 *Featherstonhaugh v Fenwick* (1810) 17 Ves 298; *Wild v Milne* (1859) 26 Beav 504. Cf *Steward v Blakeway* (1869) 4 Ch App 603.
11 *Re Bourne, Bourne v Bourne*, above.

Costs of dissolution

When a partnership is being wound up by the court, legal costs are incurred both by the plaintiff and the defendant, and the question then arises as to how those costs are to be borne. They are costs of administration; and just as the costs of administering a trust fund come out of that fund after payment of debts before either the capital or the income is distributed among the beneficiaries, so, in administering the assets of a partnership, the costs of administration must be discharged before either capital is repaid to or profits divided between the partners.

But although it is a liability of the business, ie a trade charge, it is a deferred liability[12] and can only rank after the firm's debts, for it would be obviously unjust that the creditors of the firm should be obliged to contribute to the cost of litigation between the partners.

A person who has advanced money to the firm is none the less a creditor for this purpose, because he also happens to be a member of the firm. Consequently, where one of the partners has made advances to the firm (as distinct from contributing capital for the joint adventure), such advance must be repaid to him in priority to any claims for costs, for he claims such advance as a creditor and not as a partner, ie as a debt and not as capital[13].

But where a partner owes money to the firm, eg where he has overdrawn his share of the profits, he cannot claim his costs until he has made good the debt due to the partnership estate[14]. He has in his hands what is really a part of the assets of the partnership. Although it is quite true that he is entitled to his costs, the other partner has a right to say to him: 'Pay your own costs out of that portion of the assets which you have drawn out in excess of my drawings, and which you have in your hands[15].'

If the assets, administered in the order stated above, are insufficient to pay the costs of the action or to pay them in full, the costs must be borne, like all the other liabilities which the assets are insufficient to meet, by the partners, in the proportion in which they have to bear the general losses[16]. Thus, the greater part of the costs of a partner who takes a small interest in the concern may have to be paid by the partner who hoped to take a large interest in the profits and who, therefore, impliedly undertook a correspondingly heavy responsibility for the losses.

12 Except where the dissolution action is really brought to test some disputed right, or, very rarely, where there has been gross misconduct by one partner, in which cases the unsuccessful partner, or the partner guilty of misconduct, as the case may be, may be deprived of costs or ordered to pay all the costs of the action. See *Hamer v Giles* (1879) 11 Ch D 942.

13 *Austin v Jackson* (1879) 11 Ch D 942n.; *Potter v Jackson* (1880) 13 Ch D 845, 42 LT 294.

14 *Ross v White* [1894] 3 Ch 326, 71 LT 277, CA; *Re Bear, Brewer v Bowman* [1915] WN 211.

15 *Ross v White*, above.

16 See pp 37–39, above.

Chapter 9

The insolvency of all or some of the partners

It has been hitherto assumed that where the assets of the partnership are insufficient to meet the liabilities, yet all the individual partners are solvent. In that case no questions can arise between the firm's creditors and the private creditors of the partners; they are all paid, and, in taking the partnership accounts, the joint debts thus paid will be adjusted in accordance with the terms of the partnership in relation to the bearing of losses [1].

But where a partnership business fails, it not infrequently happens that the loss is greater than one or more, or perhaps all, of the individual members of the firm can bear. A partner too often puts all his eggs into the partnership basket, staking his fortune on the success of the business.

Even where he still retains some property beyond that which he has contributed to the capital of the firm, yet if that private property proves insufficient to meet his share of the losses and also his private debts, he will be insolvent.

Now, so far as an insolvent partner is personally concerned, it is necessarily a matter of small moment to him how his private property (as distinguished from his share in the firm's assets) is administered; he, at least, will be bereft of everything.

But although it may be a matter of indifference to him personally how his estate is distributed between his private creditors on the one hand, and either the creditors of the firm or his solvent partners (who may have had to pay more than their share of the losses), on the other, it is by no means a matter of indifference to members of those classes whose interests are obviously conflicting.

Two situations must be considered:

(1) Where all the partners are insolvent.
(2) Where one or more partners are solvent.

---

1 See p 37, above.

Where all the partners are insolvent

General rule

The general rule is to be found in the Bankruptcy Act 1914, s 33(6), which states:

> In the case of partners the joint estate shall be applicable in the first instance in payment of their joint debts, and the separate estate of each partner shall be applicable in the first instance in payment of his separate debts. If there is a surplus of the separate estates, it shall be dealt with as part of the joint estate. If there is a surplus of the joint estate, it shall be dealt with as part of the respective estates in proportion to the right and interest of each partner in the joint estate.

The rule applies equally to the case of the administration of the assets of deceased partners[2].

Exceptions to the general rule

The general rule does not apply where

- (i) there is no joint estate;
- (ii) a person has been defrauded by a partner;
- (iii) where a creditor of the firm has a distinct contract for the same debt;
- (iv) where a creditor of the firm has obtained an order adjudicating one of the partners a bankrupt;
- (v) where a partner has converted the firm's property to his own use; and
- (vi) where one or more members of the partnership have carried on a distinct trade.

(i) *No joint estate*

Where there is no joint estate, the joint and separate creditors prove against the separate estate *pari passu*.

It is not easy to see the reason for this exception. It would seem however, from the judgment of Lord Loughborough in *Ex p Elton*[3] that the reason for the main rule being that where there are two funds available for distribution among creditors, a creditor will not be allowed to attach himself to one, to the prejudice of those who have no other fund, it follows that where there is only one fund, the whole foundation of the main rule is gone, and, consequently, that all the creditors (whether joint or separate) can prove *pari passu* against that fund.

This reasoning, however, does not seem to be conclusive, particularly as it has always been held that the existence of even a scintilla of joint estate (such as office furniture) is enough to negative the exception. However, it appears to be still law[4].

2 Administration of Estates Act 1925, s 34 and Sch 1, Pt I.
3 (1796) 3 Ves 238.
4 *Re Budgett, Cooper v Adams* [1894] 2 Ch 557, 71 LT 72.

(ii) *Fraud*

Where a person has been defrauded by the partners, or by any of them under such circumstances as render the firm liable, he may, at his election, prove either against the separate estate of the partners who were privy to the fraud, or against the joint estate, but not both[5].

This exception seems to rest on the principle that the fraud is that of the individual partners who committed it, and that their several liability is not affected because the firm happens also to be responsible; a principle which is also the foundation of the rule that the ordinary liability of partners for torts is joint and several.

It is true, no doubt, that demands in the nature of unliquidated damages, arising otherwise than by reason of a contract, promise, or breach of trust, are not provable in bankruptcy[6]. But where a wrongdoer has cheated another out of property which cannot be traced and restored, courts of equity have, for a long period, allowed the latter to prove for the value as an equitable debt[7].

(iii) *Distinct contract*

Where a creditor of the firm has also a contract for the same debt with the individual partners, or some of them, he may prove both against the firm estate and the separate estate.

In such cases he can prove against and receive dividends from both estates, so long, of course, as he does not get more than 100p in the £. This right is statutory, being given by the Bankruptcy Act 1914, Schedule 2, article 19, which states:

> If a debtor was at the date of the receiving order liable in respect of distinct contracts as a member of two or more distinct firms, or as a sole contractor and also as a member of a firm, the circumstance that the firms are in whole or in part composed of the same individuals, or that the sole contractor is also one of the joint contractors, shall not prevent proof in respect of the contracts against the properties respectively liable on the contracts.

Thus, in *Re Jeffrey, ex p Honey*[8]:

> A joint and several promissory note was signed by two members of the firm, by the firm and by some other persons. The firm was made bankrupt. The holder of the note sought to prove against the joint estate of the firm and also against the separate estates of the partners who had signed the note.

> *Held*, by the Court of Appeal, that he was entitled to do so and to receive dividends from all three estates[9].

5 *Re Kent County Gas Light and Coke Co Ltd* [1913] 1 Ch 92, 107 LT 641.
6 Bankruptcy Act 1914, s 30(1).
7 *Re Collie, ex p Adamson* (1878) 8 Ch D 807 at 819, 820, CA (per James LJ); *Moore v Knight* [1891] 1 Ch 547, 63 LT 831.
8 (1871) 7 Ch App 178, 25 LT 728, CA.
9 See the judgment of Mellish LJ, ibid, at 183.

(iv) Partner adjudged bankrupt

Where a creditor of the firm has obtained an order adjudicating one of the partners a bankrupt, he may prove in competition with the separate creditors of such bankrupt[10].

The reason is that it would be inequitable for the separate creditors to take advantage of the bankruptcy proceedings and yet exclude the author of them.

(v) Conversion to partner's own use

Where a partner has fraudulently converted to his own use part of the property of the firm, and his fraud has not been ratified, the firm's trustee in bankruptcy may prove for the value of such property in competition with his separate creditors[11]. And, in the converse case, the trustee in bankruptcy of the separate creditor may prove against the joint estate.

(vi) Distinct trade

Where one or more partners have carried on a distinct trade, with a distinct capital, in respect of which they have become either debtors or creditors to the firm in the ordinary way of trade, the respective trustees in bankruptcy can prove as if the two concerns were composed of distinct individuals[12].

The principle on which the exception turns seems to be that, as between the creditors of two distinct trades, it is for the benefit of commerce to consider the trades as distinct, and to neglect the fact that some or one of the partners in one may also be partners in, or the sole owner of, the other. However, as Lord Eldon remarked [13], the question what is a 'dealing in a distinct trade', is always to be looked at with great care.

Thus, where a banker is also a partner in a firm of merchants who keep their current account with him, his creditors cannot prove for the overdraft of the mercantile firm in the latter's bankruptcy; for the true nature of such a case is that there are not two distinct trades, but that one partner is financing the firm[14].

Where one or more partners are solvent

Suppose that one or more of the partners is solvent so that even although the assets of the partnership may be insufficient to pay the liabilities, the

---

10 *Ex p Ackerman* (1808) 14 Ves 604.
11 *Read v Bailey* (1877) 3 App Cas 94, 37 LT 510 HL. (See the judgment of Lord Blackburn, ibid, at 102).
12 *Re Petherbridge, ex p Cook* (1831) Mont 228.
13 *Re Goodchilds, ex p Sillitoe, ex p Hunter* (1824) 1 Gl & J 374 at 383.
14 Cf, *Re Braginton ex p Maude* (1867) 2 Ch App 550, 16 LT 577.

firm is saved from immediate bankruptcy at all events, by the solvent partner personally keeping down current liabilities—not necessarily paying them all off, because, having regard to credit, and to the fact that there might be unmatured negotiable instruments outstanding, that might be unnecessary—but paying current liabilities as they arise.

In such a case, what are the rights of such a solvent partner against the separate estates of the bankrupt partners? Can he prove for the sum which they ought to have contributed to the partnership losses (including losses of capital) in competition with their separate creditors; or is he in the same position with the creditors of the firm, for whose debts he is personally responsible, and who, under the general rule are forbidden to prove in competition with the separate creditors of his bankrupt co-partners?

General rule

There is a broad general rule that a partner cannot prove against either the joint estate, or the separate estate of his bankrupt co-partner, in competition with the firm's creditors, who are in fact his own creditors; that is to say, he cannot prove until all the partnership liabilities are discharged [15].

But this rule was not invented for the benefit of the separate creditors, to whom the solvent partner owes no duty, but for the benefit of the joint creditors who have not only a primary claim on the joint estate, but also a contingent claim on the separate estates, in the event of there being a surplus after the separate creditors have received 100p in the £.

If, however, there are no joint creditors—if, in other words, all the joint creditors have been paid by the solvent partner [16], or, if the separate estate of the co-partner is clearly insolvent [17], so that the joint creditors cannot possibly resort to it—then the reason of the rule is inapplicable.

Therefore, in such a case, the solvent partner is allowed to prove as a creditor against the separate estate of the insolvent, in competition with the separate creditors, of whom he is in fact one [18].

At first sight, this seems open to criticism, for, if the joint creditors cannot compete with the separate ones, why should the solvent partner who pays them off be in any better position? Ought he not merely to stand in their shoes by way of subrogation? Probably the true answer to such criticism is that the doctrine of subrogation does not apply. There

---

15 *Nanson v Gordon* (1876) 1 App Cas 195, 34 LT 401, HL; *Re Blythe, ex p Blythe* (1881) 16 Ch D 620. See also *Re Hind, ex p Hind* (1890) 62 LT 327; *Re Howes* [1934] Ch 49, 150 LT 95.
16 *Re Slaney, ex p Young* (1814) 2 Rose 40; *Re Elgar, ex p Taylor* (1814) 2 Rose 175.
17 *Re Levey and Robson, ex p Topping* (1865) 4 De GJ & Sm 551; *Re Head, ex p Head* [1894] 1 QB 638, 70 LT 35. Cf *Re Wright, ex p Sheen* (1877) 6 Ch D 235, 37 LT 451.
18 *Re Sheath, ex p Watson* (1819) 4 Madd 477; *Re Head, ex p Head* (above).

are no longer any joint creditors. The true relation of the parties is that of debtor and creditor, of a claim by a del credere agent against his bankrupt principal, partly for moneys paid for him, partly for moneys due to the agent under the contract of agency.

Exceptions to the general rule

There are three exceptions to the general rule:

(1) where the claim arises out of a fraud committed by the bankrupt which has not been condoned;

(2) where the bankrupt, either alone or with others, has carried on a distinct trade, which, in the ordinary course of business, has become indebted to the partnership; and

(3) where a partner has been discharged from liability for the joint debts, and has subsequently become a creditor of the firm, in which case he may prove against the firm's assets.

(i) Fraud

If Smith fraudulently induces Jones to enter into partnership with him, and to pay him a premium for the privilege, then, upon Smith becoming bankrupt, Jones may prove against his separate estate for the return of the premium, notwithstanding that the debts of the firm remain unpaid [19].

It is not easy to understand the principle of this exception as the defrauded partner is as much competing with his own creditors (ie the creditors of the firm), as if his claim arose ex contractu; and as the creditors of the firm were no parties to the fraud, it is difficult to see why they should be made to suffer. However, the principle appears to be that the equity which the partners owe to the joint creditors not to compete with them, only applies to debts owing between the partners inter se, and not to claims in the nature of fraud or breach of trust.

Indeed, the same principle applies where the claimant is solvent, as where the claimant is insolvent, and the question arises between his creditors and the firm's creditors. And if, in the latter case [20], it is just that the separate creditors of a defrauded partner should be able to prove against the separate estate of the party guilty of the fraud, so as to restore to his separate estate the amount which has been fraudulently withdrawn from it, it is equally just where the defrauded one remains solvent.

It is said that the case holds equally good where the firm, as such, is bankrupt, in which case a defrauded member of the firm may prove

---

19 *Bury v Allen* (1844) 1 Coll 589; *Re Ramsay and Aldrich, ex p Harris* (1813) 1 Rose 437, 2 Ves & B 210.

20 See p 105, above.

against the joint estate. It is, however, difficult to see how a partner can remain solvent when the firm is bankrupt, as the latter event seems to presuppose that the partners cannot jointly and severally meet the firm's liabilities. Such cases, therefore, always (or nearly always) result in disputes between respective creditors of the joint estate and the several separate estates[1].

(ii) Distinct trade by bankrupt

With regard to the exception that a solvent partner may prove against the separate estate of a bankrupt partner, where the latter has carried on privately a distinct and separate trade, and the debt has been incurred in the ordinary course of the business of that trade, the principle has already been discussed in considering the respective rights of the creditors of such distinct firms when both are bankrupt[2].

(iii) Partner discharged from firm's liabilities

The third exception, that where one of the partners has been discharged from liability for the firm's debts[3], he may prove for a debt which afterwards becomes due to him from the firm, is somewhat peculiar. For instance, a partner in a bankrupt firm obtains his discharge, and afterwards becomes the indorsee of bills of exchange on which the firm is liable. The fact that he was formerly a member of the firm does not preclude him from proving for the amount of the bills, his right to which only accrued after his discharge[4]. It would seem that the same principle would, *a fortiori*, apply where the bills were accepted by another partner and not by the firm.

By parity of reasoning, where on the death of a partner a sum was found to be due to his estate from the surviving partners in respect of which the deceased was at his death liable as a partner had been paid or settled before the firm became bankrupt, so that at that date there was no joint liability upon the deceased partner, the executors of the deceased were held entitled to prove in the bankruptcy of the firm in competition with the creditors of the firm[5].

Postponement of rights of person lending or selling in consideration of share of profits

In the event of any person, who is engaged, or about to engage, in any

---

1 See p 104, above.
2 See p 106, above.
3 Eg by lapse of time under the Limitation Act 1980 or by having obtained an order of discharge in bankruptcy.
4 *Re Atkins, ex p Atkins* (1820) Buck 479; *Re Hepburn, ex p Smith* (1884) 14 QBD 394.
5 *Re Douglas, ex p Douglas' Executors* [1930] 1 Ch 342, 142 LT 379.

business and who receives a loan under a contract stating that the lender is to receive a rate of interest varying with the profits[6],being adjudged bankrupt [7], the lender is not entitled to recover anything in respect of the share of profits contracted for until the claims of the other creditors of the borrower have been satisfied[8].

Similarly, the claims of a seller of the goodwill[9] of a business in consideration of a share of the profits[10] are also postponed, if the buyer is adjudged bankrupt[11], until the claims of the other creditors have been satisfied [12].

It is immaterial that the contract to advance the money at a rate of interest varying with the profits is only a verbal one.

Thus, in *Re Fort, ex p Schofield* [13]:

Schofield lent £3,000 to Fort, who was about to engage in business, on the terms that its net profits should be shared until the loan was repaid. The agreement was made verbally. Fort went bankrupt, and Schofield claimed that his loan should be repaid.

Held, by the Court of Appeal, that Schofield should not be paid until the claims of the other creditors had been satisfied, even though the agreement was a verbal one[14].

At first sight the above provisions seem to make the lender's security entirely dependent on the success of the business and thereby practically to make him liable for its losses to the extent of his loan, and, in fact, to place him somewhat in the position of a shareholder in a limited company.

All that the provisions mean, however, is that he cannot rank with the other creditors as a mere creditor. If he has been wise enough to obtain a collateral security for his loan, then that security is in no way prejudicially affected.

Thus, in a case decided before the Partnership Act 1890[15] Lord Lindley said[16]:

---

6 For such a loan, see Partnership Act 1890, s 2(3) and p 7, above.
7 Or entering into an arrangement to pay his creditors less than 100p in the £ or dying in insolvent circumstances.
8 Partnership Act 1890, s 3.
9 As to goodwill, see p. 93, above.
10 For the sale of goodwill in consideration of a share of the profits, see Partnership Act 1890, s 2(3) and p 160, below.
11 Or enters into an arrangement to pay his creditors less than 100p in the £ or dies in insolvent circumstances.
12 Partnership Act 1890, s 3.
13 [1897] 2 QB 495, 77 LT 274, CA.
14 See the judgment of Smith LJ, ibid, at 501 and 276, respectively. See further Ivamy *Casebook on Partnership* (2nd edn 1982) pp 11–12.
15 (1888) 38 Ch D 238.
16 Ibid, at 261.

Supposing that a person lends money upon mortgage of real estate, and stipulates that he is to have a share in the profits of some business, is it to be supposed that that mortgagee could not bring an ejectment to recover his security because of the 5th section of Bovill's Act [ie the predecessor of the Partnership Act 1890, s 3]? It is too absurd. That is not recovering his principal and interest. It is very true that unless he gets his security, he may lose the fund out of which it is to be repaid; but such a case is not within the section at all.

Whether a person has received a portion of the profits of a business in consideration of the sale by him of the goodwill of the business depends on the circumstances.

Thus, in *Re Gieve, ex p Shaw* [17]:

John Shaw was an outside stock and share dealer. He died leaving his widow his sole legatee. In 1892 she assigned the business and goodwill to Gieve and Willis under an agreement by which (inter alia) she was to be paid an annuity of £2,650 by the buyers. Gieve and Willis carried on the business until Willis died. Gieve carried it on alone until 1898 when he became bankrupt. Mrs Shaw claimed to prove in the bankruptcy for the capitalised value of the annuity, but the trustee in bankruptcy contended that her claim was postponed under s 3 of the Partnership Act 1890.

Held, by the Court of Appeal, that her claim was not postponed for she was not 'a person receiving by way of an annuity or otherwise a portion of the profits of a business in consideration of the sale by him of the goodwill of the business', since she was simply stipulating that a certain annuity should be paid to her [18].

17 (1899) 80 LT 737, CA.
18 See the judgment of Lindley MR, ibid, at 738. See further Ivamy *Casebook on Partnership* (2nd edn 1982) pp 9–11.

Chapter 10
Bankruptcy procedure

The bankruptcy procedure in the case of partnerships is generally the same as in that of individuals[1]. But certain modifications of procedure are made by the Bankruptcy Rules 1952[2].

Signature of notices in firm name

Where any notice, declaration, petition or other document requiring attestation is signed by a firm of creditors or debtors in the firm name, the partner signing for the firm must add his own signature and a statement that he is a partner in the firm[3].

Service on firm

Any notice or petition for which personal service is necessary is deemed to be duly served –

(1) on all members of a partnership firm, if it is served at the principal place of business of the firm in England on any one of the partners, or on any person having at the time of service control or management of the business there;
(2) on a person carrying on business in a name or style other than his own, if it is served on any person having at the time of service control or management of the business in England[4].

Debtor's petition by firm

A declaration of inability to pay their debts or a bankruptcy petition filed by a firm of debtors must contain the names in full of the individual partners in the firm and, if signed in the firm name, must be accompanied by an affidavit made by the partner who signs the declaration or petition, showing that all the partners concur in the filing of it[5].

1 For bankruptcy procedure generally, see Halsbury's Laws of England (4th edn) vol 3.
2 SI 1952/2113. See Appendix B, p 188, below. For the provisions relating to limited partnerships see p 121, below.
3 Bankruptcy Rules 1952 (SI 1952/2113), r 279.
4 Ibid, r 280.
5 Ibid, r 281.

Receiving order against firm

A receiving order made against a firm operates as if it were a receiving order made against each of the persons who at the date of the order is a partner in that firm[6].

Statement of affairs

Where a receiving order is made against a firm, the debtors must submit a joint statement of their partnership affairs, and each debtor must submit a statement of his separate affairs[7].

Adjudication order against partners

No order of adjudication must be made against a firm in the firm name, but must be made against the partners individually[8].

First meeting of creditors

Where a receiving order is made against a firm, the joint and separate creditors must be summoned collectively to the first meeting of creditors[9].

Acceptance of composition or scheme by joint and separate creditors

The joint creditors and each set of separate creditors may severally accept compositions or schemes of arrangement[10].

So far as circumstances allow, a proposal accepted by joint creditors may be approved notwithstanding that any proposal made by one or more of the debtors to his or their separate creditors may not be accepted[11].

Voting on composition or scheme

Where proposals for compositions or schemes are made by a firm, and by the partners in it individually, the proposal made to the joint creditors must be considered and voted upon by them apart from all separate creditors, and the proposal made to each set of separate creditors must be considered and voted upon by that set of separate creditors apart from all other creditors[12].

6 Ibid, r 285.
7 Ibid, r 287.
8 Ibid, r 288.
9 Ibid, r 291.
10 Ibid, r 292(1).
11 Ibid, r 292(2).
12 Ibid, r 293(1).

The proposals may vary in character and amount[13].

Where a composition or scheme is approved, the receiving order is discharged only so far as it relates to an estate the creditors of which have accepted the composition or scheme[14].

Trustee and committees of inspection

In the bankruptcy of a partnership the trustee appointed by the joint creditors or, in default of such appointment, by the Department of Trade and Industry, is to be the trustee of the separate estates of the partners[15].

Each set of separate creditors may appoint its own committee of inspection[16]. But the committee, if any, appointed by the joint creditors is deemed to have been appointed also by any set of separate creditors who do not appoint a separate committee[17].

Separate firms

If any two or more of the members of a partnership constitute a separate and independent firm, the creditors of such firm are deemed to be a separate set of creditors and subject to the same rules as the separate creditors of any individual member of the partnership[18].

Where any surplus remains after the administration of the assets of the separate firm, the surplus must be carried over to the separate estates of the partners in that firm according to their respective rights in it[19].

Apportionment of trustee's remuneration

Where joint and separate estates are being administered, the remuneration of the trustee in respect of the administration of the joint estate may be fixed by the creditors, or (if duly authorised) by the committee of inspection, of the joint estate, and the remuneration of the trustee in respect of the administration of any separate estate may be fixed by the creditors, or (if duly authorised) by the committee of inspection, of that separate estate[20].

13 Ibid, r 293(2).
14 Ibid, r 293(3).
15 Ibid, r 294(1).
16 Ibid, r 294(2).
17 Ibid, r 294(2).
18 Ibid, r 295(1).
19 Ibid, r 295(2).
20 Ibid, r 296.

Chapter 11

Limited partnerships

A special type of partnership known as limited partnership was introduced by the Limited Partnerships Act 1907[1], but is, in fact, little used.

Constitution of limited partnership

A limited partnership must consist of (a) one or more persons called 'general partners', who are liable for all debts and obligations of the firm; and (b) one or more persons called 'limited partners', who must at the time of entering into such a partnership contribute a sum or sums as capital or property valued at a stated amount, and who are not liable for the debts or obligations of the firm beyond the amount so contributed[2].

Thus, in *Re Barnard, Martin's Bank Ltd v Trustee*[3]:

A limited partnership under the name of W H Barnard consisted of W H Barnard, who was a general partner, and of one limited partner, and was registered in September 1928. In May 1929 another limited partnership called Scrap Metal Co was registered with W H Barnard as the only general partner and three limited partners. Between March and May 1931 five bills of exchange for £9,869 were drawn on Scrap Metal Co and were accepted by W H Barnard as managing partner of the firm. On 8 June 1931 a receiving order was made against the firm of W H Barnard and on 26 June W H Barnard was adjudicated bankrupt. On 24 July a receiving order was made against Scrap Metal Co and on the same day W H Barnard was again adjudicated bankrupt. Martin's Bank were now the holders of the bills and lodged a proof for £9,869 in the bankruptcy of Scrap Metal Co, but later withdrew the proof. In October 1931 the Bank lodged a proof for this sum in the bankruptcy of the firm of W H Barnard, but the trustee in bankruptcy rejected it on the ground that 'the bankrupt is not a party to the bills upon which the proof is made'. The Bank now moved that the proof be admitted.

1 The Act is printed, as amended, in Appendix A, p 172, below.
2 Limited Partnerships Act 1907, s 4(2).
3 [1932] 1 Ch 269, 146 LT 191.

Held, by the Chancery Division, that the proof would be admitted, for W H Barnard was personally liable under s 4(2) of the Limited Partnerships Act 1907 for all the debts and obligations of the firm, and he was a party to the bills[4].

A guarantee given by a person in respect of money advanced to the firm is not a 'contribution by him' and does not make him a limited partner, and he will be liable as though he were a general partner.

Thus, in *Rayner & Co v Rhodes*[5]:

Rhodes entered into a limited partnership with the firm of Jones & Co, who were merchants. Jones & Co sold some produce to Rayner & Co. Rayner & Co claimed damages from Rhodes on the ground that there had been a breach of contract, but Rhodes claimed that he was a limited partner within the meaning of s 4 of the Act, and could not be made liable at all, for he had contributed to the partnership the £5,000 which he had agreed to contribute. He contended that the £5,000 consisted of a running guarantee for £5,000, which he had given to Barclays Bank Ltd in respect of any advances or overdraft granted to Jones & Co, and that he had deposited as additional cover for that guarantee securities valued at £5,000.

Held, by the King's Bench Division (Liverpool Assizes), that Rhodes was not a limited partner within the meaning of s 4, for the guarantee could not be regarded as the contribution of a sum of money and he was, therefore, liable under s 5[6] of the Act to Rayner & Co, for in the statement required to be sent to the Registrar under s 8[7]—viz. 'the amount contributed by each limited partner and whether paid in cash or otherwise'—he had stated: '£5,000 paid in cash', and this was not correct[8].

A limited partner must not during the continuance of the partnership, either directly or indirectly, draw out or receive back any part of his contribution, and if he does draw out or receive back any such part, he is liable for the debts and obligations of the firm up to the amount so drawn out or received back[9].

A body corporate may be a limited partner[10].

---

4 See the judgement of Farwell J, ibid, at 272 and 192. See further Ivamy *Casebook on Partnership* (2nd edn 1982) pp 93–95.
5 (1926) 24 Ll L Rep 25.
6 See p 118, below.
7 See p 118, below.
8 See the judgment of Wright J: (1926) 24 Ll L Rep at 26. See further Ivamy *Casebook on Partnership* (2nd edn 1982) pp 95–97.
9 Ibid, s 4(3).
10 Ibid, s 4(4).

The general rule is that a limited partnership must not consist of more than twenty persons[12].

But this does not prohibit the formation of –[13]

(1) a partnership carrying on practice as solicitors and consisting of persons each of whom is a solicitor;
(2) a partnership carrying on practice as accountants and consisting of persons each of whom falls within paragraph (a)[14] or paragraph (b)[15] of the Companies Act 1985, s 389(1);
(3) a partnership carrying on business as members of a recognised stock exchange[16] and consisting of persons each of whom is a member of that stock exchange.

Further, the Secretary of State may by regulations made by statutory instrument provide that the limit of twenty persons shall not apply to a partnership carrying on business of a description specified in the regulations, being a partnership of a description so specified[17].

Thus, the Limited Partnerships (Unrestricted Size) No. 1 Regulations 1971[18] provide that the limit of twenty persons does not apply to a limited partnership carrying on one or more of the following activities: (i) surveying; (ii) auctioneering; (iii) valuing; (iv) estate agency; (v) land agency; and (vi) estate management[19]. But not less than three-quarters of the total number of the partners must be members of either (a) The Royal Institution of Chartered Surveyors or (b) The Incorporated Society of Valuers and Auctioneers, and not more than one-quarter of the total number of partners can be limited partners[20].

Registration of limited partnership

Every limited partnership must be registered as such in accordance with the provisions of the Act, and in default thereof it is deemed to be a

12 Limited Partnerships Act 1907, s 4(2).
13 Companies Act 1985, s 716(2), (3).
14 Ie a member of a body of accountants established in the United Kingdom and for the time being recognised by the Secretary of State.
15 Ie a person for the time being authorised by the Secretary of State to be appointed as an auditor either as having similar qualifications obtained outside the United Kingdom or as having obtained adequate knowledge and experience in the course of his employment by a member of a body of accountants recognised for the purposes of para (a) or as having before 6 August 1947, practised in Great Britain as an accountant.
16 A 'recognised stock exchange' means any body of persons which is for the time being a recognised stock exchange for the purposes of the Prevention of Fraud (Investments) Act 1958: Companies Act 1985, s 744.
17 Ibid, s 121(2).
18 SI 1971/782. The Regulations are set out in Appendix B, p 194, below.
19 Reg 2.
20 Reg 2.

general partnership, and every limited partner is deemed to be a general partner[1].

Manner and particulars of registration

The registration of a limited partnership is effected by sending by post or delivering to the Registrar[2] a statement containing the following particulars:

(1) the firm name;
(2) the general nature of the business;
(3) the principal place of business;
(4) the full name of each of the partners;
(5) the term, if any, for which the partnership is entered into, and the date of its commencement;
(6) a statement that the partnership is limited, and the description of every limited partner as such;
(7) the sum contributed by each limited partner, and whether paid in cash or how otherwise[3].

The fee for registration is £2[4].

Registration of change in partnerships

If during the continuance of a limited partnership any change is made or occurs in –

(1) the firm name;
(2) the general nature of the business;
(3) the principal place of business;
(4) the partners or the name of any partner;
(5) the term or character of the partnership;
(6) the sum contributed by any limited partner;
(7) the liability of any partner by reason of his becoming a limited instead of a general partner or a general instead of a limited partner,

a statement signed by the firm, specifying the nature of the change must within seven days be sent by post or delivered to the Registrar[5].

If default is made in compliance with these requirements, each of the

1 Limited Partnerships Act 1907, s 5.
2 Ie the Registrar of Companies: s 15.
3 Ibid, s 8. The form required to be used for the purpose of registration is set out in the Appendix to the Limited Partnership Rules 1907 (SR & O 1907/1020) which are set out in Appendix B, p 183, below.
4 Limited Partnership Rules 1907 (SR & O 1907/1020), r 3. See Appendix B, p 183, below.
5 Limited Partnerships Act 1907, s 9(1). The form required for the purpose of registration of changes in partnerships is set out in the Appendix to the Limited Partnership Rules 1907 (SR & O 1907/1020). See Appendix B, p 185, below.

general partners is liable on summary conviction to a fine not exceeding £1 for each day during which the default continues[6].

Filing of statement and issue of certificate of registration

On receiving any statement made in pursuance of the Act the Registrar must cause it to be filed, and must send by post to the firm from which the statement has been received a certificate of the registration[7].

Keeping of register and index

The Registrar must keep in proper books to be provided for the purpose a register and an index of all limited partnerships which have been registered and of all the statements registered in relation to them[8].

Inspection of statement

Any person may inspect the statements filed by the Registrar[9]. There must be paid for such inspection such fees as may be appointed by the Secretary of State, not exceeding 5p for each inspection[10].

Any person may require a certificate of the registration of any limited partnership, or a copy of or extract from any registered statement to be certified by the Registrar[11]. There must be paid for such certificate of registration, certified copy or extract such fees as the Secretary of State may appoint, not exceeding 10p for the certificate of registration, and not exceeding 2p for each folio of 72 words[12].

A certificate of registration or a copy of or extract from any statement registered under the Act, if duly certified to be a true copy under the hand of the Registrar or one of the assistant registrars (whom it shall not be necessary to prove to be the Registrar or assistant registrar) must be received in evidence in all legal proceedings, civil or criminal, and in all cases whatsoever[13].

Modifications of general law in case of limited partnerships

In general, the Partnership Act 1890 and the rules of equity and common

---

6 Limited Partnerships Act 1907, s 9(2).
7 Ibid, s 13.
8 Ibid, s 14.
9 Ibid, s 16(1).
10 Ibid, s 16(1).
11 Ibid, s 16(1).
12 Ibid, s 16(1).
13 Ibid, s 16(2).

law applicable to partnerships, except so far as they are inconsistent with the express provisions of that Act, apply to limited partnerships[14].

But a limited partner must not take part in the management of the partnership business and has no power to bind the firm, though he may by himself or his agent at any time inspect the books of the firm and examine into the state and prospects of the partnership business and may advise with the partners thereon[15]. If a limited partner takes part in the management of the partnership business, he is liable for all debts and obligations of the firm incurred while he so takes part in the management as though he were a general partner[16].

A limited partnership is not dissolved by the death or bankruptcy of a limited partner, and the unsoundness of mind of a limited partner is not a ground for dissolution of the partnership unless his share cannot be otherwise ascertained and realised[17].

In the event of the dissolution of a limited partnership its affairs must be wound up by the general partners unless the court otherwise orders[18].

Subject to any agreement express or implied between the partners:

(1) any difference arising as to ordinary matters connected with the partnership business may be decided by a majority of the general partners;

(2) a limited partner may, with the consent of the general partners, assign his share in the partnership, and upon such an assignment the assignee becomes a limited partner with all the rights of the assignor;

(3) the other partners are not entitled to dissolve the partnership by reason of any limited partner suffering his share to be charged for his separate debt;

(4) a person may be introduced as a partner without the consent of the existing limited partners;

(5) a limited partner is not entitled to dissolve the partnership by notice[19].

Advertisements

Notice of any arrangement or transaction under which any person will cease to be a general partner in any firm, and will become a limited partner in that firm, or under which the share of a limited partner will be assigned to any person must be forthwith advertised in *The London*

14 Ibid, s 7.
15 Ibid, s 6(1).
16 Ibid, s 6(1).
17 Ibid, s 6(2).
18 Ibid, s 6(3).
19 Ibid, s 6(4).

Gazette. Until notice of the arrangement or transaction is so advertised, the arrangement or transaction is deemed, for the purposes of the Act, to be of no effect[20].

Powers of Secretary of State

The Secretary of State may make rules (but as to fees with the concurrence of the Treasury) concerning any of the following matters:

(1) the fees to be paid to the Registrar, so that they do not exceed in the case of the original registration of a limited partnership the sum of £2, and in any other case the sum of 25p;
(2) the duties or additional duties to be performed by the Registrar for the purposes of the Act;
(3) the performance by assistant registrars and other officers of acts required by the Act to be done by the Registrar;
(4) the forms to be used for the purposes of the Act;
(5) generally the conduct and regulation of registration under the Act and any matters incidental thereto[1].

Bankruptcy

Subject to such modifications as may be made by general rules[2] the provisions of the Bankruptcy Act 1914 apply to limited partnerships in like manner as if limited partnerships were ordinary partnerships, and on all the general partners of a limited partnership being adjudged bankrupt, the assets of the limited partnership vest in the trustee[3].

A creditor's petition in bankruptcy against a limited partnership must, unless the court otherwise orders, be served at the registered principal place of business of the partnership by delivering there a sealed copy of the petition to one of the general partners or to some person having at the time of service the control or management of the partnership business[4].

20 Limited Partnerships Act 1907, s 10.
 1 Limited Partnerships Act 1907, s 17. The rules which have been made are the Limited Partnership Rules 1907 (SR & O 1907/1020) as amended by Limited Partnerships (Amendment) Rules 1972 (SI 1972/1040) and Limited Partnerships (Amendment) Rules 1974 (SI 1974/560). The rules are printed, as amended, in Appendix B, p 183, below.
 2 Bankruptcy Rules 1952 (SI 1952/2113). The relevant rules are set out in Appendix B, p 188, below.
 3 Bankruptcy Act 1914, s 127.
 4 Bankruptcy Rules 1952 (SI 1952/2113), r 282.

A limited partnership may present a petition in bankruptcy in the name of the firm[5]. The petition must be signed by a general partner and must contain the full names of the general partners and, if signed in the firm name, must be accompanied by an affidavit by the partner who signs the petition showing that all the general partners concur in filing it[6].

A petition in bankruptcy by or against a limited partnership must be presented to the court having bankruptcy jurisdiction in the place where the registered office of the partnership is situated[7]. But a High Court judge may at any time, for good cause shown, remove the proceedings to any other court having jurisdiction in bankruptcy[8].

A receiving order made against a limited partnership operates as if it were a receiving order made against each of the persons who at the date of the order is a general partner[9].

Where a receiving order is made against a limited partnership, any past or present limited partner has the same rights as a creditor who has proved his debt to inspect the file, to attend meetings of creditors, and to appear on, and take part in, the public examination of, or any application for an order of discharge by, any general partner[10].

The assets of a limited partnership which by the Bankruptcy Act 1914, s 127, are to vest in the trustee in the event of all the general partners being adjudged bankrupt, include any liability of limited partners and past general partners to contribute to the assets of the partnership, and such liability may be enforced by the trustee by motion in the bankruptcy[11].

But there are three exceptions to this rule:

(1) no person is liable as a present or past limited partner to contribute to the assets of the partnership any amount in excess of any part of his contribution as such limited partner which he may have failed to pay into or have drawn out or received back from the partnership assets since he became, or while he remained, a limited partner[12].

(2) no past general partner is liable as such to contribute to the assets of the partnership except in respect of partnership debts and obligations incurred while he continued to be a general partner[13];

(3) no past general or limited partner is liable as such to contribute to the assets of the partnership unless it appears to the court that the

---

5 Ibid, r 283(1).
6 Ibid, r 283(2).
7 Ibid, r 284.
8 Ibid, r 284.
9 Ibid, r 286.
10 Ibid, r 289.
11 Ibid, r 290.
12 Ibid, r 290, proviso (a).
13 Ibid, r 290, proviso (b).

partnership assets otherwise available are insufficient for the payment in full of the partnership liabilities and the costs, charges and expenses of the administration in bankruptcy of the partnership estate[14].

Sex discrimination

It is unlawful for a firm consisting of six or more general partners in relation to a position as general partner in the firm to discriminate against a woman –

(1) in the arrangements they make for the purpose of determining who should be offered that position[15], or
(2) in the terms on which they offer her that position[16], or
(3) by refusing or deliberately omitting to offer her that position[17], or
(4) in a case where the woman already holds that position
    (a) in the way they afford her access to any benefits, facilities or services, or by refusing or deliberately omitting to afford her access to them, or
    (b) by expelling her from that position or subjecting her to any other detriment[18].

The above provisions apply also in relation to persons proposing to form themselves into a limited partnership[19].

14 Ibid, r 290, proviso (c).
15 Sex Discrimination Act 1975, s 11(1)(a). This subsection does not apply to a position as partner where, if it was employment, being a man would be a genuine occupational qualification for the job: ibid, s 11(3).
16 Ibid, s 11(1)(b). This subsection does not apply to provision made in relation to death or retirement: ibid, s 11(4).
17 Ibid, s 11(1)(c). This subsection does not apply to a position as partner where, if it was employment, being a man would be a genuine occupational qualification for the job: ibid, s 11(3).
18 Ibid, s 11(1)(d). This subsection does not apply to provision made in relation to death or retirement: ibid, s 11(4).
19 Ibid, s 11(2).

Chapter 12

Partnership taxation

Income tax

Taxation of partnership income

Unlike a company, a partnership is not a separate legal person. For tax purposes however, it is to a certain extent treated as if it were, in that the Revenue uses the entity as a medium through which the income tax of the separate partners is assessed and collected. Thus, where a partnership exists, tax in respect of it must be computed jointly and a joint assessment made in the partnership name[1]. The liability of the partners to tax on their earnings is a joint liability of all the partners and not the several liability of each[2].

Computation of profit

The income of the firm is computed in accordance with the rules applicable to individuals. The relevant charging Schedule is therefore Schedule D Cases I and II of the Income and Corporation Taxes Act 1970, which catches annual profits or gains of a trade, profession or vocation[3]. In this context, the word 'annual' means that only profits of an income nature are chargeable. For tax purposes, annual profits are the firm's taxable receipts less its deductible expenses. Strictly, Schedule D Case I applies to trades, and Case II to professions or vocations, but little practical importance attaches to the distinction other than in relation to the basis on which profits are computed, where the Revenue allows greater flexibility to professions.

Profits of a trade must normally be computed on an earnings basis, treating as income all sums earned in the accounting period as opposed to those merely received. Correspondingly, its expenses are deductible for the period in which the obligation arises as opposed to when payment is made. Adjustments are made to reflect the value of work in hand. The earnings basis also applies to professions and vocations and indeed is the

1 Income and Corporation Taxes Act (ICTA) 1970, s 152.
2 *Harrison v Willis Bros (Willis and Executors of Willis)* [1966] Ch 619, [1965] 3 All ER 753, CA.
3 ICTA 1970, ss 108–109.

only basis accepted by the Revenue for the first three tax years of any new business. Thereafter, however, the Revenue may allow profits to be calculated by reference to a cash basis, ie actual cash received less cash paid out in the accounting period, on the taxpayer undertaking to render bills promptly. Another basis, fairly widely allowed to solicitors, is the bills delivered or bills rendered basis, where profit is determined by the value of bills sent out in the period and unbilled work is ignored.

The basis of assessing profit

Under Schedule D Cases I and II the normal basis for assessing profits is the 'preceding year basis'; ie the assessment for the year is based on the profits of the accounting period ending in the preceding year of assessment.

Thus –

A firm's accounting period runs from 1 January to 31 December. In 1981/82 its assessment is based on the profits of its accounting year ended 31 December 1980.

The preceding year basis is however, clearly inappropriate for the first year of a business and could be inconvenient to the Revenue in the closing years of a business. Accordingly, there are special provisions in the Income and Corporation Taxes Act 1970 to cover both the opening years of a business[4], and its closing years[5].

The opening year rules

In the first year of assessment, assessment is on profits from the date of commencement until the end of the tax year on 5 April. In the second year, assessment is on profits for the first twelve months of the business[6]. In the third year, the normal preceding year basis applies[7].

Thus –

A firm commences trading on 6 January 1981. Its profits for its first three years trading are:

	£
Accounting year ended 5 January 1982	12,000
Accounting year ended 5 January 1983	20,000
Accounting year ended 5 January 1984	30,000

---

4 ICTA 1970, ss 115–117.
5 ICTA 1970, s 118.
6 ICTA 1970, s 116(1).
7 ICTA 1970, s 116(2).

Assessments will be as follows: £

First tax year: 1980/81 (3 months)	3,000
Second tax year: 1981/82 (12 months)	12,000
Third tax year: 1982/83 (normal)	12,000
Fourth tax year: 1983/84 (normal)	20,000

The result, as can be seen, is that opening profits are the basis for more than one assessment and the taxpayer will benefit from keeping them low. Where the taxpayer finds this difficult, in particular where the trade is profitable at first but then declines, he will probably prefer to take advantage of an option allowed him under s 117 with regard to the second and third tax years. The option is to have assessments for both those years based on actual profits of those years, ie from 6 April to 5 April in each of those years, calculated where necessary by apportioning profits on a time basis. The option is exercisable by notice to the Inspector of Taxes within seven years from the end of the second tax year and is also revocable during that period, should the decision, with hindsight, prove disadvantageous.

The closing year rules

On a permanent discontinuance, assessment of profits for the last three tax years of the firm's existence is governed by the so called 'cessation provisions' of s 118.

In the final tax year, assessment is on profits from the start of the tax year on 6 April until the date of discontinuance[8]. The assessments for the penultimate and antepenultimate tax years should have been made already on a normal preceding year basis[9]. If however, the aggregate of the actual profits of those two years from 6 April to 5 April in each year, is greater than the aggregate of the profits as computed on the preceding year basis then the Revenue will revise their assessments for those tax years on an actual basis, again by apportionment of profits on a time basis if necessary, and adjust their previous assessments, so charging more tax[10].

Thus –

The business of a firm was permanently discontinued on 15 October 1984. The final year's profits had been:

	£
Accounting year ending 5 October 1981	30,000
Accounting year ending 5 October 1982	36,000
Accounting year ending 5 October 1983	48,000
Accounting year ending 5 October 1984	40,000
Period 5 October to 15 October 1984	500

8 ICTA 1970, s 118(1)(a).
9 ICTA 1970, s 115.
10 ICTA 1970, s 118(1)(b).

Assessments will be as follows:

		Eventual assess-ment
		£
Final year 1984/85 (6 months & 10 days)		20,500
(Actual basis)		
	£	
Penultimate year 1983/84 (Normal basis)	36,000	
(Actual basis)	44,000	44,000
Antepenultimate year 1982/83 (Normal basis)	30,000	
(Actual basis)	42,000	42,000

An actual basis here produces an aggregate of £86,000, a total £20,000 in excess of the total on a normal preceding year basis for those years and the Revenue accordingly will revise their previous assessments.

The assessment

The income tax payable in respect of the trading income of the firm is computed and stated jointly in one sum. It is separate and distinct from any other tax chargeable on the partners and a joint assessment is made in the firm's name. To this end a joint return of partnership income must be made by the precedent acting partner on behalf of the others[11]. He is generally the first named partner in the partnership agreement. Each partner is also obliged to make a personal return of his own income to establish his entitlement to reliefs and of his total income for the purpose of enabling the Revenue to charge additional tax where appropriate[12].

When the trading income is determined, it must be allocated to each partner by reference to the share of profits to which he is entitled in the year of assessment in which those profits are the basis of assessment[13]. It is not necessarily allocated in accordance with the way those profits were actually shared by the partners. This at first sight can be confusing. It is however a feature of the application of the preceding year basis to partnership taxation, that the current partners in any year, are being assessed on the basis of profits attributable to an earlier period.

Thus –

Profits for the firm James and John for the year ended 31 December 1978 were £30,000. They shared that income in their partnership ratios at that time of 2:1, ie £20,000 and £10,000. John became an equal partner on 1 January 1979. The £30,000 is the statutory income of the firm for 1979/80 and was divided between the partners in the assessment, in accordance with their entitlement

11 Taxes Management Act 1970, s 9(1).
12 Taxes Management Act 1970, s 8.
13 ICTA 1970, s 26.

for that tax year, ie equally. James and John may well of course, be prepared to rectify privately what potentially may seem unfair.

Salaries and interest on capital credited to full partners are fairly common items in partnership accounts. It is often specified in the partnership agreement that they are to be a preferential charge on profits before division of the balance between partners in the profit sharing ratio. In the eyes of the Revenue, however, they are nonetheless mere allocations of profit and no deduction is allowed from profits in respect of them. They are included in the profits of the partnership and not separately taxed as income of the individual partners.

The following example illustrates how these items are dealt with in a computation of partnership assessable income.

The firm Brown and Jones has two partners sharing profits in the ratio: Brown 3/5, Jones 2/5. Brown is entitled to a salary of £8,000 p.a. in lieu of rent for the premises used by the firm, which he owns. Interest on capital for the year of assessment 1984/85 is agreed at: Brown £3,200, Jones £2,500. Adjusted profits less capital allowances for their trading year ended 31 December 1983 were £50,000. Their 1984/85 assessment is computed as follows:

		Firm	*Brown*	*Jones*
		£		
Adjusted profits to 31 Dec 1983		50,000		
Less interest on capital	5,700			
salary	8,000	13,700		
Net divisible profit		36,300	21,780	14,520
Add back interest on capital		5,700	3,200	2,500
„ „ salary		8,000	8,000	
Assessment		50,000	32,980	17,020

The tax liability of Brown and Jones is now computed, credit being given for their respective personal allowances and reliefs, and the total is assessed in the partnership name.

It should however be noted that the foregoing does not apply as regards interest on loans from a partner to the firm where there is no reason why the interest should not constitute a normal business expense. It may also be that the salary of a so called salaried partner may, in some instances, be a deductible expense. Where, in reality, his status is that of an employee and in particular where his salary is paid under deduction of tax under PAYE, the Revenue will treat him as an employee whose salary and attendant costs are deductible trading expenses and not as a partner whose salary is an appropriation of profit.

Deposit interest

It is of course possible that the profits of a partnership include income which is chargeable to tax other than under Case I or II of Schedule D, for instance rent, or interest paid to the firm. Such items are in fact excluded from the adjusted profit of the firm and taxed separately. Thus, tax on investment income chargeable under Schedule D Case III will be payable in January, unlike the Schedule D Case I or II assessment on the firm which is payable by two instalments, in January and July.

Firms of solicitors commonly raise interest on client money held by them, by placing on deposit in an undesignated deposit account such sums as they estimate may safely be so placed. After accounting to clients for interest where appropriate, a healthy surplus is likely to remain and constitute a welcome supplement to the income of the partners. Such interest constitutes investment income taxable under Schedule D Case III. By agreement with the Revenue[14], only the net balance actually retained by the firm is regarded as its investment income. Sums actually paid out to clients in lieu of interest where appropriate, are to be regarded as income of those clients and not the firm. The actual payments to clients are made gross, and interest on the undesignated deposit account is exempted from the composite rate scheme and also paid gross to the solicitor[15].

Partnership losses

A firm may well suffer a loss instead of making a profit. If so, the adjusted loss is calculated in exactly the same way as an adjusted profit and is apportioned between the partners according to how they agreed to share losses during the accounting period. Each partner deals with his share of loss as a matter personal to him. He may claim loss relief under ss 168 or 171 of the Income and Corporation Taxes Act 1970 in the usual way, and terminal loss relief under s 174 of the same Act can apply. The effect of ss 168 and 171, is that the loss suffering partner can choose to take immediate relief under s 168 by setting off his loss against his other statutory income of that year, and then the next year of assessment if he is still carrying on the same business. Alternatively, he may carry forward his loss under s 171 against his share of profits in subsequent years of assessment.

This will in fact apply, even where there is technically a discontinuance on a change of partners, provided the partner in question continues in the business[16]. Otherwise, on a discontinuance, including a statutory discontinuance following a change of partners, a partner who retires from his business can claim terminal loss relief in respect of his share of the losses sutained by his firm in its last twelve months prior to

14 See *Law Society's Gazette* of 19 April 1978.
15 FA 1984, Sch 8, para 3(3)(dd) inserted by FA 1985, s 38.
16 ICTA 1970, s 171(4).

discontinuance. Such relief can be taken against assessments of the three years preceding that in which the business was discontinued.

Loss relief and limited partners

An interesting point in relation to loss relief and limited partners arose in a case *Reed v Young* [17]. The Court of Appeal held that notwithstanding the limitation of the limited partner's liability to the amount of capital contributed by him to the firm, he was in terms of loss relief, entitled to relief for the full amount of the losses borne by him under the partnership agreement, whether or not that exceeded his capital contribution. It may be that this decision will not meet with the accord of the House of Lords but in any event the Finance Act 1985 now imposes specific restrictions by s 48 and Schedule 12 of the Act on the share of partnership losses, interest charges and allowances for expenditure for which a limited partner (as somewhat widely defined by Schedule 12, Paragraph 1) can claim relief. It applies to chargeable periods beginning after 19 March 1985 (and periods straddling that date in which the taxpayer became a limited partner after that date).

Change of partners

A change in the constitution of the firm can have drastic effects upon the tax assessment. Section 154 of the Income and Corporation Taxes Act 1970 provides that where there is a change in the persons engaged in carrying on any trade, profession or vocation, then the amount of profits on which tax is chargeable and the persons on whom it is chargeable shall be determined as if the business had been permanently discontinued at the date of the change and a new business then set up and commenced. This provision will apply on death or retirement of a partner, on admission of a new partner, or where a sole trader takes into partnership another person.

In view of the frequency with which the section could apply to a firm and the potentially grave consequences of discontinuance where post cessation legislation comes into play, a right of election is given to exclude s 154(1) and treat a firm as a continuing entity despite a change in its constitution.

The election

The election provisions are contained in s 154(2) of the Income and Corporation Taxes Act 1970, which provides that where there is a change in the persons engaged in carrying on a business, and a person so

17 [1985] STC 25.

engaged immediately before the change continues to be so engaged immediately thereafter, all the persons so engaged immediately before and after the change may, by notice, elect that s 154(1) shall not apply. All relevant persons must sign, including personal representatives of a deceased partner[18] and the notice must be sent to the Inspector of Taxes within two years after the date of the change[19]. The election is not irrevocable. In practice a notice of revocation signed by all interested parties and given before the expiry of the same time limit will be accepted by the Tax Inspector[20].

Because all partners must join in the election, firms not uncommonly find it desirable to specify in the partnership agreement that a majority of the partners shall be entitled to insist on the others joining in an election on a partnership change, and the terms on which an incoming partner joins the firm are likely to include his agreement to sign the election. This will have distinct advantages where a firm's profits are steadily increasing, because taxation remains on a preceding year basis and the cessation and opening years rules are not brought into play. In other words, on an election, assessments on the firm are made as if no change had occurred, although there will of course be an apportionment of profits between the partners themselves, generally on a time basis. The effect of assessments continuing on a preceding year basis, in principle, will of course mean that the incoming partner's share of his first assessment is based on profits in which he personally did not share, and it can sometimes be thought appropriate to provide for indemnities to safeguard his position. In other circumstances, in particular where it is uncertain whether or not an election may be advantageous, the firm may find it prudent to have all relevant parties sign both a notice of election and a notice of subsequent revocation in advance, leaving discretion to decide at a later date, in conjunction with the firm's accountant, on the appropriate course of action.

There are, moreover, circumstances in which the election can be nullified. They arise where there has been an election for continuance under s 154(2) in respect of a change of partners, and before the end of the second year of assessment following that in which the change occurred there is a permanent discontinuance. Such discontinuance brings into effect the cessation provisions and allows the Revenue the option to assess the penultimate and antepenultimate years on an actual basis so that its revised assessments reach back into the original partnership[1]. It can lead to additional assessments being raised on the former partners, and enhances the desirability of including an election clause in

---

18 ICTA 1970, s 154(6).
19 Finance Act 1971, s 17.
20 See Inland Revenue Press Notice of 17 January 1973.
 1 ICTA 1970, s 154(3)(b).

partnership agreements, together with, perhaps, appropriately drafted indemnities.

Although the predominant motive to any partnership election is invariably that of saving tax, the Revenue do not find this unacceptable.

Changes leading to a discontinuance after 19 March 1985

A device which the Revenue has found offensive and sought to counteract is that of deliberately operating a business in cycles of five or six years with a view to using the opening year rules to advantage. FA 1985, s 47 provides for new rules to apply to discontinuances after 19 March 1985.

For discontinuances on a partnership change before 20 March 1985, the rules provided, subject to the above described right of election for continuance, for a discontinuance of the old business bringing into operation the closing year rules, and the commencment of a new business to which the opening year rules applied.

It can probably be appreciated that one consequence ensuing from the rules governing the periods which form the basis of assessment is that in relation to a business of a limited lifespan, the opening year rules for assessment on the early profits of the business for more than one tax year, entail some other accounting period dropping out of the net of assessment. Thus, so long as a partnership change constituted a discontinuance and the commencement of a new business under the normal rules, it offered scope for a business which could appropriately regulate its profits, to use this factor to advantage by operating in cycles of five years or more. Some partnerships have succeeded in using the device over the years to considerable advantage.

FA 1985, s 47 seeks to nullify such devices by substituting an alternative s 116 in I&CTA 1970 to provide a different method of charging the profits of the 'new partnership' to tax in the years immediately following the change. It applies to changes after 19 March 1985 where the right to make a continuance election was available to the partners but no election was made. It makes no change to the rules on an election, or to the closing year rules as they apply on the discontinuance.

The new rules apply as follows: in the year of assessment in which the change occurs, tax (as in the past), is charged on the actual profits arising that year after the date of change. The tax liability in each of the following three years of assessment is also determined by reference to the actual profits arising in those years of assessment. The new firm, in its first four tax years, is thus assessed throughout on an actual basis.

Thereafter, the normal preceding year basis applies although the firm can elect for the fifth and sixth year also to be taxed on an actual basis.

Thus:

A partnership change occurs on the admission of a new partner on 1 January 1986. Its accounting year runs from 1 January – 31 December.
Accounts for various years are:

Calendar year		
	1985	54,000
	1986	52,000
	1987	56,000
	1988	58,000
	1989	60,000
	1990	68,000
	1991	70,000

If a continuance election is not made, its (approximate) assessments will be as follows:

Old firm	£	*Assessment* £
Final year 1985/86	$\frac{9}{12} \times 54{,}000$	40,500
New firm		
First year 1985/86	$\frac{3}{12} \times 52{,}000$	13,000
Second year 1986/87	$\frac{9}{12} \times 52{,}000 + \frac{3}{12} \times 56{,}000$	53,000
Third year 1987/88	$\frac{9}{12} \times 56{,}000 + \frac{3}{12} \times 58{,}000$	56,500
Fourth year 1988/89	$\frac{9}{12} \times 58{,}000 + \frac{3}{12} \times 60{,}000$	58,500
Fifth year 1989/90	(The rise in profits means the firm would not elect to be taxed on actual profits and therefore the preceding year basis will apply)	58,000
Sixth year 1990/91		60,000

The above rules apply to deemed discontinuances where the business is a partnership both before and after the change and the two firms have at least one partner in common.

Interest relief on loans to acquire a partnership share

Tax relief is available for interest on a loan made to acquire a share in a firm or to provide capital or an advance to be used in it. Relief takes the form of a charge on the borrower's income[2]. Interest in relation to borrowings by the firm on the other hand, qualify for relief as a deductible business expense on normal principles.

---

2 Finance Act 1974, s 19(2), Sch 1, paras 11 & 12.

Provision for retirement

Partners may well take the attitude that self help is the best form of provision for retirement and that each partner should safeguard his future by adequate insurance or by entering into a retirement annuity scheme designed to produce benefits on death or retirement of the partner, or indeed both. Otherwise, there are circumstances where it is appropriate that the continuing partners should pay annual sums to a retired or deceased partner or his dependants, perhaps by way of payment to him for goodwill or for the transfer of his share of the firm.

Retirement Annuities under Income and Corporation Taxes Act 1970, ss 226–229

Before 1956, self-employed persons could not provide for their retirement out of untaxed income, unlike employees under an approved pension scheme. Provisions were introduced by the Finance Act 1956 to rectify this discrimination, so that an individual could make arrangements to secure a retirement annuity from an insurance company or through a professional body and obtain tax relief in respect of his contributions. The relevant provisions are now contained in ss 226–229 of the Income and Corporation Taxes Act 1970, as amended.

Section 226 allows tax relief to an individual chargeable to income tax in respect of relevant earnings from his business occupation, and who pays a qualifying premium under an annuity contract approved by the Board of the Inland Revenue. To obtain approval, the contract must have as its main object, the provision of a life annuity for the individual in old age. The Board may also approve under s 226A, a contract intended to benefit dependants, being either a contract, the main object of which is the provision of an annuity for the spouse of the individual, or for any one or more dependants of the individual, or a contract, the sole object of which is the provision of a lump sum on the death of the individual before he attains the age of 75. Various other conditions have to be satisfied before approval will be granted. Approved contracts can give the right to the individual to commute part of his annuity into a lump sum not exceeding three times the annual amount of the remaining part of the annuity and it has since 1978 been possible to obtain approval of a retirement annuity contract under which the individual may transfer the value of his accrued benefits to another life office.

The benefits deriving from approval of a retirement annuity contract are twofold. The annuity, when eventually paid, reaches the annuitant as earned income[3]. The payments made by the individual by way of

---

3 The practical significance of this, however has considerably diminished with the disappearance of an investment income surcharge (Finance Act 1984, s 17).

premium may be fully deductible from his relevant earnings in assessing his tax liability for the year of assessment in which the premium is paid. Under s 227 of the Income and Corporation Taxes Act 1970, relief is given only on a claim being made for the purpose[4], and takes the form of allowing against his relevant earnings a deduction of the amount of the premium, subject to limits. The current limit is $17\frac{1}{2}\%$[5] of the individual's net relevant earnings[6] for the year, and non business charges on income are now ignored in calculating such net relevant earnings. No more than 5% of his net relevant earnings may be deducted in respect of a contract under section 226A. There are provisions allowing unused relief to be carried forward for up to six years[7].

Annuities paid to former partners

As we have seen, another form of provision for retirement is to arrange that continuing partners pay an annuity to a former partner. Such payments, whether paid to the former partner or his widow or dependants will be paid under deduction of tax at the basic rate under the provisions of ss 52 or 53 of the Income and Corporation Taxes Act 1970. Of more importance to the paying partners, is the question of whether or not such payments will qualify for tax relief as a total deduction from their income for tax purposes. To do so, they must fall outside the restrictions imposed by s 457 of the Income and Corporation Taxes Act 1970. They can do so in two ways. Annual payments made under a partnership agreement to or for the benefit of a former partner or to the widow or dependants of a deceased former partner will escape the restrictions of s 457 if the payments are made under a liability incurred for full consideration[8]. Similarly, payments to an individual, or if deceased, to his widow or dependants, and made in connection with the acquisition of the whole or part of a business under a liability incurred for full consideration also fall outside the restrictions of s 457[9].

The deduction takes the form of a charge on the income of the paying partners.

While the requirement in both cases, that there be full consideration, is satisfied in an easily ascertainable form when there is a disposal of a business or a partnership share, its existence may be less obvious when the annuity is a payment under the terms of the partnership agreement. Consideration then, however, might well consist of the mutual

4 ICTA 1970, s 227(1).
5 Finance Act 1980, s 31.
6 Defined by ICTA 1970, s 227(5) as amended by Finance Act 1980, s 33(3).
7 ICTA. s 227A.
8 ICTA 1970, s 457(1)(a).
9 ICTA 1970, s 457(2).

undertakings by the partners to contribute to paying annuities in return for the right to receive one on their own retirement.

It is unlikely that the continuing partners would seriously contemplate an annuity designed to extend without time limit beyond the life of their former partner. Generous intentions are inhibited by s 457(4) which provides that the paying partners will cease to obtain full tax relief after their former partner's death, if such an annuity continues for more than ten years after he had ceased to be a partner. It is thought that the subsection applies only where the annuity devolves upon persons other than the widow or dependants of the retired partner but common sense urges that in any event, annuities should from a practical point of view be subject to some time limit.

The removal of an investment income surcharge by the 1984 Finance Act has meant that at present, the question of whether or not the annuity constitutes earned or investment income of the recipient is of far less significance than in the past. In principle, the annuity should constitute investment income. Section 16 of the Finance Act 1974 however allows the annuity scope for being taxed as earned income. It provides that within certain limits an annuity paid either to a person who has ceased to be a partner because of age, ill health or death, or to his widow or dependants shall be treated as earned income. The annuity must be paid under the partnership agreement itself or under an agreement supplementing or replacing it or an agreement for the acquisition of the whole or part of the business. Any such annuity is treated as earned income to the extent it does not exceed 50 per cent of the former partner's average share of profits for the best three out of the last seven years of assessment in which he was required to devote substantially the whole of his time to acting as a partner. Moreover, the Revenue has recognised the effect of inflation in this area. There are provisions allowing the index linking of the limits of the annuity for s 16 purposes, instead of freezing as of the date of the partner's retirement the maximum amount which can qualify for relief[10].

It is probably relatively unlikely that continuing partners would choose to pay to former partners sums in excess of the s 16 limits. To the extent that they do however, the excess will be investment income of the annuitant[11].

Consultancy arrangements

A further method of provision for a retired partner, and one which has the advantage of retaining his connection with the firm, is some form of consultancy. Consultancy fees will be a deductible expense for the firm

10 Finance Act 1980, s 34(4).
11 See *Pegler v Abell* [1973] 1 All ER 52, [1973] 1 WLR 155.

under Schedule D Case II. In the hands of the consultant they will be earned income and it may be possible to persuade the Revenue that they be taxed under Schedule D as opposed to Schedule E. There are however minor pitfalls to avoid.

In the event of the fees being excessive in proportion to work actually done, the Revenue might take the attitude that they are not expenses incurred wholly and exclusively for the purposes of the business and as a result, disallow the excessive element in the firm's Schedule D Case II assessment. To be safe, the consultant should be in a position to earn his fees[12].

Apart from this, the firm, although the consultancy may be intended as part of an overall 'package' on retirement, should take care to avoid any linking of a consultancy agreement with the transfer of the retired partner's share. The consultancy fee will in that event be potentially taxable as investment income[13], and although the limits of s 16 of the Finance Act 1974 are applicable, it might be that a combination of the consultancy fee with any annuity payment could produce a total in excess of the relevant limits which would be taxable as investment income.

While this may be of no consequence to the recipient, the payment, if linked with the acquisition by the continuing partners of their former partner's share in the firm, could not constitute a deductible expense of the partnership because it would not be an expense wholly and exclusively incurred in carrying on the business of the firm in that it may be said to form partial consideration for the retired partner's share in the firm.

Capital gains tax

Whether the draftsman of the Finance Act 1965 ignored the implications of capital gains tax for partnerships by inadvertence, or by design, is a question which may interest the cynically inclined. Certainly, the lack of a comprehensive code which did relate to partnerships caused the Inland Revenue, almost ten years later, to resort to issuing on 17 January 1975, an agreed Statement of Practice, after consultation with the Law Society and the Allied Accountancy Bodies. The Statement itself does not carry the force of law. It is, of course, the Revenue's own interpretation of how it intended the legislation to apply to this area and may not entirely accord with the interpretation placed on the actual legislation by other persons. However, as an indication of the Revenue view of how

---

12 *Copeman v William Flood & Sons Ltd* [1941] 1 KB 202, 24 TC 53.
13 *Hale v Shea* [1965] 1 All ER 155, [1965] 1 WLR 290.

partnerships are affected by capital gains tax it is of paramount importance and in practice is relatively unlikely to be queried. Where it is not strictly in accordance with the legislation the better view is probably that it is concessionary.

The statute

Capital gains tax catches gains accruing to a person on a disposal of chargeable assets. The tax was introduced by the Finance Act 1965 and is now contained in a consolidating Act, the Capital Gains Tax Act 1979. Chargeable gains are gains arising on the disposal of most assets, but individuals in any tax year are entitled to an annually increased exemption in respect of their gains for that tax year[14]. A disposal which gives rise to a chargeable gain can similarly give rise to an allowable loss. There has since 1982 been an indexation allowance for disposals on or after 6 April 1982 to attempt to neutralise the inflation element in gains. The allowance applies in the partnership context to the kinds of disposal described in the following pages and in practice its application, particularly where partnership shares are acquired by stages, may prove complicated. Another Practice Statement seems called for.

The general rule is that the tax is charged by reference to the excess of the actual consideration received over the relevant expenditure on the asset[15]. There are however, provisions under which the Revenue can substitute market value if there is not a bargain at arm's length[16]. In this context, transfers between connected person are treated as not being at arm's length, but fortunately, although partners come within the category of connected persons, they do not do so 'in relation to acquisitions or disposals of partnership assets pursuant to bona fide commercial arrangements'[17]. There need therefore be no great risk in the provision for partners if their arrangement is on a commercial basis and they are not otherwise connected, eg by consanguinity.

Another provision which might have proved inconvenient in the partnership context is s 29A(1) of the Capital Gains Tax Act 1979, which enables the Revenue to substitute market value for actual consideration where disposal is for a consideration which cannot be valued. Happily again, the Revenue do not seek to apply it to partnership dealings in general and do not refer to it in the Practice Statement.

Assessment of tax is treated on a basis different to that used for income tax. Partnership dealings are treated as dealings by the individual partners, tax being charged on them by reference to their share of any

14 Capital Gains Tax Act (CGTA) 1979, s 5.
15 CGTA 1979, s 30.
16 CGTA 1979, s 29A(1)(a).
17 CGTA 1979, s 63(4).

overall gain[18]. The tax is the personal liability of each partner and not a joint liability although returns of capital gains are in fact made by the firm[19].

The statement

The basic premise of the Inland Revenue Statement of Practice of 17 January 1975 is the principle that each partner is to be treated as owning a fractional share of the value of the total partnership interest in any partnership asset. In other words, for the purposes of capital gains tax he owns not so much a part of the firm as a part of each of its underlying assets. The distinct advantage for partners, of this approach, is that tax will not be based on amounts withdrawn from the partnership merely because they exceed the original contribution of the partner to the firm. The tax will be chargeable only insofar as the whole or part of a payment to a partner is attributable to an increase in chargeable assets, and therefore moneys taken out by a partner, eg on retirement, attributable to his retained profits and other contributions to capital, do not attract capital gains tax.

Capital gains may arise in the partnership context in two types of circumstance. The first is the disposal of a chargeable asset by the partnership. The second is where there is a change in the constitution of the firm. Thus, gains can arise where a partner leaves the firm and disposes of his interest in the partnership assets to the others, or where a new partner joins the firm and acquires from the other partners a share in the partnership assets. They can also arise where there is a change in the ratio in which partners share asset surpluses, which entails an acquisition by the partners whose shares increase from the partners whose shares have decreased. The earlier paragraphs of the Statement of Practice indicate the Revenue's attitude toward the above disposals.

Acquisition costs

Every acquisition by the firm of a partnership asset, must be allocated to the partners in accordance with the ratio in which they share in asset surpluses at that time, or, in other words, the ratio in which they expect to share capital profits and losses. It is a matter for the partners to agree upon and may well coincide with the income profit sharing ratio, but if not specifically laid down, follows the treatment of gains in the firm's accounts.

Thus:

If the firm A B and C, which equally shares both its income and capital profits and losses, bought its premises since 1965 for £15,000, the partners are each

18 CGTA 1979, s 60.
19 Taxes Management Act 1970, s 12(4).

treated as having acquired a one third share therein for £5,000. This figure is their base cost.

It is quite possible that the ratio in which they share capital profits differs from their income profit sharing ratio. This can come about (although it does not necessarily follow) because of an imbalance in capital.
Thus:

The firm D, E and F has a senior partner, D, whose capital exceeds that of his partners. They have agreed to share income profits equally but capital profits in the ratio 2:1:1. They purchased their premises in 1966 for £18,000. The base costs for each partner are:

D   £9,000
E   £4,500
F   £4,500

Disposals by a partnership to an outside party[20]

Disposals are treated on a similar basis. So, the proceeds of disposal are allocated to the partners in accordance with the ratio in which they share in asset surpluses *at the time of disposal*.
Thus:

If in the example above, the firm D, E and F were to sell the premises in 1981 for £60,000, the proceeds of disposal would be allocated between the partners:

D	E	F
30,000	15,000	15,000

D has therefore realised a gain of £21,000 (£30,000 less £9,000) and E and F have each realised a gain of £10,500 (£15,000 less £4,500).

By the same token, where the asset is sold for a consideration less than the acquisition cost, there is an allowable loss which is allocated in the same way between the partners.

Disposal of an asset to or among the partners[1]

If a partnership disposes of an asset to a partner, eg on dissolution, the acquiring partner is not regarded as actually disposing of his own fractional share in it. The asset is treated as disposed of at its market value, with the result that a gain or a loss may accrue to the partners. The gains of the other partners are chargeable. As regards the acquiring partner, the base cost of the asset to be carried forward will be its market value at the date of the disposal as reduced by the amount of his notional gain. The above will also apply on a sale to a partner of one of the firm's assets.

20 Practice Statement, para 2.
 1 Practice Statement, para 3.

Thus:

In the previous example, assume that the purchaser of the premises from the firm for £60,000 was partner D. Partners E and F make a gain of £10,500 each, chargeable at that time.

D, who 'paid' £60,000 for the premises has a base cost in respect of them to carry forward, of £39,000 (£60,000 less £21,000). This reflects what has really happened because in reality of course, D will have paid £30,000 to his two partners.

Changes in partnership sharing ratios[2]

An occasion of charge also arises where there is a change in asset surplus sharing ratios. This can occur when a partner leaves a firm, or a new partner joins a firm, or where the partners merely decide to alter the ratio in which they are to share asset surpluses (and, in all likelihood, income profits). In these circumstances, the partner who reduces or gives up his share in asset surpluses is treated as making a disposal of part or the whole of his share in each of the partnership assets while the partner whose share increases makes an acquisition. Disposal consideration, according to the Statement, provided there is no direct payment of consideration outside the agreement, will normally be the appropriate fraction of current balance sheet value of each chargeable asset.

Thus:

The firm G, H and I shared all its profits in the ratio: G one half, H and I one quarter each. Their assets included premises which they bought for £18,000. In 1981 the partners decided that *all* profits were henceforward to be shared equally.

G's position is that his share in asset surpluses fell from a half to one third. He has disposed of the difference between his interest in this asset (and others) before the change and after the change, a difference between his former half and current one third. This is one third of his original share in the premises, or to put it differently, one sixth of the value of the premises.

H and I of course, correspondingly each made an acquisition of one twelfth of the value of the premises.

In fact, it does not necessarily follow that there will be a charge to tax. Whether or not there is a 'gain' will generally depend on whether the assets in question have been revalued in the balance sheet. Where they have been revalued upwards, the disponor partners will make a chargeable gain.

Thus:

In the previous example, partner G made a disposal of one third of his interest or, put otherwise, of one sixth of the value of the premises. His co-partners correspondingly acquired that interest equally between them.

If the premises had been revalued and appeared in the balance sheet at £60,000, the position would be as follows:

2 Practice Statement, para 4.

	£
G: Disposal of one sixth of value of premises	10,000
His base value for one sixth of value of premises	3,000
Chargeable gain	7,000

Moreover, his former base value of £9,000 for his share now drops by £3,000, the base value of the part disposed of, to leave him with a new base value of £6,000.

H and I, whose previous base values were £4,500 each, have made an acquisition of the £10,000 equally between them and their new base values for their shares in the premises are £9,500 each.

Overall base value for the premises is now £25,000, made up as follows:

G	H	I
£6,000	£9,500	£9,500

This merely reflects the fact that in relation to any prospective gain the firm may make in the future, an element has already produced a chargeable gain on this change of ratios.

However, it seems that tax is not inevitable. Capital gains tax can only bite where there is an increase in value. If the item in question remains in the balance sheet at cost, disposal is likewise at cost and no gain will have arisen. The question then arises of whether the Revenue can regard the partnership change as a disposal otherwise than by way of bargain made at arm's length and substitute market value for the consideration based on current balance sheet value[3]. Unless there is consideration for the partnership change this would clearly appear to be the case and the Revenue, subject to the provisions in s 79 of the Finance Act 1980 relating to deferment of liability on gifts (see below) could charge capital gains tax on the basis of actual market value.

This can however be avoided, by showing that there is a bona fide commercial transaction and the acquiring partners are providing consideration for their increased share. Such consideration might take the form of a variety of arrangements, expressly agreed or implicit, such as agreement to pay retirement annuities or to allow the disponor partner to reduce his work load or as to the assumption of responsibilities by the acquiring partners. These arrangements can provide consideration[4] and the partnership change can be by way of bargain made at arm's length.

Adjustments through the accounts[5]

A revaluation of partnership assets is not itself an occasion of charge, for

3 CGTA 1979, s 19(3).
4 See *A-G v Boden* [1912] 1 KB 539, 105 LT 247, discussed later under capital transfer tax.
5 Practice Statement, para 5.

no disposal is necessarily entailed, but only an adjustment to the value shown in the partners' capital accounts. Thus, in our earlier example, a mere revaluation of the premises owned by the firm G, H and I before any change, would have resulted in their shares therein being £30,000, £15,000, £15,000 respectively, but without any tax charge. On a subsequent partnership change, however, the revaluation will be reflected in the values deemed to pass, and may create a capital gains tax liability for the partner whose share decreases.

Payments outside the accounts[6]

Payments into the firm by way of capital, retentions of capital in the firm, and subsequent withdrawal of such capital on retirement or death, have no bearing on capital gains tax liability.

Payments outside the accounts however, between partners on a change of partnership sharing ratios, represent and are treated as, consideration for the disposal of the whole or part of the partner's share in partnership assets in addition to any consideration calculated on the basis of balance sheet value. The payment could be for goodwill not included in the balance sheet. In that event, the partner receiving payment will generally have no base cost to set against it and will be liable to capital gains tax on the whole amount, unless he himself made a similar payment, which will be treated as an acquisition cost.

Transfers between persons not at arm's length[7]

No charge will arise in connection with a change in partnership sharing ratio provided no payment is made through or outside the accounts, unless the transaction can be said to be otherwise than by way of bargain made at arm's length, when the Revenue may substitute market value for current balance sheet value. However, the provision that transfers between partners are not regarded as transactions between connected persons if they are pursuant to bona fide commercial arrangements does not apply if the partners are connected other than by partnership, or are otherwise not at arm's length. This could be of concern to a family partnership.

Nonetheless, paragraph 7 of the statement provides that market value will not be substituted either where nothing would have been paid had the parties been at arm's length, or where, in the event of consideration being less than market value it is not less than would have been paid by parties at arm's length. In short, there are no peculiar capital gains tax

---

6 Practice Statement, para 6.
7 Practice Statement, para 7.

problems for family partnerships who can show that their members are being treated in the same way as any unrelated partner.

In the light of the relief for gifts contained in s 79 of the Finance Act 1980 this may no longer be of real practical significance.

Annuities provided by the partnership[8]

We have seen that a lump sum paid to a partner on a partnership change may constitute consideration for the disposal of assets. The same treatment applies where a firm buys for a partner a purchased life annuity. Consideration is the actual cost to them of the annuity. Generally, there can be no question of a sum attracting both income tax and capital gains tax liability. It may therefore seem unsatisfactory that the statute should contain a provision that in respect of annuity payments provided by the continuing partners to a former partner, the capitalised value of such annuity can also be treated by the Revenue as consideration on the disposal of assets[9]. The Statement of Practice makes an invaluable concession in this area however.

Paragraph 8 provides that it will not be so treated unless it is 'more than can be regarded as a reasonable recognition of the past contribution of work and effort by the partners to the partnership'. In the case of a partner who had been in the firm for at least ten years, an annuity of no more than two thirds of his average share of profits in the best three of the last seven years in which he acted as a full-time partner will be regarded as reasonable. A sliding scale operates to cover partners who have not completed ten years in partnership and partners in a merged firm can include pre-merger periods as part of their qualification period.

The concession is generous, and few firms are likely to be troubled by the provision as a consequence. It is of course possible, that the outgoing partner receives payment in the form of a lump sum as well as annual payments, and the Revenue attitude to this is set out in a further Statement of Practice[10], which broadly, repeats the concession as regards the annuity payment, provided the aggregate of annuity payment and one-ninth of the lump sum does not exceed the two-thirds or other appropriate fraction.

Reliefs in connection with business property

In the infancy of capital gains tax, it was fairly true to say that in order to qualify for reliefs in relation to business property it was essential that the

8 Practice Statement, para 8.
9 CGTA 1979, s 31(3).
10 Statement of 12 January 1979 (SP 1/79).

property be vested in the firm. The position has gradually changed over the years.

Relief on replacement of business assets (Capital Gains Tax Act 1979, s 115)

This relief, widely known as 'roll-over relief', applies where a trader disposes of assets used solely in his trade and uses the proceeds to acquire replacement assets for the trade. He may deduct from the cost of the new assets any gain realised, thus producing a lower base cost for the assets, and defer payment of tax on his gain until the assets are disposed of and not replaced. Business assets[11] include land and buildings used only for the purposes of a trade, fixed plant and machinery and goodwill. There may be scope for proportionate relief.

The relief clearly applies to business assets owned by the firm, and its application should be straightforward, unless, between disposal of the asset and reinvestment of the proceeds in a replacement asset, there has been a change of asset surplus sharing ratios. Such a change can have the effect of restricting the amount of gain a disponor partner can roll-over.

It has for some years been the view of the Inland Revenue that the relief is also available where assets used by the firm actually belong to an individual partner, provided the proceeds of disposal of such an asset are reinvested in another business asset used by the firm. Whether or not rent was charged for use of the assets seems irrelevant.

Retirement relief (Finance Act 1985, ss 69, 70 and Sch 20)

The Finance Act 1985 introduced a new, more wide-ranging form of retirement relief to replace the provisions previously contained in s 124 of the Capital Gains Tax Act 1979.

Section 69 allows relief to individuals over the age of 60 in respect of new gains realised on the disposal by way of sale or gift of business assets. Business assets can comprise the whole or part of a business, and, where a business is carried on in partnership, includes the disponor's interest in the assets of the partnership which carries on the business.

The minimum qualifying period of ownership is one year, rising to a maximum of ten years. A person who has been a partner for ten years will qualify for maximum relief of £100,000.

The relief is now also available to an individual below the age of 60 forced to retire by virtue of his ill health.

The new code makes specific provision for a matter previously covered by a published Statement of Practice, namely that the relief applies to disposal of an asset belonging to a partner rather than the firm

11 Listed in CGTA 1979, ss 18 and 19.

but which was used for the purpose of the partnership business, if it is associated with the disposal of the business or part of the business and the other requirements of the relief are satisfied. Relief however will be restricted if a rent was charged, and a partner whose firm uses premises owned by him, may well find this material in deciding whether or not the firm should be charged rent as such. He may prefer a larger profit share.

Reliefs for gifts of business assets

Section 126 of the Capital Gains Tax Act contains a relief for gifts of business assets. It is now largely superseded by the wider relief of s 79 of the Finance Act 1980, which allows relief on gifts of all assets, but will still be relevant if a disposal is to a non-individual, eg to a company or to trustees.

Both reliefs work in essentially the same manner. The transferor and transferee jointly claim to have the otherwise chargeable element of gain on the gift deducted from acquisition cost to the transferee. The transferor thus suffers no capital gains tax, and the lowered base cost of the transferee means that the held over gain is potentially chargeable in his hands on his subsequent disposal. In both cases, credit is first given for any retirement relief due to the transferor and only the non-exempt excess is held over.

Section 79 will generally be the appropriate relief. It operates more favourably to the taxpayer in that under its provisions, any capital transfer tax payable by either transferor or transferee is deductible by the transferee in computing any capital gain on a later disposal by him[12]. Section 126 will however, still be relevant if the disposal is not to an individual.

The reliefs should be particularly useful where the Revenue can claim that a transaction is not a bargain at arm's length, in particular where the partners are parent and child, and would seek to substitute market value for consideration actually passing. Their disadvantage lies in the fact that when they are used, the reduced base value will be the basis on which indexation is allowed.

Capital transfer tax

The tax

Capital transfer tax was introduced by the Finance Act 1975 and applies to dispositions made after 26 March 1974 which reduce the value of the transferor's estate and are not exempt transfers. It operates both as a tax

12 Finance Act 1980, s 79(5).

upon lifetime gifts and as a tax on the property comprised in a person's estate on his death. The Capital Transfer Tax Act 1984 now consolidates the provisions of the Finance Act 1975 and other enactments. There are various exemptions; in particular, an exemption for transfers between spouses both in lifetime and on death[13]; and dispositions without donative intent are protected by s 10 of the Act, which applies to transactions where there is no intention to confer any gratuitous benefit on any person and the transaction either is a transaction at arm's length between unconnected persons, or is such a transaction as might be expected to be made in an arm's length transaction between unconnected persons.

Relevance of the tax to partnerships

There are few direct references to partnerships in the capital transfer tax legislation, and general principles apply. Clearly, anything payable on a partner's death to his estate will form part of it and hence, except where it passes to his spouse, may attract capital transfer tax. Similarly, lifetime gifts by the partner, including a gift of his partnership share could give rise to a charge to tax. Where there is no donative intention, s 10 should apply with the result that there will be no charge to tax.

There are, of course, other circumstances in which the tax is relevant to the partnership field and dealings between the partners could give rise to capital transfer tax. As was true of capital gains tax, the circumstances are likely to relate to changes in either the constitution of the firm or of profit or asset surplus sharing ratios.

Thus, when a new partner joins a firm and is to have a share in assets, absence of consideration from him in some such tangible form as cash, could indicate a gift element in the arrangement. A similar assumption could arise where partners agree to a variation in asset sharing ratios or to a variation of one or more of the terms of the partnership agreement. The abolition of goodwill, which in professional firms has of recent years become increasingly common, could denote a gift element in the absence of some consideration for the partners who owned it. If partners are allowed to purchase assets from the firm at a preferential price this should constitute a transfer at an undervalue. Perhaps most important of all, if a partner's share automatically accrues to his surviving partners on his death or retirement without payment there is at least the suggestion of a present or previous transfer of value.

In practice in fact, it seems generally possible to avoid tax liability. In many cases the circumstances will fall within the scope of s 10 for although for capital transfer tax purposes partners, as for capital gains tax, are connected persons[14], there is an exception, as for capital gains

13 Capital Transfer Tax Act 1984, s 18.
14 CTTA 1984, s 270.

tax, in relation to acquisitions or disposals of partnership assets pursuant to bona fide commercial arrangements. In practice, it is thought that a change in partner's interests in the firm's assets by reason of a change in partnership ratio can fall within s 10.

Thus:

> If partner Tom's profit share decreases from 50 per cent to 40 per cent and partner Ian's share increases from 20 per cent to 30 per cent then an interest in 10 per cent of the firm's goodwill will presumably have shifted from Tom to Ian and there is a disposition. It nonetheless may be perfectly appropriate to argue that the arrangement is part of a bona fide commercial bargain and made without gratuitous intent. Consideration from Ian may well be agreement by him to work harder and/or to pay an annuity to Tom on Tom's eventual retirement.

The same principle should apply to most dealings between partners. In reality, there is relatively little likelihood of intention to confer truly gratuitous benefit (other than between relatives) and it should be possible, for instance, to invoke s 10 to cover the introduction of a new partner or the abolition of goodwill. It may even be that annuity provisions have been designed to cover the very eventuality. This would only strengthen the contention that there is consideration in any event emanating from the mutual covenants by the partners to work in the business.

A common feature of partnership agreements is a clause providing that a deceased or retired partner's share is to accrue automatically to the remaining partners or that the remaining partners have an option to purchase that share. At first sight, this might appear to lead to difficulties in the light of s 163 of the Capital Transfer Tax Act which provides that where by a contract, the right to dispose of any property has been excluded or restricted, then in valuing that property, the exclusion or restriction is effectively ignored except to the extent that consideration in money or money's worth has been given for it. In other words, if the share, or rather the exclusion or restriction, has not been purchased, then on the partner's retirement or death, he will, for capital transfer tax purposes, be treated as owning his share in the partnership assets as if the restriction did not affect it. ·There could also be a charge to capital transfer tax when the partnership agreement containing the clause in question is entered into, although in that event, then on subsequently calculating liability on death or retirement, credit will be given for the value transferred on entry into the agreement.

Fortunately, there is the possibility that the partners can show that consideration in money or money's worth has been given. It was established in cases on estate duty, *A-G v Boden*[15] and *A-G v Ralli*[16] that

---

15 [1912] 1 KB 539, 105 LT 247.
16 (1936) 15 ATC 523.

purchase, for this sort of circumstance does not necessarily entail cash consideration. If the partnership agreement contains mutual covenants providing that goodwill is to pass on death to surviving partners without payment or even with some type of payment, those mutual covenants will normally amount to a consideration in money or money's worth. In practice, it seems that where agreement is clear and there is between the partners a genuine commercial bargain without an element of bounty, the Revenue will normally accept that only the amount the former partner's estate receives from the firm and no more, forms part of his estate for capital transfer tax.

It is wrong to assume that the foregoing cannot apply to relatives, for instance, where a father and son are in partnership. It is true that there is a greater likelihood of bounty in any arrangements between them, and the Revenue are unlikely to be oblivious to that possibility. They are also connected persons for the purpose of the legislation by virtue of their consanguinity and not merely their partnership. On the other hand, *A-G v Boden* itself concerned a partnership between a father and sons and s 10 is not restricted to transactions between unconnected persons, but includes such transactions as might have been expected between unconnected persons. If therefore, the partners can persuade the Revenue that the terms of their arrangement are those which would have prevailed even where no related persons were involved, their problem may well be one of overcoming Revenue suspicions rather than one of satisfying totally different criteria.

Exemptions and reliefs for business property

Apart from s 10, and the interspouse exemption, which will relieve the estates of many deceased partners from liability, the most significant relief from capital transfer tax for partners is likely to be the relief for relevant business property contained in ss 103 to 114 of the Act. The relief is available to a partner in relation to his interest in his firm and takes the form of a reduction in the value of the property transferred. It applies to lifetime transfers and to those on death. The relief is one of 50 per cent in relation to property consisting of a business or an interest in a business, eg the partner's interest, however insignificant, in his firm.

Assets owned by the partner privately but which are used in the business can qualify for relief in a separate category as 'any land or building, machinery or plant which immediately before the transfer, was used wholly or mainly for the purposes of a business carried on . . . by a partnership in which he was then a partner'. Relief for such assets is however, at the lower figure of 30 per cent[17].

The above relief is particularly useful, not on a transfer between

17 CTTA 1984, s 104(1)(b).

spouses which already qualifies for exemption, but rather on the transfer to some other recipient, eg a son. In this context, it may be appropriate to consider an ancillary form of relief. Under s 227 of the Act, payment of capital transfer tax on death or on life transfers where the transferee pays the tax, may be paid by instalments over a period of up to ten years. The provision applies to a business or interest in a business[18], and where the value transferred represents a business, the instalments are free of interest, which can be of significant importance. This latter facility does not apply to land which is used in the business but is not a partnership asset, although such land does qualify for the instalment facility. The result is that interest is charged on the whole of the unpaid tax at each instalment date which considerably detracts from the attraction of being able to spread the tax payments. The inference from these reliefs is that purely from a capital transfer tax point of view, property is perhaps best vested in the partnership and represented by the interest of the partner in his business.

It is also important to appreciate that the Revenue will not allow the above business property reliefs if at the time of transfer a partner's share is subject to a binding contract for sale[19]. Thus, buy and sell agreements, under which outgoing partners are obliged to sell and continuing partners purchase, and (presumably) automatic accrual clauses, carry with them this disadvantage. An option to purchase is however not so treated by the Revenue and preserves the right to these reliefs.

18 Ibid, s 227(2)(b).
19 See Practice Statement SP 12/80.

Chapter 13

Business names

It was mentioned earlier that, in general, a partnership is free to use any name that it chooses, but that it must conform with the provisions of the Business Names Act 1985[1].

This Act applies to certain persons only. It prohibits the use of certain business names. Some words and expressions require the Secretary of State's approval. Disclosure is required by persons using business names. There are civil remedies for breach of the Act's requirements on this point. Regulations under the Act must be made by statutory instrument. Various punishments may be imposed for contravention of the Act.

Persons to whom Business Names Act 1985 applies

The Act applies to any person who has a place of business[2] in Great Britain and who carries on business in Great Britain under a name which, in the case of a partnership[3], does not consist of the surnames[4] of all partners who are individuals and the corporate names of all partners who are bodies corporate without any addition other than an addition permitted by the Act[5].

In the case of a partnership the permitted additions are –
(1) the forenames of individual partners or the initials[6] of those forenames or, where two or more individual partners have the same surname, the addition of 's' at the end of that surname; and
(2) any addition merely indicating that the business is carried on in succession to a former owner of the business.[7]

---

1 See p 20, above.
2 'Business' includes a profession: Business Names Act 1985, s 8(1).
3 'Partnership' includes a foreign partnership: ibid, s 8(1).
4 'Surname' in relation to a peer or person usually known by a British title different from his surname means the title by which he is known: ibid, s 8(1).
5 Ibid, s 1(1).
6 'Initial' includes any recognised abbreviation of a name: ibid, s 8(1).
7 Ibid, s 1(2).

Prohibition of use of certain business names

A person to whom the Act applies[8] must not, without the written approval of the Secretary of State, carry on business in Great Britain under a name which –

(1) would be likely to give the impression that the business is connected with Her Majesty's Government or with any local authority[9]; or
(2) includes any word or expression for the time being specified in regulations made under the Act[10].

A person who contravenes this provision is guilty of an offence[11].

Words and expressions requiring Secretary of State's approval

The Secretary of State may by regulations –

(1) specify words or expressions for the use of which as or as part of a business name his approval is required[12]; and
(2) in relation to such word or expression specify a Government department or other body as the body which a person to whom the Act applies [13] and who wishes to carry on a business under a name which is or includes such a word or expression, must contact[14].

8 See p 151, above.
9 'Local authority' means any local authority within the meaning of the Local Government Act 1972, the Common Council of the City of London or the Council of the Isles of Scilly: ibid, s 8(1).
10 Ibid, s 2(1). This subsection does not apply to the carrying on of a business by a person –
  (a) to whom the business has been transferred on or after 26 February 1982; and
  (b) who carries on the business under the name which was its lawful business name immediately before that transfer, during the period of 12 months beginning with the date of that transfer: ibid, s 2(2). 'Lawful business name', in relation to a business, means a name under which the business was carried on without contravening the Business Names Act 1985, s 2(1) or the Registration of Business Names Act 1916, s 2: ibid, s 8(1). Further, s 2(1) of the Business Names Act 1985 does not apply to the carrying on of business by a person who –
  (a) carried on that business immediately before 26 February 1982; and
  (b) continues to carry it on under the name which immediately before that date was its lawful business name; ibid, s 2(3)
11 Ibid, s 2(4). For offences, see p 155, below.
12 Under s 2(1)(b).
13 See p 151, above.
14 Business Names Act 1985, s 3(1). The regulations at present in force are the Company and Business Names Regulations 1981 (SI 1981/1685) and the Company and Business Names (Amendment) Regulations 1982 (SI 1982/1653). See Appendix B, pp 195–200, below.

That person must –

(1) request (in writing) the relevant body to indicate whether (and if so, why) it has any objections to the proposal; and
(2) submit to the Secretary of State a statement that such a request has been made and a copy of any response from the relevant body[15].

Disclosure by person using business name

(a) Disclosure on business letters, written orders etc

A person to whom the Act applies[16] must state in legible characters on all business letters, written orders for goods or services to be supplied to the business, invoices and receipts issued in the course of the business and written demands for payment of debts arising in the course of the business –

(1) the name of each partner; and
(2) in relation to each person so named, an address in Great Britain at which service of any document relating in any way to the business will be effective[17].

A person who without reasonable cause fails to make the statement concerning the names and addresses of the partners is guilty of an offence[18].

But the above provisions do not apply in relation to any document issued by a partnership of more than 20 persons which maintains at its principal place of business a list of the names of all the partners if –

(1) none of the names of the partners appears in the document otherwise than in the text or as a signatory; and
(2) the document states in legible characters the address of the partnership's principal place of business and that the list of the partners' names is open to inspection at that place[19].

Where a partnership maintains a list of the partners' names, any person may inspect the list during office hours[20].

Where an inspection required by any person is refused, any partner of the partnership concerned who without reasonable excuse refused that inspection, or permitted it to be refused, is guilty of an offence[1].

15 Business Names Act 1985, s 3(2).
16 See p 151, above.
17 Business Names Act 1985, s 4(1)(a).
18 Ibid, s 4(6).
19 Ibid, s 4(3).
20 Ibid, s 4(4).
 1 Ibid, s 4(7). For offences, see p 155, below.

(b) Disclosure by display of notice

A person to whom the Act applies[2] must in any premises where the business is carried on and to which the customers of the business or suppliers of any goods or services to the business have access, display in a prominent position so that it may easily be read by such customers or suppliers a notice containing the names and addresses of each partner[3].

The Secretary of State may by regulations[4] require notices to be displayed in a specified form[5].

A person who without reasonable excuse fails to display the notice or contravenes the regulations is guilty of an offence[6].

(c) Disclosure to persons on request

A person to whom the Act applies[7] must secure that the names and addresses of each partner are immediately given by written notice to any person with whom anything is done or discussed in the course of the business and who asks for such names and addresses[8].

The Secretary of State may by regulations require notices to be given in a specified form[9].

A person who without reasonable excuse fails to give the notice or contravenes the regulations is guilty of an offence[10].

Civil remedies

Any legal proceedings brought by a person to whom the Act applies[11] to enforce a right arising out of a contract made in the course of a business in respect of which he was, at the time the contract was made, in breach of s 4(1)[12] or (2)[13] must be dismissed if the defendant to the proceedings shows –

(1) that he has a claim against the plaintiff arising out of that contract

2 See p 151, above.
3 Business Names Act 1985, s 4(1)(b).
4 As to regulations, see p 155, below.
5 Business Names Act 1985, s 4(5).
6 Ibid, s 4(6).
7 See p 151, above.
8 Ibid, s 4(2).
9 Ibid, s 4(5).
10 Ibid, s 4(6). For offences, see p 155, below.
11 See p 151, above.
12 See p 153, above.
13 See above.

which he has been unable to pursue by reason of such breach by the plaintiff; or

(2) that he has suffered some financial loss in connection with the contract by reason of such breach by the plaintiff,

unless the court before which the proceedings are brought is satisfied that it is just and equitable to permit them to continue[14].

The above provision is without prejudice to the right of any person to enforce such rights as he may have against another person in any proceedings brought by that person[15].

Regulations

Regulations under the Act must be made by statutory instrument and may contain such savings as the Secretary of State thinks appropriate, and may make different provision for different cases or classes of cases[16].

In the case of regulations made under s 3[17] the statutory instrument containing them must be laid before Parliament after they are made and ceases to have effect at the end of the period of 28 days beginning with the day on which they were made[18] unless during that period they are approved by a resolution of each House of Parliament[19].

In the case of regulations made under s 4[20] the statutory instrument containing them is subject to annulment in pursuance of a resolution of either House of Parliament[1].

Offences

Offences under the Act are punishable on summary conviction[2].

A person guilty of an offence under the Act is liable to a fine not exceeding one-fifth of the statutory maximum[3].

14 Business Names Act 1985, s 5(1).
15 Ibid, s 5(2).
16 Ibid, s 6(1).
17 See p 152, above.
18 But without prejudice to anything previously done by virtue of them or to the making of new regulations.
19 Business Names Act 1985, s 6(2). In reckoning the period of 28 days no account is to be taken of any time during which Parliament is dissolved or prorogued, or during which both Houses are adjourned for more than 4 days: ibid, s 6(2).
20 See p 154, above.
 1 Business Names Act 1985, s 6(3).
 2 Ibid, s 7(1).
 3 Ibid, s 7(2). 'Statutory maximum' means the prescribed sum under the Magistrates' Courts Act 1980, s 32: ibid, s 8(1).

If after a person has been convicted summarily of an offence under s 2[4] or s 4(6)[5] the original contravention is continued, he is liable on a second or subsequent summary conviction of the offence to a fine not exceeding one-fiftieth of the statutory maximum for each day on which the contravention is continued[6].

4 See p 152, above.
5 See p 153, above.
6 Business Names Act 1985, s 7(3).

Appendices

Appendix A

Statutes

Partnership Act 1890[1]

53 & 54 Vict c. 39

An Act to declare and amend the Law of Partnership.

[14 August 1890]

Be it enacted by the Queen's most Excellent Majesty, by and with the advice and consent of the Lords Spiritual and Temporal, and Commons, in this present Parliament assembled, and by the authority of the same, as follows:

NATURE OF PARTNERSHIP

1. Definition of partnership

(1) Partnership is the relation which subsists between persons carrying on a business in common with a view of profit.

(2) But the relation between members of any company or association which is—

(a) Registered as a company under the Companies Act 1862, or any other Act of Parliament for the time being in force and relating to the registration of joint stock companies; or

(b) Formed or incorporated by or in pursuance of any other Act of Parliament or letters patent, or Royal Charter; or

(c) A company engaged in working mines within and subject to the jurisdiction of the Stannaries:

is not a partnership within the meaning of this Act.

2. Rules for determining existence of partnership

In determining whether a partnership does or does not exist, regard shall be had to the following rules:

(1) Joint tenancy, tenancy in common, joint property, common property, or part ownership does not of itself create a partnership as

1 The Act is printed as amended.

to anything so held or owned, whether the tenants or owners do or do not share any profits made by the use thereof.

(2) The sharing of gross returns does not of itself create a partnership, whether the persons sharing such returns have or have not a joint or common right or interest in any property from which or from the use of which the returns are derived.

(3) The receipt by a person of a share of the profits of a business is prima facie evidence that he is a partner in the business, but the receipt of such a share, or of a payment contingent on or varying with the profits of a business, does not of itself make him a partner in the business; and in particular—

(a) The receipt by a person of a debt or other liquidated amount by instalments or otherwise out of the accruing profits of a business does not of itself make him a partner in the business or liable as such:

(b) A contract for the remuneration of a servant or agent of a person engaged in a business by a share of the profits of the business does not of itself make the servant or agent a partner in the business or liable as such:

(c) A person being the widow or child of a deceased partner, and receiving by way of annuity a portion of the profits made in the business in which the deceased person was a partner, is not by reason only of such receipt a partner in the business or liable as such:

(d) The advance of money by way of loan to a person engaged or about to engage in any business on a contract with that person that the lender shall receive a rate of interest varying with the profits, or shall receive a share of the profits arising from carrying on the business, does not of itself make the lender a partner with the person or persons carrying on the business or liable as such. Provided that the contract is in writing, and signed by or on behalf of all the parties thereto:

(e) A person receiving by way of annuity or otherwise a portion of the profits of a business in consideration of the sale by him of the goodwill of the business is not by reason only of such receipt a partner in the business or liable as such.

3. Postponement of rights of person lending or selling in consideration of share of profits in case of insolvency
In the event of any person to whom money has been advanced by way of loan upon such a contract as is mentioned in the last foregoing section or of any buyer of a goodwill in consideration of a share of the profits of the business, being adjudged a bankrupt, entering into an arrangement to pay his creditors less than twenty shillings in the pound, or dying in

insolvent circumstances, the lender of the loan shall not be entitled to recover anything in respect of his loan, and the seller of the goodwill shall not be entitled to recover anything in respect of the share of profits contracted for, until the claims of the other creditors of the borrower or buyer for valuable consideration in money or money's worth have been satisfied.

4. Meaning of firm

(1) Persons who have entered into partnership with one another are for the purposes of this Act called collectively a firm, and the name under which their business is carried on is called the firm-name.

(2) In Scotland a firm is a legal person distinct from the partners of whom it is composed, but an individual partner may be charged on a decree or diligence directed against the firm, and on payment of the debts is entitled to relief *pro rata* from the firm and its other members.

RELATIONS OF PARTNERS TO PERSONS DEALING WITH THEM

5. Power of partner to bind the firm

Every partner is an agent of the firm and his other partners for the purpose of the business of the partnership; and the acts of every partner who does any act for carrying on in the usual way business of the kind carried on by the firm of which he is a member bind the firm and his partners, unless the partner so acting has in fact no authority to act for the firm in the particular matter, and the person with whom he is dealing either knows that he has no authority, or does not know or believe him to be a partner.

6. Partners bound by acts on behalf of firm

An act or instrument relating to the business of the firm and done or executed in the firm-name, or in any other manner showing an intention to bind the firm, by any person thereto authorised whether a partner or not, is binding on the firm and all the partners.

Provided that this section shall not affect any general rule of law relating to the execution of deeds or negotiable instruments.

7. Partner using credit of firm for private purposes

Where one partner pledges the credit of the firm for a purpose apparently not connected with the firm's ordinary course of business, the firm is not bound, unless he is in fact specially authorised by the other partners: but this section does not affect any personal liability incurred by an individual partner.

8. Effect of notice that firm will not be bound by acts of partner

If it has been agreed between the partners than any restriction shall be placed on the power of any one or more of them to bind the firm, no act done in contravention of the agreement is binding on the firm with respect to persons having notice of the agreement.

9. Liability of partners

Every partner in a firm is liable jointly with the other partners, and in Scotland severally also, for all debts and obligations of the firm incurred while he is a partner; and after his death his estate is also severally liable in a due course of administration for such debts and obligations, so far as they remain unsatisfied, but subject in England or Ireland to the prior payment of his separate debts.

10. Liability of the firm for wrongs

Where, by any wrongful act or omission of any partner acting in the ordinary course of the business of the firm, or with the authority of his co-partners, loss or injury is caused to any person not being a partner in the firm, or any penalty is incurred, the firm is liable therefor to the same extent as the partner so acting or omitting to act.

11. Misapplication of money or property received for or in custody of the firm

In the following cases; namely—

(a) Where one partner acting within the scope of his apparent authority receives the money or property of a third person and misapplies it; and

(b) Where a firm in the course of its business receives money or property of a third person, and the money or property so received is misapplied by one or more of the partners while it is in the custody of the firm;

the firm is liable to make good the loss.

12. Liability for wrongs joint and several

Every partner is liable jointly with his co-partners and also severally for everything for which the firm while he is a partner therein becomes liable under either of the two last preceding sections.

13. Improper employment of trust property for partnership purposes

If a partner, being a trustee, improperly employs trust property in the business or on the account of the partnership, no other partner is liable for the trust property to the persons beneficially interested therein:

Provided as follows:

(1) This section shall not affect any liability incurred by any partner by reason of his having notice of a breach of trust; and

(2) Nothing in this section shall prevent trust money from being followed and recovered from the firm if still in its possession or under its control.

14. Persons liable by 'holding out'

(1) Every one who by words spoken or written or by conduct represents himself, or who knowingly suffers himself to be represented, as a partner in a particular firm, is liable as a partner to any one who has on the faith of any such representation given credit to the firm, whether the representation has or has not been made or communicated to the person so giving credit by or with the knowledge of the apparent partner making the representation or suffering it to be made.

(2) Provided that where after a partner's death the partnership business is continued in the old firm-name, the continued use of that name, or of the deceased partner's name as part thereof shall not of itself make his executors or administrators estate or effects liable for any partnership debts contracted after his death.

15. Admissions and representations of partners

An admission or representation made by any partner concerning the partnership affairs, and in the ordinary course of its business, is evidence against the firm.

16. Notice to acting partner to be notice to the firm

Notice to any partner who habitually acts in the partnership business of any matter relating to partnership affairs operates as notice to the firm, except in the case of a fraud on the firm committed by or with the consent of that partner.

17. Liabilities of incoming and outgoing partners

(1) A person who is admitted as a partner into an existing firm does not thereby become liable to the creditors of the firm for anything done before he became a partner.

(2) A partner who retires from a firm does not thereby cease to be liable for partnership debts or obligations incurred before his retirement.

(3) A retiring partner may be discharged from any existing liabilities, by an agreement to that effect between himself and the members of the firm as newly constituted and the creditors, and this agreement may be either express or inferred as a fact from the course of dealing between the creditors and the firm as newly constituted.

18. Revocation of continuing guaranty by change in firm

A continuing guaranty or cautionary obligation given either to a firm or to a third person in respect of the transactions of a firm is, in the absence of agreement to the contrary, revoked as to future transactions by any change in the constitution of the firm to which, or of the firm in respect of the transactions of which, the guaranty or obligation was given.

RELATIONS OF PARTNERS TO ONE ANOTHER

19. Variation by consent of terms of partnership

The mutual rights and duties of partners, whether ascertained by agreement or defined by this Act, may be varied by the consent of all the partners, and such consent may be either express or inferred from a course of dealing.

20. Partnership property

(1) All property and rights and interests in property originally brought into the partnership stock or acquired, whether by purchase or otherwise, on account of the firm, or for the purposes and in the course of the partnership business, are called in this Act partnership property, and must be held and applied by the partners exclusively for the purposes of the partnership and in accordance with the partnership agreement.

(2) Provided that the legal estate or interest in any land, or in Scotland the title to and interest in any heritable estate, which belongs to the partnership shall devolve according to the nature and tenure thereof, and the general rules of law thereto applicable, but in trust, so far as necessary, for the persons beneficially interested in the land under this section.

(3) Where co-owners of an estate or interest in any land, or in Scotland of any heritable estate, not being itself partnership property, are partners as to profits made by the use of that land or estate, and purchase other land or estate out of the profits to be used in like manner, the land or estate so purchased belongs to them, in the absence of an agreement to the contrary, not as partners, but as co-owners for the same respective estates and interests as are held by them in the land or estate first mentioned at the date of the purchase.

21. Property bought with partnership money

Unless the contrary intention appears, property bought with money belonging to the firm is deemed to have been bought on account of the firm.

22. Conversion into personal estate of land held as partnership property

Where land or any heritable interest therein has become partnership property, it shall, unless the contrary intention appears, be treated as between the partners (including the representatives of a deceased partner), and also as between the heirs of a deceased partner and his executors or administrators, as personal or movable and not real or heritable estate.

23. Procedure against partnership property for a partner's separate judgment debt

(1) . . . a writ of execution shall not issue against any partnership property except on a judgment against the firm.

(2) The High Court, or a judge thereof, . . . (a) or a county court may, on the application by summons of any judgment creditor of a partner, make an order charging that partner's interest in the partnership property and profits with payment of the amount of the judgment debt and interest thereon, and may by the same or a subsequent order appoint a receiver of that partner's share of profits (whether already declared or accruing), and of any other money which may be coming to him in respect of the partnership, and direct all accounts and inquiries, and give all other orders and directions which might have been directed or given if the charge had been made in favour of the judgment creditor by the partner, or which the circumstances of the case may require.

(3) The other partner or partners shall be at liberty at any time to redeem the interest charged, or, in case of a sale being directed, to purchase the same.

(4) This section shall apply in the case of a cost-book company as if the company were a partnership within the meaning of this Act.

(5) This section shall not apply to Scotland.

24. Rules as to interests and duties of partners subject to special agreement

The interests of partners in the partnership property and their rights and duties in relation to the partnership shall be determined, subject to any agreement express or implied between the partners, by the following rules:

(1) All the partners are entitled to share equally in the capital and profits of the business, and must contribute equally towards the losses whether of capital or otherwise sustained by the firm.

(2) The firm must indemnify every partner in respect of payments made and personal liabilities incurred by him—
   (a) In the ordinary and proper conduct of the business of the firm; or
   (b) In or about anything necessarily done for the preservation of the business or property of the firm.

(3) A partner making, for the purpose of the partnership, any actual payment or advance beyond the amount of capital which he has agreed to subscribe, is entitled to interest at the rate of five per cent per annum from the date of the payment or advance.

(4) A partner is not entitled, before the ascertainment of profits, to interest on the capital subscribed by him.

(5) Every partner may take part in the management of the partnership business.

(6) No partner shall be entitled to remuneration for acting in the partnership business.

(7) No person may be introduced as a partner without the consent of all existing partners.

(8) Any difference arising as to ordinary matters connected with the partnership business may be decided by a majority of the partners, but no change may be made in the nature of the partnership business without the consent of all existing partners.

(9) The partnership books are to be kept at the place of business of the partnership (or the principal place, if there is more than one), and every partner may, when he thinks fit, have access to and inspect and copy any of them.

25. Expulsion of partner
No majority of the partners can expel any partner unless a power to do so has been conferred by express agreement between the partners.

26. Retirement from partnership at will
(1) Where no fixed term has been agreed upon for the duration of the partnership, any partner may determine the partnership at any time on giving notice of his intention so to do to all the other partners.

(2) Where the partnership has originally been constituted by deed, a notice in writing, signed by the partner giving it, shall be sufficient for this purpose.

27. Where partnership for term is continued over, continuance on old terms presumed
(1) Where a partnership entered into for a fixed term is continued after the term has expired, and without any express new agreement, the rights and duties of the partners remain the same as they were at the expiration of the term, so far as is consistent with the incidents of a partnership at will.

(2) A continuance of the business by the partners or such of them as habitually acted therein during the term, without any settlement or liquidation of the partnership affairs, is presumed to be a continuance of the partnership.

28. Duty of partners to render accounts, etc.
Partners are bound to render true accounts and full information of all things affecting the partnership to any partner or his legal representatives.

29. Accountability of partners for private profits
(1) Every partner must account to the firm for any benefit derived by him without the consent of the other partners from any transaction concerning the partnership, or from any use by him of the partnership property, name or business connection.

(2) This section applies also to transactions undertaken after a partnership has been dissolved by the death of a partner, and before the affairs thereof have been completely wound up, either by any surviving partner or by the representatives of the deceased partner.

30. Duty of partner not to compete with firm
If a partner, without the consent of the other partners, carries on any business of the same nature as and competing with that of the firm, he must account for and pay over to the firm all profits made by him in that business.

31. Rights of assignee of share in partnership
(1) An assignment by any partner of his share in the partnership, either absolute or by way of mortgage or redeemable charge, does not, as against the other partners, entitle the assignee, during the continuance of the partnership, to interfere in the management or administration of the partnership business or affairs, or to require any accounts of the partnership transactions, or to inspect the partnership books, but entitles the assignee only to receive the share of profits to which the assigning partner would otherwise be entitled, and the assignee must accept the account of profits agreed to by the partners.

(2) In case of a dissolution of the partnership, whether as respects all the partners or as respects the assigning partner, the assignee is entitled to receive the share of the partnership assets to which the assigning partner is entitled as between himself and the other partners, and, for the purpose of ascertaining that share, to an account as from the date of the dissolution.

DISSOLUTION OF PARTNERSHIP, AND ITS CONSEQUENCES

32. Dissolution by expiration or notice
Subject to any agreement between the partners, a partnership is dissolved—

(a) If entered into for a fixed term, by the expiration of that term:
(b) If entered into for a single adventure or undertaking, by the termination of that adventure or undertaking:
(c) If entered into for an undefined time, by any partner giving notice to the other or others of his intention to dissolve the partnership.

In the last-mentioned case the partnership is dissolved as from the date mentioned in the notice as the date of dissolution, or, if no date is so mentioned, as from the date of the communication of the notice.

33. Dissolution by bankruptcy, death or charge
(1) Subject to any agreement between the partners, every partnership is dissolved as regards all the partners by the death or bankruptcy of any partner.

(2) A partnership may, at the option of the other partners, be dissolved if any partner suffers his share of the partnership property to be charged under this Act for his separate debt.

34. Dissolution by illegality of partnership
A partnership is in every case dissolved by the happening of any event which makes it unlawful for the business of the firm to be carried on or for the members of the firm to carry it on in partnership.

35. Dissolution by the court
On application by a partner the court may decree a dissolution of the partnership in any of the following cases:

(a) [*Repealed*]
(b) When a partner, other than the partner suing, becomes in any other way permanently incapable of performing his part of the partnership contract:
(c) When a partner, other than the partner suing, has been guilty of such conduct as, in the opinion of the Court, regard being had to the nature of the business, is calculated to prejudicially affect the carrying on of the business:
(d) When a partner, other than the partner suing, wilfully or persistently commits a breach of the partnership agreement, or otherwise so conducts himself in matters relating to the partnership business that it is not reasonably practicable for the other partner or partners to carry on the business in partnership with him:
(e) When the business of the partnership can only be carried on at a loss:
(f) Whenever in any case circumstances have arisen, which, in the opinion of the Court, render it just and equitable that the partnership be dissolved.

36. Rights of persons dealing with firm against apparent members of firm

(1) Where a person deals with a firm after a change in its constitution he is entitled to treat all apparent members of the old firm as still being members of the firm until he has notice of the change.

(2) An advertisement in the London Gazette as to a firm whose principal place of business is in England or Wales, in the Edinburgh Gazette as to a firm whose principal place of business is in Scotland, and in the Dublin Gazette as to a firm whose principal place of business is in Ireland [2], shall be notice as to persons who had not dealings with the firm before the date of the dissolution or change so advertised.

(3) The estate of a partner who dies, or who becomes bankrupt, or of a partner who, not having been known to the person dealing with the firm to be a partner, retires from the firm, is not liable for partnership debts contracted after the date of the death, bankruptcy, or retirement respectively.

37. Right of partners to notify dissolution

On the dissolution of a partnership or retirement of a partner any partner may publicly notify the same, and may require the other partner or partners to concur for that purpose in all necessary or proper acts, if any, which cannot be done without his or their concurrence.

38. Continuing authority of partners for purposes of winding up

After the dissolution of a partnership the authority of each partner to bind the firm, and the other rights and obligations of the partners, continue notwithstanding the dissolution so far as may be necessary to wind up the affairs of the partnership, and to complete transactions begun but unfinished at the time of the dissolution, but not otherwise.

Provided that the firm is in no case bound by the acts of a partner who has become bankrupt; but this proviso does not affect the liability of any person who has after the bankruptcy represented himself or knowingly suffered himself to be represented as a partner of the bankrupt.

39. Rights of partners as to application of partnership property

On the dissolution of a partnership every partner is entitled, as against the other partners in the firm, and all persons claiming through them in respect of their interests as partners, to have the property of the partnership applied in payment of the debts and liabilities of the firm, and to have the surplus assets after such payment applied in payment of what may be due to the partners respectively after deducting what may be due from them as partners to the firm; and for that purpose any

2 Now the 'Belfast Gazette' for Northern Ireland (see SR & O 1921/1804, art 7; SR & O 1923/405, art 2).

partner or his representatives may on the termination of the partnership apply to the court to wind up the business and affairs of the firm.

40. Apportionment of premium where partnership prematurely dissolved

Where one partner has paid a premium to another on entering into a partnership for a fixed term, and the partnership is dissolved before the expiration of that term otherwise than by the death of a partner, the court may order the repayment of the premium, or of such part thereof as it thinks just, having regard to the terms of the partnership contract and to the length of time during which the partnership has continued; unless

(a) the dissolution is, in the judgment of the court, wholly or chiefly due to the misconduct of the partner who paid the premium, or

(b) the partnership has been dissolved by an agreement containing no provision for a return of any part of the premium.

41. Rights where partnership dissolved for fraud or misrepresentation

Where a partnership contract is rescinded on the ground of the fraud or misrepresentation of one of the parties thereto, the party entitled to rescind is, without prejudice to any other right, entitled—

(a) to a lien on, or right of retention of, the surplus of the partnership assets, after satisfying the partnership liabilities, for any sum of money paid by him for the purchase of a share in the partnership and for any capital contributed by him, and is

(b) to stand in the place of the creditors of the firm for any payments made by him in respect of the partnership liabilities, and

(c) to be indemnified by the person guilty of the fraud or making the representation against all the debts and liabilities of the firm.

42. Right of outgoing partner in certain cases to share profits made after dissolution

(1) Where any member of a firm has died or otherwise ceased to be a partner, and the surviving or continuing partners carry on the business of the firm with its capital or assets without any final settlement of accounts as between the firm and the outgoing partner or his estate, then, in the absence of any agreement to the contrary, the outgoing partner or his estate is entitled at the option of himself or his representatives to such share of the profits made since the dissolution as the court may find to be attributable to the use of his share of the partnerships assets, or to interest at the rate of five per cent per annum on the amount of his share of the partnership assets.

(2) Provided that where by the partnership contract an option is given to surviving or continuing partners to purchase the interest of a deceased or outgoing partner, and that option is duly exercised, the estate of the

deceased partner, or the outgoing partner or his estate, as the case may be, is not entitled to any further or other share of profits; but if any partner assuming to act in exercise of the option does not in all material respects comply with the terms thereof, he is liable to account under the foregoing provisions of this section.

43. Retiring or deceased partner's share to be a debt

Subject to any agreement between the partners, the amount due from surviving or continuing partners to an outgoing partner or the representatives of a deceased partner in respect of the outgoing or deceased partner's share is a debt accruing at the date of the dissolution or death.

44. Rule for distribution of assets on final settlement of accounts

In settling accounts between the partners after a dissolution of partnership, the following rules shall, subject to any agreement, be observed:

(a) Losses, including losses and deficiencies of capital, shall be paid first out of profits, next out of capital, and lastly, if necessary, by the partners individually in the proportion in which they were entitled to share profits.

(b) The assets of the firm, including the sums, if any, contributed by the partners to make up losses or deficiencies of capital, shall be applied in the following manner and order:

1. In paying the debts and liabilities of the firm to persons who are not partners therein:
2. In paying to each partner rateably what is due from the firm to him for advances as distinguished from capital:
3. In paying to each partner rateably what is due from the firm to him in respect of capital:
4. The ultimate residue, if any, shall be divided among the partners in the proportion in which profits are divisible.

SUPPLEMENTAL

45. Definitions of 'court' and 'business'

In this Act, unless the contrary intention appears,—

The expression 'court' includes every court and judge having jurisdiction in the case:

The expression 'business' includes every trade, occupation or profession.

46. Saving for rules of equity and common law

The rules of equity and of common law applicable to partnership shall continue in force except so far as they are inconsistent with the express provisions of this Act.

47. Provision as to bankruptcy in Scotland

(1) In the application of this Act to Scotland the bankruptcy of a firm or of an individual shall mean sequestration under the Bankruptcy (Scotland) Acts, and also in the case of an individual the issue against him of a decree of cessio bonorum.

(2) Nothing in this Act shall alter the rules of the law of Scotland relating to the bankruptcy of a firm or of the individual partners thereof.

48. [*Repealed.*]

49. [*Repealed.*]

50. Short title

This Act may be cited as the Partnership Act 1890.

SCHEDULE

[*Repealed*]

Limited Partnerships Act 1907[3]

7 Edw 7, c. 24

An Act to establish Limited Partnerships.   [28 August 1907]

Be it acted by the King's most Excellent Majesty, by and with the advice and consent of the Lords Spiritual and Temporal, and Commons, in this present Parliament assembled and by the authority of the same, as follows:

1. Short title

This Act may be cited for all purposes as the Limited Partnerships Act 1907.

2. [*Repealed.*]

3. Interpretation of terms

In the construction of this Act the following words and expressions shall have the meanings respectively assigned to them in this section, unless

3 The Act is printed as amended.

there be something in the subject or context repugnant to such construction:

'Firm', 'firm name', and 'business' have the same meanings as in the Partnership Act 1890:

'General partner' shall mean any partner who is not a limited partner as defined by this Act.

4. Definition and constitution of limited partnership

(1)... Limited partnerships may be formed in the manner and subject to the conditions by this Act provided.

(2) A limited partnership shall not consist ... of more than twenty persons, and must consist of one or more persons called general partners, who shall be liable for all debts and obligations of the firm, and one or more persons to be called limited partners, who shall at the time of entering into such partnership contribute thereto a sum or sums as capital or property valued at a stated amount, and who shall not be liable for the debts or obligations of the firm beyond the amount so contributed.

(3) A limited partner shall not during the continuance of the partnership, either directly or indirectly, draw out or receive back any part of his contribution, and if he does so draw out or receive back any such part, shall be liable for the debts and obligations of the firm up to the amount so drawn out or received back.

(4) A body corporate may be a limited partner.

5. Registration of limited partnership required

Every limited partnership must be registered as such in accordance with the provisions of this Act, or in default thereof it shall be deemed to be a general partnership, and every limited partner shall be deemed to be a general partner.

6. Modifications of general law in case of limited partnerships

(1) A limited partner shall not take part in the management of the partnership business, and shall not have power to bind the firm:

Provided that a limited partner may by himself or his agent at any time inspect the books of the firm and examine into the state and prospects of the partnership business, and may advise with the partners thereon.

If a limited partner takes part in the management of the partnership business, he shall be liable for all debts and obligations of the firm incurred while he so takes part in the management as though he were a general partner.

(2) A limited partnership shall not be dissolved by the death or bankruptcy of a limited partner, and the lunacy of a limited partner shall not be a ground for dissolution of the partnership by the Court unless the lunatic's share cannot be otherwise ascertained and realised.

(3) In the event of the dissolution of a limited partnership its affairs shall be wound up by the general partners unless the court otherwise orders.

(4) [*Repealed.*]

(5) Subject to any agreement expressed or implied between the partners—

(a) Any difference arising as to ordinary matters connected with the partnership business may be decided by a majority of the general partners;

(b) A limited partner may, with the consent of the general partners, assign his share in the partnership, and upon such an assignment the assignee shall become a limited partner with all the rights of the assignor;

(c) The other partners shall not be entitled to dissolve the partnership by reason of any limited partner suffering his share to be charged for his separate debt;

(d) A person may be introduced as a partner without the consent of the existing limited partners;

(e) A limited partner shall not be entitled to dissolve the partnership by notice.

7. Law as to private partnership to apply where not excluded by this Act

Subject to the provisions of this Act, the Partnership Act 1890, and the rules of equity and of common law applicable to partnerships, except so far as they are inconsistent with the express provisions of the last-mentioned Act, shall apply to limited partnerships.

8. Manner and particulars of registration

The registration of a limited partnership shall be effected by sending by post or delivering to the registrar at the register office in that part of the United Kingdom in which the principal place of business of the limited partnership is situated or proposed to be situated a statement signed by the partners containing the following particulars:

(a) The firm name;

(b) The general nature of the business;

(c) The principal place of business;

(d) The full name of each of the partners;

(e) The term, if any, for which the partnership is entered into, and the date of its commencement;

(f) A statement that the partnership is limited, and the description of every limited partner as such;

(g) The sum contributed by each limited partner, and whether paid in cash or how otherwise.

9. Registration of changes in partnerships

(1) If during the continuance of a limited partnership any change is made or occurs in—

(a) The firm name,
(b) The general nature of the business,
(c) The principal place of business,
(d) The partners or the name of any partner,
(e) The term or character of the partnership,
(f) The sum contributed by any limited partner,
(g) The liability of any partner by reason of his becoming a limited instead of a general partner or a general instead of a limited partner,

a statement, signed by the firm, specifying the nature of the change shall within seven days be sent by post or delivered to the registrar at the register office in that part of the United Kingdom in which the partnership is registered.

(2) If default is made in compliance with the requirements of this section each of the general partners shall on conviction under the Summary Jurisdiction Acts be liable to a fine not exceeding one pound for each day during which the default continues.

10. Advertisement in Gazette of statement of general partner becoming a limited partner and of assignment of share of limited partner

(1) Notice of any arrangement or transaction under which any person will cease to be a general partner in any firm, and will become a limited partner in that firm, or under which the share of a limited partner in a firm will be assigned to any person, shall be forthwith advertised in the Gazette, and until notice of the arrangement or transaction is so advertised, the arrangement or transaction shall, for the purposes of this Act, be deemed to be of no effect.

(2) For the purposes of this section, the expression 'the Gazette' means—

In the case of a limited partnership registered in England, the London Gazette;
In the case of a limited partnership registered in Scotland the Edinburgh Gazette;
In the case of a limited partnership registered in Ireland, the Dublin Gazette [4].

11. [*Repealed.*]

12. [*Repealed.*]

4 As respects Northern Ireland this means the 'Belfast Gazette' (SR & O 1921/1804, art 7).

13. Registrar to file statement and issue certificate of registration

On receiving any statement made in pursuance of this Act the registrar shall cause the same to be filed, and he shall send by post to the firm from whom such statement shall have been received a certificate of the registration thereof.

14. Register and index to be kept

At each of the register offices hereinafter referred to the registrar shall keep, in proper books to be provided for the purpose, a register and an index of all the limited partnerships registered as aforesaid, and of all the statements registered in relation to such partnerships.

15. Registrar of joint stock companies to be registrar under Act

The registrar of joint stock companies shall be the registrar of limited partnerships, and the several offices for the registration of joint stock companies in London, Edinburgh, and Belfast shall be the offices for the registration of limited partnerships carrying on business within those parts of the United Kingdom in which they are respectively situated.

16. Inspection of statements registered

(1) Any person may inspect the statements filed by the registrar in the register offices aforesaid, and there shall be paid for such inspection such fees as may be appointed by the Board of Trade, not exceeding one shilling for each inspection; and any person may require a certificate of the registration of any limited partnership, or a copy of or extract from any registered statement, to be certified by the registrar, and there shall be paid for such certificate of registration, certified copy, or extract such fees as the Board of Trade may appoint, not exceeding [10p] for the certificate of registration, and not exceeding [2p] for each folio of seventy-two words, or in Scotland for each sheet of two hundred words.

(2) A certificate of registration, or a copy of or extract from any statement registered under this Act, if duly certified to be a true copy under the hand of the registrar or one of the assistant registrars (whom it shall not be necessary to prove to be the registrar or assistant registrar) shall, in all legal proceedings, civil or criminal, and in all cases whatsoever be received in evidence.

17. Power to Board of Trade to make rules

The Board of Trade may make rules (but as to fees with the concurrence of the Treasury) concerning any of the following matters—

(a) The fees to be paid to the registrar under this Act, so that they do not exceed in the case of the original registration of a limited partnership the sum of two pounds, and in any other case the sum of [25p];

(b) The duties or additional duties to be performed by the registrar for the purposes of this Act;

(c) The performance by assistant registrars and other officers of acts by this Act required to be done by the registrar;
(d) The forms to be used for the purposes of this Act;
(e) Generally the conduct and regulation of registration under this Act and any matters incidental thereto.

Sex Discrimination Act 1975

(c. 65)

11. Partnerships

(1) It is unlawful for a firm consisting of six or more partners, in relation to a position as partner in the firm, to discriminate against a woman—

(a) in the arrangements they make for the purpose of determining who should be offered that position, or
(b) in the terms on which they offer her that position, or
(c) by refusing or deliberately omitting to offer her that position, or
(d) in a case where the woman already holds that position—

    (i) in the way they afford her access to any benefits, facilities or services, or by refusing or deliberately omitting to afford her access to them, or
    (ii) by expelling her from that position, or subjecting her to any other detriment.

(2) Subsection (1) shall apply in relation to persons proposing to form themselves into a partnership as it applies in relation to a firm.

(3) Subsection (1) (a) and (c) do not apply to a position as partner where, if it were employment, being a man would be a genuine occupational qualification for the job.

(4) Subsection (1) (b) and (d) do not apply to provision made in relation to death or retirement.

(5) In the case of a limited partnership references in subsection (1) to a partner shall be construed as references to a general partner as defined in section 3 of the Limited Partnerships Act 1907[5].

---

5 See p 172, above.

Business Names Act 1985

(1985 c. 7)

An Act to consolidate certain enactments relating to the names under which persons may carry on business in Great Britain.   [11 March 1985]

Be it enacted by the Queen's most Excellent Majesty, by and with the advice and consent of the Lords Spiritual and Temporal, and Commons, in this present Parliament assembled, and by the authority of the same, as follows—

1. Persons subject to this Act

(1) This Act applies to any person who has a place of business in Great Britain and who carries on business in Great Britain under a name which—

(a) in the case of a partnership, does not consist of the surnames of all partners who are individuals and the corporate names of all partners who are bodies corporate without any addition other than an addition permitted by this Act;

(b) in the case of an individual, does not consist of his surname without any addition other than one so permitted;

(c) in the case of a company, being a company which is capable of being wound up under the Companies Act 1985, does not consist of its corporate name without any addition other than one so permitted.

(2) The following are permitted additions for the purposes of subsection (1)—

(a) in the case of a partnership, the forenames of individual partners or the initials of those forenames or, where two or more individual partners have the same surname, the addition of 's' at the end of that surname; or

(b) in the case of an individual, his forename or its initial;

(c) in any case, any addition merely indicating that the business is carried on in succession to a former owner of the business.

2. Prohibition of use of certain business names

(1) Subject to the following subsections, a person to whom this Act applies shall not, without the written approval of the Secretary of State, carry on business in Great Britain under a name which—

(a) would be likely to give the impression that the business is connected with Her Majesty's Government or with any local authority; or

(b) includes any word or expression for the time being specified in regulations made under this Act.

(2) Subsection (1) does not apply to the carrying on of a business by a person—

(a) to whom the business has been transferred on or after 26 February 1982; and

(b) who carries on the business under the name which was its lawful business name immediately before that transfer,

during the period of 12 months beginning with the date of that transfer.

(3) Subsection (1) does not apply to the carrying on of a business by a person who—

(a) carried on that business immediately before 26 February 1982; and

(b) continues to carry it on under the name which immediately before that date was its lawful business name.

(4) A person who contravenes subsection (1) is guilty of an offence.

3. Words and expressions requiring Secretary of State's approval

(1) The Secretary of State may by regulations—

(a) specify words or expressions for the use of which as or as part of a business name his approval is required by section 2(1)(b); and

(b) in relation to any such word or expression, specify a Government department or other body as the relevant body for purposes of the following subsection. ʻ

(2) Where a person to whom this Act applies proposes to carry on a business under a name which is or includes any such word or expression, and a Government department or other body is specified under subsection (1)(b) in relation to that word or expression, that person shall—

(a) request (in writing) the relevant body to indicate whether (and if so why) it has any objections to the proposal; and

(b) submit to the Secretary of State a statement that such a request has been made and a copy of any response received from the relevant body.

4. Disclosure required of persons using business names

(1) A person to whom this Act applies shall—

(a) subject to subsection (3), state in legible characters on all business letters, written orders for goods or services to be supplied to the business, invoices and receipts issued in the course of the business and written demands for payment of debts arising in the course of the business—

(i) in the case of a partnership, the name of each partner.

(ii) in the case of an individual, his name,

      (iii) in the case of a company, its corporate name, and

      (iv) in relation to each person so named, an address in Great Britain at which service of any document relating in any way to the business will be effective; and

(b) in any premises where the business is carried on and to which the customers of the business or suppliers of any goods or services to the business have access, display in a prominent position so that it may easily be read by such customers or suppliers a notice containing such names and addresses.

(2) A person to whom this Act applies shall secure that the names and addresses required by subsection (1)(a) to be stated on his business letters, or which would have been so required but for the subsection next following, are immediately given, by written notice to any person with whom anything is done or discussed in the course of the business and who asks for such names and addresses.

(3) Subsection (1)(a) does not apply in relation to any document issued by a partnership of more than 20 persons which maintains at its principal place of business a list of the names of all the partners if—

(a) none of the names of the partners appears in the document otherwise than in the text or as a signatory; and

(b) the document states in legible characters the address of the partnership's principal place of business and that the list of the partners' names is open to inspection at that place.

(4) Where a partnership maintains a list of the partners' names for purposes of subsection (3), any person may inspect the list during office hours.

(5) The Secretary of State may by regulations require notices under subsection (1)(b) or (2) to be displayed or given in a specified form.

(6) A person who without reasonable excuse contravenes subsection (1) or (2), or any regulations made under subsection (5), is guilty of an offence.

(7) Where an inspection required by a person in accordance with subsection (4) is refused, any partner of the partnership concerned who without reasonable excuse refused that inspection, or permitted it to be refused, is guilty of an offence.

5. Civil remedies for breach of s 4

(1) Any legal proceedings brought by a person to whom this Act applies to enforce a right arising out of a contract made in the course of a business in respect of which he was, at the time the contract was made, in breach of subsection (1) or (2) of section 4 shall be dismissed if the defendant (or, in Scotland, the defender) to the proceedings shows—

(a) that he has a claim against the plaintiff (pursuer) arising out of that contract which he has been unable to pursue by reason of the latter's breach of section 4(1) or (2), or

(b) that he has suffered some financial loss in connection with the contract by reason of the plaintiff's (pursuer's) breach of section 4(1) or (2),

unless the court before which the proceedings are brought is satisfied that it is just and equitable to permit the proceedings to continue.

(2) This section is without prejudice to the right of any person to enforce such rights as he may have against another person in any proceedings brought by that person.

6. Regulations

(1) Regulations under this Act shall be made by statutory instrument and may contain such transitional provisions and savings as the Secretary of State thinks appropriate, and may make different provision for different cases or classes of case.

(2) In the case of regulations made under section 3, the statutory instrument containing them shall be laid before Parliament after the regulations are made and shall cease to have effect at the end of the period of 28 days beginning with the day on which they were made (but without prejudice to anything previously done by virtue of them or to the making of new regulations) unless during that period they are approved by a resolution of each House of Parliament.

In reckoning this period of 28 days, no account is to be taken of any time during which Parliament is dissolved or prorogued, or during which both Houses are adjourned for more than 4 days.

(3) In the case of regulations made under section 4, the statutory instrument containing them is subject to annulment in pursuance of a resolution of either House of Parliament.

7. Offences

(1) Offences under this Act are punishable on summary conviction.

(2) A person guilty of an offence under this Act is liable to a fine not exceeding one-fifth of the statutory maximum.

(3) If after a person has been convicted summarily of an offence under section 2 or 4(6) the original contravention is continued, he is liable on a second or subsequent summary conviction of the offence to a fine not exceeding one-fiftieth of the statutory maximum for each day on which the contravention is continued (instead of to the penalty which may be imposed on the first conviction of the offence).

(4) Where an offence under section 2 or 4(6) or (7) committed by a body corporate is proved to have been committed with the consent or connivance of, or to be attributable to any neglect on the part of, any director, manager, secretary or other similar officer of the body corporate, or any person who was purporting to act in any such

capacity, he as well as the body corporate is guilty of the offence and liable to be proceeded against and punished accordingly.

(5) Where the affairs of a body corporate are managed by its members, subsection (4) applies in relation to the acts and defaults of a member in connection with his functions of management as if he were a director of the body corporate.

(6) For purposes of the following provisions of the Companies Act 1985—

(a) section 731 (summary proceedings under the Companies Acts), and
(b) section 732(3) (legal professional privilege),

this Act is to be treated as included in those Acts.

8. Interpretation

(1) The following definitions apply for purposes of this Act—

'business' includes a profession;
'initial' includes any recognised abbreviation of a name;
'lawful business name', in relation to a business, means a name under which the business was carried on without contravening section 2(1) of this Act or section 2 of the Registration of Business Names Act 1916;
'local authority' means any local authority within the meaning of the Local Government Act 1972 or the Local Government (Scotland) Act 1973, the Common Council of the City of London or the Council of the Isles of Scilly;
'partnership' includes a foreign partnership;
'statutory maximum' means—

(a) in England and Wales the prescribed sum under section 32 of the Magistrates' Courts Act 1980, and
(b) in Scotland, the prescribed sum under section 289B of the Criminal Procedure (Scotland) Act 1975;

and 'surname', in relation to a peer or person usually known by a British title different from his surname, means the title by which he is known.

(2) Any expression used in this Act and also in the Companies Act 1985 has the same meaning in this Act as in that.

9. Northern Ireland

This Act does not extend to Northern Ireland.

10. Commencement

This Act comes into force on 1 July 1985.

11. Citation

This Act may be cited as the Business Names Act 1985.

Appendix B
Statutory instruments

Limited Partnership Rules 1907[1]

SR & O 1907/1020

1. 'The Act' means the Limited Partnerships Act 1907.

2. Whenever any act is by the Act directed to be done to or by the Registrar such act shall be done in England to or by the Registrar of Joint Stock Companies or in his absence to or by such person as the Board of Trade may for the time being authorise; in Scotland to or by the existing Registrar of Joint Stock Companies in Scotland; and in Ireland to or by the existing Assistant Registrar of Joint Stock Companies for Ireland or by such person as the Board of Trade may for the time being authorise in Scotland or Ireland in the absence of the Registrar; but in the event of the Board of Trade altering the constitution of the existing Joint Stock Companies Registry Office such act shall be done to or by such officer or officers and at such place or places with reference to the local situation of the principal place of business of the limited partnership to be registered as the Board of Trade may appoint.

3. The fees to be paid to the Registrar under the Act shall be as follows:

(a) on the original registration of a limited partnership the sum of two pounds,
(b) [*Repeated.*]
(c) by any person inspecting the statements filed by the Registrar in the Register Office the sum of one shilling for each inspection,
(d) by any person requiring a Certificate of the registration of any limited partnership or a certified copy of or extract from any registered statement the sum of [10p] for each certificate and for such certified copy or extract the sum of [2p] for each folio of seventy-two words or in Scotland for each sheet of two hundred words.

4. The forms in the Appendix hereto with such variations as the

1 The Rules are printed as amended.

circumstances of each case may require shall be the forms to be used for the purposes of the Act.

D. Lloyd George.

Board of Trade,
17 December 1907.

Approved, so far as relating to Fees.

Joseph A. Pease.
J. H. Whitley.

APPENDIX

Forms to be used for the purposes of the Act and for the purposes of Section 47 of the Finance Act 1973

Registration No.

Form No. L.P.5
(Registration fee £2)
(Capital duty also payable)

LIMITED PARTNERSHIPS ACT 1907

Application for Registration of a Limited Partnership and

Statement of particulars and of the amounts contributed
(in cash or otherwise) by the Limited Partners

(Pursuant to Section 8 of the Limited Partnerships Act 1907
and Section 47 of the Finance Act 1973)

Name of firm or partnership

We, the undersigned, being the partners of the above-named firm, hereby apply for registration as a limited partnership and for that purpose supply the following particulars:

The general nature of the business	
The principal place of business	
The term, if any, for which the partnership is entered into	

If no definite term, the conditions
of existence of the partnership

Date of commencement

The partnership is limited and the full name and address of each of the partners are as follows:
General partners

Limited partners	Amounts Contributed (1)	Capital duty payable (2)
	Total	

Signatures of all ⎫
the partners   ⎬

Date.........................

Presented by:
Presentor's reference:

Notes

(1) State amount contributed by each limited partner, and whether paid in cash, or how otherwise.

(2) The capital duty is £1 for every £100, or part of £100, contributed by each limited partner.

Registration No...............   Form No. L.P.6

LIMITED PARTNERSHIPS ACT 1907

Statement specifying the nature of a change in the
Limited Partnership
and Statement of increase in the amount contributed (in cash
or otherwise) by limited partners

(Pursuant to Section 9 of the Limited Partnerships Act 1907
and Section 47 of the Finance Act 1973)

Name of firm or partnership

Notice is hereby given that the changes specified below have occurred in this limited partnership:

(please see Notes overleaf)

(a) The firm name	{	Previous name New name
(b) General nature of the business	{	Business previously carried on Business now carried on
(c) Principal place of business	{	Previous place of business New place of business
(d) Change in the partners or the name of a partner (Note 1)	{	
(e) Term or character of the partnership (Note 2)	{	Previous term New term
(f) Change in the sum contributed by any limited partner (Note 3) (particulars of any increase in capital contributions must be provided at (h) overleaf)	{	
(g) Change in the liability of any partner by reason of his becoming a limited instead of a general partner, or vice versa	{	

(h) Statement of increase in capital contributions

Names of Limited Partners	Increase or additional sum now contributed (If otherwise than in cash, that fact, with particulars, must be stated)	Total amount contributed (If otherwise than in cash, that fact, with particulars, must be stated)	Capital duty payable on increase, etc.

Total capital duty payable

Signature of firm ....

Date ....

Presented by:

Presentor's reference:

Notes

(1) Changes brought about by death, by transfer of interests, by increase in the number of partners, or by change of name of any partner, must be notified here.

(2) If there is, or was, no definite term, then state against 'previous term' the conditions under which the partnership was constituted and against 'new term' the conditions under which it is now constituted.

(3) Any variation in the sum contributed by any limited partner must be stated at (f) overleaf. A statement of any increase in the amount of the partnership capital, whether arising from increase of contributions, or

from introduction of fresh partners must also be made at (h) above. Capital duty is payable at £1 for every £100, or part of £100, on any increase in the amounts of contributions made, in cash or otherwise, by a limited partner.

(4) Each change must be entered in the proper division (a), (b), (c), (d), (e), (f), (g) or (h), as the case may be. Provision is made in this form for notifying all the changes required by the Act to be notified, but it will frequently happen that only one item of change has to be notified. In any such case, the word 'Nil' should be inserted in the other divisions.

(5) The statement must be signed at the end by the firm, and delivered for registration within seven days of the change or changes taking place.

Bankruptcy Rules 1952
SI 1952/2113

279. Signature of notices etc. in firm name
Where any notice, declaration, petition, or other document requiring attestation is signed by a firm of creditors or debtors in the firm name, the partner signing for the firm shall add his own signature and a statement that he is a partner in the firm.

280. Service on firm
Any notice or petition for which personal service is necessary shall be deemed to be duly served –

(a) on all members of a partnership firm, if it is served at the principal place of business of the firm in England on any one of the partners, or on any person having at the time of service control or management of the partnership business there;
(b) on a person carrying on business in a name or style other than his own, if it is served on any person having at the time of service control or management of the business in England.

281. Debtor's petition by firm
A declaration of inability to pay their debts or a bankruptcy petition filed by a firm of debtors shall contain the names in full of the individual partners in the firm and, if signed in the firm name, shall be accompanied by an affidavit made by the partner who signs the declaration or petition, showing that all the partners concur in the filing thereof.

282. Service of creditor's petition on limited partnership
A creditor's petition against a limited partnership registered as such under the Limited Partnerships Act 1907, shall, unless the court other-

wise orders, be served at the registered principal place of business of the partnership by delivering there a sealed copy of the petition to one of the general partners or to some person having at the time of service the control or management of the partnership business.

283. Petition by limited partnership

(1) A limited partnership may present a petition in bankruptcy in the name of the firm.

(2) The petition shall be signed by a general partner and shall contain the full names of the general partners and, if signed in the firm name, shall be accompanied by an affidavit made by the partner who signs the petition showing that all the general partners concur in filing it.

284. Court having jurisdiction in case of limited partnership

A petition in bankruptcy by or against a limited partnership shall be presented to the court having bankruptcy jurisdiction in the place where the registered office of the partnership is situate, but the Judge of the High Court may at any time, for good cause shown, remove the proceedings to any other court having jurisdiction in bankruptcy.

285. Receiving order against firm

A receiving order made against a firm shall operate as if it were a receiving order made against each of the persons who at the date of the order is a partner in that firm.

286. Receiving order against limited partnership

A receiving order made against a limited partnership shall operate as if it were a receiving order made against each of the persons who at the date of the order is a general partner in the firm.

287. Statement of affairs

Where a receiving order is made against a firm, the debtors shall submit a joint statement of their partnership affairs, and each debtor shall submit a statement of his separate affairs.

288. Adjudication order against partners

No order of adjudication shall be made against a firm in the firm name, but it shall be made against the partners individually.

289. Rights of limited partners

Where a receiving order is made against a limited partnership, any past or present limited partner shall have the same rights as a creditor who has proved his debt to inspect the file, to attend meetings of creditors, and to appear on, and take part in, the public examination of, or any application for an order of discharge by, any general partner.

290. Liability of limited partners
The assets of a limited partnership which, by section 127 of the Act, are to vest in the trustee in the event of all the general partners being adjudged bankrupt, shall include any liability of limited partners and past general partners to contribute to the assets of the partnership, and such liability may be enforced by the trustee by motion in the bankruptcy:

Provided that –

(a) no person shall be liable as a present or past limited partner to contribute to the assets of the partnership any amount in excess of any part of his contribution as such limited partner which he may have failed to pay into or have drawn out or received back from the partnership assets since he became, or while he remained, a limited partner;

(b) no past general partner shall be liable as such to contribute to the assets of the partnership except in respect of partnership debts and obligations incurred while he continued to be a general partner;

(c) no past general or limited partner shall be liable as such to contribute to the assets of the partnership unless it appears to the court that the partnership assets otherwise available are insufficient for the payment in full of the partnership liabilities and the costs, charges and expenses of the administration in bankruptcy of the partnership estate.

291. First meeting of creditors
Where a receiving order is made against a firm, the joint and separate creditors shall be summoned collectively to the first meeting of creditors.

292. Acceptance of composition or scheme by joint and separate creditors
(1) The joint creditors and each set of separate creditors may severally accept compositions or schemes of arrangement.

(2) So far as circumstances will allow, a proposal accepted by joint creditors may be approved notwithstanding that any proposal made by one or more of the debtors to his or their separate creditors may not be accepted.

293. Voting on composition or scheme
(1) Where proposals for compositions or schemes are made by a firm, and by the partners therein individually, the proposal made to the joint creditors shall be considered and voted upon by them apart from all separate creditors, and the proposal made to each set of separate creditors shall be considered and voted upon by that set of separate creditors apart from all other creditors.

(2) The proposals may vary in character and amount.

(3) Where a composition or scheme is approved, the receiving order shall be discharged only so far as it relates to an estate the creditors of which have accepted the composition or scheme.

294. Trustee and committees of inspection

(1) In the bankruptcy of a partnership the trustee appointed by the joint creditors or, in default of such appointment, by the Board of Trade, shall be the trustee of the separate estates of the partners.

(2) Each set of separate creditors may appoint its own committee of inspection:

Provided that the committee (if any) appointed by the joint creditors shall be deemed to have been appointed also by any set of separate creditors who do not appoint a separate committee.

295. Separate firms

(1) If any two or more of the members of a partnership constitute a separate and independent firm, the creditors of such firm shall be deemed to be a separate set of creditors and subject to the same rules as the separate creditors of any individual member of the partnership.

(2) Where any surplus remains after the administration of the assets of the separate firm, the surplus shall be carried over to the separate estates of the partners in that firm according to their respective rights therein.

296. Apportionment of trustee's remuneration

Where joint and separate estates are being administered, the remuneration of the trustee in respect of the administration of the joint estate may be fixed by the creditors, or (if duly authorised) by the committee of inspection, of the joint estate, and the remuneration of the trustee in respect of the administration of any separate estate may be fixed by the creditors, or (if duly authorised) by the committee of inspection, of that separate estate.

Partnerships (Unrestricted Size) No. 1 Regulations 1968

SI 1968/1222

The Board of Trade in pursuance of the powers conferred upon them by section 120(2) of the Companies Act 1967 hereby make the following Regulations:

1. Section 434 of the Companies Act 1948 shall not apply to the formation—

(a) for the purpose of carrying on practice as patent agents, of a partnership consisting of persons each of whom is registered as a patent agent in the register of patent agents maintained pursuant to the Patents Act 1949;

(b) for the purpose of carrying on one or more of the activities mentioned in Part I of the Schedule hereto, of a partnership consisting of persons not less than three-quarters of the total number of whom are members of one or more of the bodies mentioned in Part II of that Schedule.

2. These Regulations may be cited as the Partnerships (Unrestricted Size) No. 1 Regulations 1968 and shall come into operation on 7th August 1968.

C. W. Jardine,
An Under-Secretary
30 July 1968.   of the Board of Trade.

SCHEDULE

Part I

1. Surveying.
2. Auctioneering.
3. Valuing.
4. Estate Agency.
5. Land Agency.
6. Estate Management.

Part II

1. The Royal Institution of Chartered Surveyors.
2. The Chartered Land Agents' Society.
3. The Chartered Auctioneers' and Estate Agents' Institute.
4. The Incorporated Society of Valuers and Auctioneers.

Partnerships (Unrestricted Size) No. 2 Regulations 1970

SI 1970/835

The Board of Trade in pursuance of the powers conferred upon them by section 120(2) of the Companies Act 1967 hereby make the following Regulations:

1. These Regulations may be cited as the Partnerships (Unrestricted Size) No. 2 Regulations 1970.

2. Section 434 of the Companies Act 1948 shall not apply to the formation for the purpose of carrying on practice as actuaries of a partnership consisting of persons each of whom is either a Fellow of the Institute of Actuaries or a Fellow of the Faculty of Actuaries.

C. W. Jardine,
An Under-Secretary
of the Board of Trade.

28 May 1970.

Partnerships (Unrestricted Size) No. 3 Regulations 1970

SI 1970/992

The Board of Trade in pursuance of the powers conferred upon them by section 120(2) of the Companies Act 1967 hereby make the following Regulations:

1. These Regulations may be cited as the Partnerships (Unrestricted Size) No. 3 Regulations 1970.

2. Section 434 of the Companies Act 1948 shall not apply to the formation for the purpose of carrying on practice as consulting engineers of a partnership consisting of persons the majority of whom are recognised by the Council of Engineering Institutions as Chartered Engineers.

C. W. Jardine,
An Under-Secretary
of the Board of Trade.

1 July 1970.

Partnerships (Unrestricted Size) No. 4 Regulations 1970

SI 1970/1319

The Board of Trade in pursuance of the powers conferred upon them by section 120(2) of the Companies Act 1967 hereby make the following Regulations:

1. These Regulations may be cited as the Partnerships (Unrestricted Size) No. 4 Regulations 1970.

2. Section 434 of the Companies Act 1948 shall not apply to the formation for the purpose of carrying on practice as building designers of a partnership consisting of persons not less than three-quarters of whom are persons each of whom is either registered under the Architects (Registration) Act 1931 or is recognised by the Council of Engineering Institutions as a Chartered Engineer or by the Royal Institution of Chartered Surveyors as a Chartered Surveyor.

J. B. Smith,
An Assistant Secretary
4 September 1970.   of the Board of Trade.

Limited Partnerships (Unrestricted Size) No. 1 Regulations 1971

SI 1971/782

The Secretary of State, in exercise of his powers under section 121(2) of the Companies Act 1967, hereby orders as follows:

1. These Regulations may be cited as the Limited Partnerships (Unrestricted Size) No. 1 Regulations 1971.

2. So much of section 4(2) of the Limited Partnerships Act 1907 as provides that a limited partnership (other than a partnership carrying on the business of banking) shall not consist of more than twenty persons shall not apply to a limited partnership carrying on one or more of the activities mentioned in Part I of the Schedule hereto and consisting of persons not less than three-quarters of the total number of whom are members of one of the bodies mentioned in Part II of that Schedule and not more than one-quarter of the total number of whom are limited partners within the meaning of section 4 of the Limited Partnerships Act 1907.

J. B. Smith,
An Assistant Secretary.
11 May 1971.   Department of Trade and Industry.

SCHEDULE

Part I

1. Surveying.
2. Auctioneering.
3. Valuing.
4. Estate Agency.
5. Land Agency.
6. Estate Management.

Part II

1. The Royal Institution of Chartered Surveyors.
2. The Incorporated Society of Valuers and Auctioneers.

Company and Business Names Regulations 1981[2]

SI 1981/1685

The Secretary of State, in exercise of his powers under sections 31 and 32 of the Companies Act 1981 hereby makes the following Regulations:

1. These Regulations may be cited as the Company and Business Names Regulations 1981 and shall come into operation on 26 February 1982.

2. In these Regulations, unless the context otherwise requires, 'the Act' means the Companies Act 1981.

3. The words and expressions stated in column (1) of the Schedule hereto are hereby specified as words and expressions for the registration of which as or as part of a company's corporate name the approval of the Secretary of State is required by section 22(2)(b) of the Act or for the use of which as or as part of a business name his approval is required by section 28(2)(b) of the Act.

4. Subject to Regulation 5, each Government department or other body stated in column (2) of the Schedule hereto is hereby specified as the relevant body for the purposes of section 31(2) and (3) of the Act in relation to the word or expression opposite to it in column (1).

5. Where two Government departments or other bodies are specified in the alternative in Column (2) of the Schedule hereto the second alternative is to be treated as specified,

(a) in the case of the corporate name of a company,
    (i) if the company has not yet been registered and its principal or only place of business in Great Britain is to be in Scotland or, if it will have no place of business in Great Britain, its proposed registered office is in Scotland, and
    (ii) if the company is already registered and its principal or only place of business in Great Britain is in Scotland or, if it has no

2 The Regulations are printed as amended.

place of business in Great Britain, its registered office is in Scotland, and

(b) in the case of a business name, if the principal or only place of the business carried on or to be carried on in Great Britain is or is to be in Scotland,

and the first alternative is to be treated as specified in any other case.

Reginald Eyre,
Parliamentary Under Secretary of State,
24 November 1981.   Department of Trade.

SCHEDULE   Regulations 3, 4 and 5.

SPECIFICATION OF WORDS, EXPRESSIONS AND RELEVANT BODIES

Column (1)	Column (2)
Word or expression	Relevant body
Abortion	Department of Health and Social Security
Apothecary	Worshipful Society of Apothecaries of London or Pharmaceutical Society of Great Britain
Association	
Assurance	
Assurer	
Authority	
Benevolent	
Board	
Breed	
Breeder	Ministry of Agriculture, Fisheries and Food
Breeding	
British	
Building Society	
Chamber of Commerce	
Chamber of Industry	
Chamber of Trade	
Charitable	Charity Commission or Scottish Home and Health Department
Charity	
Charter	
Chartered	
Chemist	
Chemistry	
Contact Lens	General Optical Council
Co-operative	

Column (1)	Column (2)
Word or expression	Relevant body
Council Dental Dentistry	} General Dental Council
District Nurse	Panel of Assessors in District Nurse Training
Duke	Home Office or Scottish Home and Health Department
England English European Federation Friendly Society Foundation Fund Giro Great Britain Group	
Health Centre Health Service	} Department of Health and Social Security
Health Visitor	Council for the Education and Training of Health Visitors
Her Majesty His Majesty	} Home Office or Scottish Home and Health Department
Holding Industrial and Provident Society Institute Institution Insurance Insurer International Ireland Irish	
King	Home Office or Scottish Home and Health Department
Midwife Midwifery	} Central Midwives Board or Central Midwives Board for Scotland
National	
Nurse Nursing	} General Nursing Council for England and Wales or General Nursing Council for Scotland
Nursing Home	Department of Health and Social Security

Column (1)	Column (2)
Word or expression	Relevant body
Patent	
Patentee	
Police	Home Office or Scottish Home and Health Department
Polytechnic	Department of Education and Science
Post Office	
Pregnancy Termination	Department of Health and Social Security
Prince	Home Office or Scottish Home and Health Department
Princess	
Queen	
Reassurance	
Reassurer	
Register	
Registered	
Reinsurance	
Reinsurer	
Royal	Home Office or Scottish Home and Health Department
Royale	
Royalty	
Scotland	
Scottish	
Sheffield	
Society	
Special School	Department of Education and Science
Stock Exchange	
Trade Union	
Trust	
United Kingdom	
University	Department of Education and Science
Wales	
Welsh	
Windsor	Home Office or Scottish Home and Health Department

Partnerships (Unrestricted Size) No. 5 Regulations 1982

SI 1982/530

The Secretary of State, in exercise of the powers conferred by section 120(2) of the Companies Act 1967 and now vested in him, hereby makes the following Regulations:

1. These Regulations may be cited as the Partnerships (Unrestricted Size) No. 5 Regulations 1982 and shall come into operation on 4 May 1982.

2. Section 434 of the Companies Act 1948 shall not apply to the formation for the purpose of carrying on practice as loss adjusters of a partnership consisting of persons not less than three-quarters of the total number of whom are members of the Chartered Institute of Loss Adjusters.

E. M. Llewellyn-Smith,
An Under Secretary,
6 April 1982.   Department of Trade.

Company and Business Names (Amendment) Regulations 1982

SI 1982/1653

The Secretary of State, in exercise of his powers under sections 31 and 32 of the Companies Act 1981 hereby makes the following Regulations:

1. These Regulations may be cited as the Company and Business Names (Amendment) Regulations 1982 and shall come into operation on 1st January 1983.

2. [Amends SI 1981/1685[3].]

3. – (1) Section 28(2) of the Companies Act 1981 shall not prohibit a person from carrying on any business under a name which includes any of the words specified in the said Schedule by virtue of the amendments contained in paragraphs (b) and (c) of Regulation 2 if—

(a) he carried on that business immediately before 1 January 1983, and
(b) he continues to carry it on under the name which immediately before that day was its lawful business name.

(2) Nor shall the said section 28(2) prohibit a person to whom a business has been transferred on or after 1 January 1983 from carrying on that business during the period of twelve months beginning with the

3 See p 195, above.

date of transfer so long as he continues to carry it on under the name which was its lawful business name immediately before that transfer.

Gerard Vaughan,
Minister of State,
23 November 1982.　　　　　　　　　　　　Department of Trade.

Appendix C

Rules of the Supreme Court

Order 81[1]

Actions by and against firms within jurisdiction

1. Subject to the provisions of any enactment, any two or more persons claiming to be entitled, or alleged to be liable, as partners in respect of a cause of action and carrying on business within the jurisdiction may sue, or be sued, in the name of the firm (if any) of which they were partners at the time when the cause of action accrued.

Disclosure of partners' names

2.—(1) Any defendant to an action brought by partners in the name of a firm may serve on the plaintiffs or their solicitor a notice requiring them or him forthwith to furnish the defendant with a written statement of the names and places of residence of all the persons who were partners in the firm at the time when the cause of action accrued; and if the notice is not complied with the court may order the plaintiffs or their solicitor to furnish the defendant with such a statement and to verify it on oath or otherwise as may be specified in the order, or may order that further proceedings in the action be stayed on such terms as the court may direct.

(2) When the names of the partners have been declared in compliance with a notice or order given or made under paragraph (1), the proceedings shall continue in the name of the firm but with the same consequences as would have ensued if the persons whose names have been so declared had been named as plaintiffs in the writ.

(3) Paragraph (1) shall have effect in relation to an action brought against partners in the name of a firm as it has effect in relation to an action brought by partners in the name of a firm but with the substitution, for references to the defendant and the plaintiffs, of references to the plaintiff and the defendants respectively, and with the omission of the words 'or may order' to the end.

Service of writ

3.—(1) Where by virtue of rule 1 partners are sued in the name of a firm,

---

1 The Order is printed as amended.

the writ may, except in the case mentioned in paragraph (3), be served—

(a) on any one or more of the partners, or
(b) at the principal place of business of the partnership within the jurisdiction, on any person having at the time of service the control or management of the partnership business there; or
(c) by sending a copy of the writ by ordinary first-class post (as defined in Order 10, rule 1(2) to the firm at the principal place of business of the partnership within the jurisdiction

and subject to paragraph (2) where service of the writ is effected in accordance with this paragraph, the writ shall be deemed to have been duly served on the firm, whether or not any member of the firm is out of the jurisdiction.

(2) Where a writ is served on a firm in accordance with sub-paragraph (1)(c)—

(a) the date of service shall, unless the contrary is shown, be deemed to be the seventh day (ignoring Order 3, rule 2(5)) after the date on which the copy was sent to the firm; and
(b) any affidavit proving due service of the writ must contain a statement to the effect that—
  (i) in the opinion of the deponent (or, if the deponent is plaintiff's solicitor or an employee of that solicitor, in the opinion of the plaintiff) the copy of the writ, if sent to the firm at the address in question, will have come to the knowledge of one of the persons mentioned in paragraph (1)(a) or (b) within 7 days thereafter, and
  (ii) the copy of the writ has not been returned to the plaintiff through the post undelivered to the addressee.

(3) Where a partnership has, to the knowledge of the plaintiff, been dissolved before an action against the firm is begun, the writ by which the action is begun must be served on every person within the jurisdiction sought to be made liable in the action.

(4) Every person on whom a writ is served under paragraph (1)(a) or (b) must at the time of service be given a written notice stating whether he is served as a partner or as a person having the control or management of the partnership business or both as a partner and as such a person; and any person on whom a writ is so served but to whom no such notice is given shall be deemed to be served as a partner.

Acknowledgment of service in an action against firm

4.—(1) Where persons are sued as partners in the name of their firm, service may not be acknowledged in the name of the firm but only by the partners thereof in their own names, but the action shall nevertheless continue in the name of the firm.

(2) Where in an action against a firm the writ by which the action is

begun is served on a person as a partner, that person, if he denies that he was a partner or liable as such at any material time, may acknowledge service of the writ in the action and state in his acknowledgment that he does so as a person served as a partner in the defendant firm but who denies that he was a partner at any material time.

An acknowledgment of service given in accordance with this paragraph shall, unless and until it is set aside, be treated as an acknowledgment by the defendant firm.

(3) Where an acknowledgment of service has been given by a defendant in accordance with paragraph (2), then—

(a) the plaintiff may either apply to the court to set it aside on the ground that the defendant was a partner or liable as such at a material time or may leave that question to be determined at a later stage of the proceedings;

(b) the defendant may either apply to the court to set aside the service of the writ on him on the ground that he was not a partner or liable as such at a material time or may at the proper time serve a defence on the plaintiff denying in respect of the plaintiff's claim either his liability as a partner or the liability of the defendant firm or both.

(4) The court may at any stage of the proceedings in an action in which a defendant has acknowledged service in accordance with paragraph (2), on the application of the plaintiff or of that defendant, order that any question as to the liability of that defendant or as to the liability of the defendant firm be tried in such manner and at such time as the court directs.

(5) Where in an action against a firm the writ by which the action is begun is served on a person as a person having the control or management of the partnership business, that person may not acknowledge service of the writ in the action unless he is a member of the firm sued.

Enforcing judgment or order against firm

5.—(1) Where a judgment is given or order made against a firm, execution to enforce the judgment or order may, subject to rule 6, issue against any property of the firm within the jurisdiction.

(2) Where a judgment is given or order made against a firm, execution to enforce the judgment or order may, subject to rule 6 and to the next following paragraph issue against any person who—

(a) acknowledged service of the writ in the action as a partner, or

(b) having been served as a partner with the writ of summons, failed to acknowledge service of it in the action, or

(c) admitted in his pleading that he is a partner, or

(d) was adjudged to be a partner.

(3) Execution to enforce a judgment or order given or made against a firm may not issue against a member of the firm who was out of the jurisdiction when the writ of summons was issued unless he—

(a) acknowledged service of the writ in the action as a partner, or
(b) was served within the jurisdiction with the writ as a partner, or
(c) was, with the leave of the court given under Order 11, served out of the jurisdiction with the writ, or notice of the writ, as a partner;

and, except as provided by paragraph (1) and by the foregoing provisions of this paragraph, a judgment or order given or made against a firm shall not render liable, release or otherwise affect a member of the firm who was out of the jurisdiction when the writ was issued.

(4) Where a party who has obtained a judgment or order against a firm claims that a person is liable to satisfy the judgment or order as being a member of the firm, and the foregoing provisions of this rule do not apply in relation to that person, that party may apply to the court for leave to issue execution against that person, the application to be made by summons which must be served personally on that person.

(5) Where the person against whom an application under paragraph (4) is made does not dispute his liability, the court hearing the application may, subject to paragraph (3), give leave to issue execution against that person, and, where that person disputes his liability, the court may order that the liability of that person be tried and determined in any manner in which any issue or question in an action may be tried and determined.

Enforcing judgment or order in actions between partners, etc.
6.—(1) Execution to enforce a judgment or order given or made in—

(a) an action by or against a firm in the name of the firm against or by a member of the firm, or
(b) an action by a firm in the name of the firm against a firm in the name of the firm where those firms have one or more members in common,

shall not issue except with the leave of the court.

(2) The court hearing an application under this rule may give such directions, including directions as to the taking of accounts and the making of inquiries, as may be just.

Attachment of debts owed by firm
7.—(1) An order may be made under Order 49, rule 1, in relation to debts due or accruing due from a firm carrying on business within the jurisdiction notwithstanding that one or more members of the firm is resident out of the jurisdiction.

(2) An order to show cause under the said rule 1 relating to such debts as aforesaid must be served on a member of the firm within the

jurisdiction or on some other person having the control or management of the partnership business.

(3) Where an order made under the said rule 1 requires a firm to appear before the court, an appearance by a member of the firm constitutes a sufficient compliance with the order.

Actions begun by originating summons
8. Rules 2 to 7 shall, with the necessary modifications, apply in relation to an action by or against partners in the name of their firm begun by originating summons as they apply in relation to such an action begun by writ.

Application to person carrying on business in another name
9. An individual carrying on business within the jurisdiction in a name or style other than his own name, may whether or not he is within the jurisdiction be sued in that name or style as if it were the name of a firm, and rules 2 to 8 shall, so far as applicable, apply as if he were a partner and the name in which he carries on business were the name of his firm.

Applications for orders charging partner's interest in partnership property, etc.
10.—(1) Every application to the court by a judgment creditor of a partner for an order under section 23 of the Partnership Act, 1890 (which authorises the High Court or a judge thereof to make certain orders on the application of a judgment creditor of a partner, including an order charging the partner's interest in the partnership property), and every application to the court by a partner of the judgment debtor made in consequence of the first mentioned application must be made by summons.

(2) A master or the Admiralty Registrar or a district registrar may exercise the powers conferred on a judge by the said section 23.

(3) Every summons issued by a judgment creditor under this rule, and every order made on such a summons, must be served on the judgment debtor and on such of his partners as are within the jurisdiction or, if the partnership is a cost book company, on the judgment debtor and the purser of the company.

(4) Every summons issued by a partner of a judgment debtor under this rule, and every order made on such a summons, must be served—

(a) on the judgment creditor, and
(b) on the judgment debtor, and
(c) on such of the other partners of the judgment debtor as do not join in the application and are within the jurisdiction or, if the partnership is a cost book company, on the purser of the company.

(5) A summons or order served in accordance with this rule on the

purser of a cost book company or, in the case of a partnership not being such a company, on some only of the partners thereof, shall be deemed to have been served on that company or on all the partners of that partnership, as the case may be.

Index